20⁰⁰ NET

Simultaneous and Successive
Cognitive Processes

EDUCATIONAL PSYCHOLOGY

Allen J. Edwards, Series Editor
Department of Psychology
Southwest Missouri State University
Springfield, Missouri

In preparation:

Gary D. Phye and Daniel J. Reschly (eds.). School Psychology: Perspectives and Issues

Published

Norman Steinaker and M. Robert Bell. The Experiential Taxonomy: A New Approach to Teaching and Learning

J. P. Das, John R. Kirby, and Ronald F. Jarman. Simultaneous and Successive Cognitive Processes

Herbert J. Klausmeier and Patricia S. Allen. Cognitive Development of Children and Youth: A Longitudinal Study

Victor M. Agruso, Jr. Learning in the Later Years: Principles of Educational Gerontology

Thomas R. Kratochwill (ed.). Single Subject Research: Strategies for Evaluating Change

Kay Pomerance Torshen. The Mastery Approach to Competency-Based Education

Harvey Lesser. Television and the Preschool Child: A Psychological Theory of Instruction and Curriculum Development

Donald J. Treffinger, J. Kent Davis, and Richard E. Ripple (eds.). Handbook on Teaching Educational Psychology

Harry L. Hom, Jr. and Paul A. Robinson (eds.). Psychological Processes in Early Education

J. Nina Lieberman. Playfulness: Its Relationship to Imagination and Creativity

Samuel Ball (ed.). Motivation in Education

Erness Bright Brody and Nathan Brody. Intelligence: Nature, Determinants, and Consequences

The list of titles in this series continues on the last page of this volume

Simultaneous and Successive Cognitive Processes

J.P. DAS

Centre for the Study of Mental Retardation
The University of Alberta
Edmonton, Alberta, Canada

JOHN R. KIRBY

Division of Educational Psychology
University of Newcastle
Shortland, N.S.W., Australia

RONALD F. JARMAN

Department of Educational Psychology
University of British Columbia
Vancouver, B.C., Canada

With a chapter by James P. Cummins

ACADEMIC PRESS   New York   San Francisco   London   1979

A Subsidiary of Harcourt Brace Jovanovich, Publishers

ACADEMIC PRESS, INC.
111 Fifth Avenue, New York, New York 10003

United Kingdom Edition published by
ACADEMIC PRESS, INC. (LONDON) LTD.
24/28 Oval Road, London NW1 7DX

Library of Congress Cataloging in Publication Data

Das, Jagannath Prasad.
    Simultaneous and successive cognitive processes.

    Bibliography: p.
    1. Cognition. 2. Cognition in children.
I. Kirby, J. R., joint author. II. Jarman, R. F., joint
author. III. Title.
BF311.D34   153.4   78–20039
ISBN 0–12–203150–4

PRINTED IN THE UNITED STATES OF AMERICA
79 80 81 82   9 8 7 6 5 4 3 2 1

To our parents

Contents

3
A Model of Simultaneous and Successive Processing

4
Simultaneous and Successive Processing in Children

5
Relationship of Simultaneous and Successive Coding to School Achievement

6
Understanding Mental Retardation and Learning Disability

7
Cross-Cultural Studies

8
Comparison with Alternate Models

9
Can Strategies Be Taught?

10
Language Functions and Cognitive Processing
James P. Cummins

11
Retrospect and Prospect

APPENDIX
A General Manual for Tests of Simultaneous and Successive Processing and Speed of Processing

Preface

This book presents some innovative ideas. Since the manuscript was set into type, our model and some of our experiments have come to the attention of critics. It has made us think about the questions raised by them and generally about our line of research. We wish to share some of our thoughts with the reader before the book is read.

One approach to the study of abilities is to apply as many tests as possible that measure general cognitive ability and factor analyze them. Subsequently, the factors are examined to provide meaningful labels for tests that load on them. We did not proceed in this fashion. Our purpose was not to tap as many abilities as possible, but to discover processes that might parsimoniously describe what was involved in those abilities. Thus, our tests were deliberately not numerous. We have tried to conceptualize the basic cognitive functions as *coding* and *planning*. Within coding, two major processes, simultaneous and successive, have been identified. Armed with these assumptions we have attempted to define cognitive processes by choosing certain tasks which would elicit the use of coding and planning processes. How did we select these basic processes?

It will be apparent to the reader after he or she has read the first three chapters that the basic cognitive functions were suggested by Luria after he observed numerous cases of brain lesions. The coding and planning processes, therefore, embody a vast number of cognitive functions related to different parts of the cortex. We have used factor analysis as a tool to confirm our hypothesis in regard to the organization of cognitive functions in terms of coding and planning. In our factor-analytic work we have found that very similar tests describe different processes. Apparently these similar tests may be approached through separate processes. Likewise, apparently dissimilar tests may share similar processes. Further, inconsistent with the ability approach to tests, we have shown that the same test may load on, say, the simultaneous process in a white Canadian sample, whereas it loads on both simultaneous and successive processes in a culturally different sample.

Having established that one may be able to isolate coding and planning processes by using a battery of tasks, we are now extending our research into complex cognitive areas such as reading, word association, and sentence comprehension. We believe that the two coding processes, simultaneous and successive, and planning are, in fact, metaprocesses which subsume a variety of cognitive skills that are required in reading comprehension and number work. The significance of the planning process has not been explored by us as it relates to intelligent behavior. It is perhaps reasonable to assume that the usual intelligence tests measure very little, if any, of planning behavior. One should also explore the relationship between coding and planning, on the one hand, and hemisphericity, on the other. Above all, we think that it is of great potential importance to understand how coding and planning interact with motivation.

We believe that the line of work described in this book will prove a significant contribution to the understanding of intellectual behavior. The basic conceptualization of the functions of the brain in terms of arousal, coding, and planning would prove to be a useful approach to understanding the interaction between motivation, cognitive processes (such as perception, memory, and thinking), and executive functions (such as decision making, planning, and goal setting).

1

Intelligence:
Tradition and Change

1.1 HISTORY OF INTELLIGENCE: A MATTER OF DEFINITION

The attempt to define intelligence can be traced back to Aristotle, who divided mental functions into the *cognitive* (cybernetic) and the *orectic* (dynamic) categories. Whereas the cognitive functions are essentially thought processes, the orectic functions comprise emotional and moral aspects. A similar dichotomy is found in the Hindu system of logic: Purusa, literally, the male energy, is thought which acts as a catalyst for Prakriti, the female energy, which is emotion and action. The former is passive, the latter is active. Currently, we separate intelligence from personality or the cognitive from the affective domain, although such separation is recognized to be impossible at a practical level.

Cyril Burt (1955) defines intelligence as an innate, general, cognitive ability. Every term in the definition is open to debate. Perhaps the least controversial description is that intelligence is cognitive, although historically even this has been questioned. Because performance varies greatly given the same intelligence, one wonders if extracognitive factors do not play a dominant role in behavior. Current techniques for improving the performance of mentally retarded individuals have been so successful that a recognition of cognitive limitations has been discarded (see Bijou, 1966). It is claimed that there is no mental retardation; what exists is retarded behavior.

Is intelligence innate? Burt, along with many contemporary researchers, thinks that, largely, it is. The nature–nurture debate is a particularly lively one at the moment, and will be discussed later in this book. One may step back a little and consider with Burt why the early geneticists could not accept intelligence to be innate. Single traits such as eye color can be inherited. But the geneticists questioned the inheritance of a trait that is normally distributed. Multifactorial inheritance of intelligence had to be proven. Apparently, the pioneering work of Tryon on selective breeding of rats into two groups, the maze-bright and the maze-dull, demonstrated that a normally distributed trait can be inherited. Incidentally, selective breeding, as a technique, has been used subsequently to separate intelligence from emotionality (Das, G. & Broadhurst, 1959). As far as rats are concerned, emotionality is orthogonal to maze-brightness.

Is intelligence a general ability? Burt, following Spearman, has maintained that it is. "All branches of intellectual activity have in common one fundamental function, whereas the remaining or specific elements of the activity seem in every case to be wholly different from that in all others [Spearman, 1904, p. 284]." Beside general ability, Spearman recognized at least two specific ones, which were verbal ability and fluency. Fluency has emerged as divergent thinking in Guilford's model, whereas verbal ability occupies an important place among Thurstone's primary mental abilities.

Thurstone was the chief challenger to Spearman's notion of a general factor. An examination of his factor-analytic argument in favor of specific group factors reveals how vulnerable factor-analytic evidence is to the biases of its user. Thurstone (1938) could not find any trace of a general factor; instead several primary abilities such as verbal reasoning, spatial, numerical reasoning, and rote learning could be identified. These primary abilities were related to one another. Ideally, factor solution should aim at orthogonality *and* simple structure. Thurstone sacrificed the first for the second, and by doing so, opened himself to criticism. Since the primary abilities were factors arrived at through oblique rotation, what would the result be if one imposed an orthogonal rotation on his data? In a review of Thurstone's book a year after its publication, Eysenck (1939) presented a reanalysis of Thurstone's correlation matrix. He discovered a general factor which explains 30.8% of the variance. The remaining specific factors, eight in number, are indeed less significant; the strongest among these explains 6.6% of the variance. Apparently Thurstone's oblique method of rotation not only destroys the general factor, but gives undue importance to tests which correlate little with each other. Prior to Thurstone's book, Alexander in 1935 (cited in Eysenck, 1939) had also confirmed the existence of a strong general factor, and three other factors—a verbal, an arithmetic, and a practical (visual–spatial?) factor—which are somewhat similar to Thurstone's. Much later, Vernon (1960) came upon the same factors—

verbal–educational, spatial–mechanical, and numerical, in addition to a general factor.

The notion of a general factor, although not a monolithic one as Spearman had supposed, survives to this day. McNemar (1964) finds no strong reason to discard g in favor of primary abilities which are essentially tests of different aptitudes. Jensen (1969), in his otherwise controversial review, revived the notion of a two-tier system—of associative (rote) learning and reasoning. Cattell (see Horn, 1968) found evidence for general ability, although he divided it into fluid and crystallized intelligence.

The conflict between the Spearman school and Thurstone cannot be characterized as one between the British and the Americans. Cattell was of course very much a product of the British school. But his notions of fluid and crystallized intelligence can be traced to Thorndike's distinction of altitude and width of intelligence (Thorndike, Bergman, Cobb, & Woodyard, 1926). Altitude refers to the complexity of mental functions whereas width refers to the number of intellectual tasks a person can solve. Altitude was largely determined by nature, width by nurture. Later, these distinctions were abandoned, and Thorndike recognized one intellectual ability which varied in a continuum. Higher forms of intellectual operations were thought to be identical with more associations. Thorndike wrote that the essential difference between them was the number of "connections." Perhaps, "connections" would be called gnostic assemblies (Bindra, 1976) in contemporary terminology.

Is intelligence an ability? Returning to Burt's definition, one may consider what intelligence tests do measure and what they should measure. These questions are of greatest importance for our book. Our bias may as well be stated early in the book. Intelligence tests, as they exist presently, measure schooling; they provide an alternative measure of school attainment. As Thorndike observed in the 1921 symposium (1921), intelligence scores on Binet give an indication of how well a child will do in the school system for the next few months, and perhaps to a lesser extent, his attainment through the school years. We also believe that intelligence tests should be looked upon as measures of ability and that they do not indicate clearly the intellectual processes whose end products are these abilities. By focusing solely on measures of ability, the essential functions of the mind—the perceptual, associative, and relational functions, as Herbert Spencer described them—have been neglected. Research in these areas has had little influence on the psychometricians. We will attempt to present the view, with evidence, that mental functions can be looked upon as coding and decision-making processes. Coding, broadly considered, represents input, recoding, and storage of information. Decision processes refer to the formation and realization of plans, which regulate human behavior. The notion of the three blocks of the brain (Luria, 1969) representing arousal, coding, and decision making have provided a background for our research on simultaneous and successive processes.

1.2   THE NATURE OF INTELLIGENCE

The psychological study of intelligence or mental ability can be traced back to Sir Francis Galton in the late nineteenth century. Due in part, perhaps, to the influence of his half-cousin Charles Darwin, Galton chose an evolutionary perspective for this study; this bias was strengthened by his data which showed the tendency to high achievement to be largely inherited (Galton, 1883). Furthermore, Galton proposed that achievement was due to an underlying, unitary construct, general mental ability or intelligence, which was genetically determined. In addition to demonstrating the heritability of genius, his research also attempted to specify more accurately the nature of this underlying general ability: Galton believed that it was based upon the fineness with which the individual could make sensory discriminations. While his particular definition of the nature of intelligence has not been successful, Galton's work is important because it introduced two basic ideas about intelligence: It is a unitary construct, and it is largely genetically determined.

Galton's immediate successor was Charles Spearman, who accepted the idea of a unitary, general intelligence (g), but proposed it in the context of what he called the Theory of Two Factors. According to Spearman (1904, 1923, 1927), any cognitive operation is served by the general factor g which is peculiar to that cognitive operation. The general factor was conceived of as an energy or power that served the whole nervous system, and that could be concentrated upon any specific group of neurons, which were represented by the s factors. Thus, whereas g was the energy, the various s's were the engines which actually accomplished the cognitive operations.

The s factors which Spearman added to the theory of intelligence were necessitated by factor analysis (which Spearman had largely developed). Galton's evidence for his unitary general intelligence had been the substantial correlations which he had observed among a variety of cognitive tests. When Spearman applied the new technique of factor analysis to these high correlations, he extracted one factor (g) but found that some of the variance of each test remained unexplained as is bound to happen when correlations are less than 1.0. He deemed that his specific (or, as it is sometimes called, error) variance was due to the s factors.

Disagreements about the nature of that specific variance were to characterize the psychological study of intelligence for a long time. As will be seen later, rival techniques of factor analysis were developed that tended to produce a larger number of factors. At the same time, new theories were developed that saw intelligence not as a unitary construct, but rather as the aggregation of a number of diverse abilities or skills. These factors were intermediate in generality between Spearman's g and s factors, in a sense giving more importance to the specific variance by de-emphasizing the variance explained by one general factor.

Though it may now be amusing to examine Spearman's Industrial-Revolution-inspired model of energies and engines, it is important to realize that his efforts to define the nature of intelligence were very much the spirit of differential psychology in the 1920s. During a time when experimental psychology fell increasingly under the influence of Watson's radical Behaviorism, it is significant to note that psychologists studying intelligence were opting for what would now be termed *cognitive models,* ones which attempted to specify the hypothetical constructs which produced intelligent action. Though much was written on the subject (Spearman, 1923; Thurstone, 1926; Thorndike et al., 1921) no successful theory emerged from this period.

Why was a theory of intelligence so difficult to produce? Looking back at that period there seem to have been at least three reasons. The first was that experimental psychology, which should have provided a rich supply of cognitive constructs for inclusion in a theory of intelligence, was at that time almost devoid of appropriate constructs. Attempts to define intelligence as learning ability, for instance, failed because no distinction was made between simple stimulus–response learning and complex cognitive learning. When the former did not correlate with tests of intelligence, those theories were discarded (Woodrow, 1946).

A second hurdle for a definition of the nature of intelligence was some uncertainty as to which behavior could be called intelligent. Before a model could be produced that effectively simulated intelligent action, those intelligent actions had to be specified. Whereas Galton had chosen to study genius and extraordinary accomplishment, intelligence tests of the 1920s (and of the present) stressed the inclusion of items that discriminated between average children of various ages. Which of these phenomena were to be modeled?

A third factor related to the others was the gradual evolution of differential psychology into a technology of selection and prediction, a trend which had started with Binet's early work. With increased concern for the development of more and more precise tests, interest in what those tests were supposed to measure decreased. It was during this period that intelligence came to be described as "whatever intelligence tests measure."

1.3   OLD PIONEERS AND NEW MESSIAHS

One way of illustrating the evolution of the concept of intelligence is to consider some notable workers in the field. The following are capsule treatments of their contributions.

Cyril Burt

What E. L. Thorndike was to American psychology, Cyril Burt was to British psychology. He was more influential than Thorndike in changing the practice of educational psychology, at least in Britain. What is now called the British School in the field of intelligence is largely identified with Spearman and Burt who were co-workers in the first project directed at the measurement of intellectual characteristics of school children in Britain.

Burt lived until he was 89, and was contributing to the field of intelligence even in his old age. In fact, some of his important writings on the inheritance of intelligence were done after he was 70 (Jensen, 1974b). During some 60 years of activity in the field, he looked at two questions thoroughly: What is the nature of intelligence? How is it inherited? The question of interest to us in this book is whether or not he was aware of intelligence as a process, although recognizing it as an ability. If it were the end product of processes that can be improved upon, then intelligence would not be immutable. We will discuss this here. One cannot neglect to discuss also an unrelated issue. Was Burt inaccurate in reporting his empirical investigations, and if he was, does this make these reports suspect?

Intelligence, according to Burt, is a general cognitive ability which is largely inherited. In regarding intelligence as such he (Burt, 1972) was following up Galton's idea. Binet has also accepted Galton's view. The origin of g or a general ability running through all aspects of intellectual behavior was not founded in Spearman. According to Burt, Spearman came to accept the notion while working on the project with Burt and others under McDougall's general sponsorship.

Emergence of g was the result of factor analysis. And the strength and weakness of this statistical procedure are a part of it. Essentially, these reflect the nature of correlational analysis: Factors are apt to change with different samples, and with different tests. Additionally, they also change by adopting different methods of rotation. As far as the *notion* of a general cognitive ability is concerned, it may survive in spite of the weaknesses of factor analysis as a statistical technique—at least this is apparent from Burt's writing. Factor analysis seems to be an elegant window dressing for the notion.

Burt considers three general characteristics in humans—physical, intellectual, and temperamental. An adequate investigation of the last characteristic has not been completed according to him (Burt, 1972) although temperaments play an important role in the expression of intelligence.

Are mental characteristics inherited? It is clear in Burt's writings that these are largely inherited. In a sense, Burt was engaged in delineating how they are inherited. His research on kinship was directed to a systematic study of the mechanism of inheritance. Inheritance of intelligence is largely multifactorial; but to a certain extent, it is also unifactorial. There is no doubt that individual differences in ability are determined by a number of factors, and hence their distribution conforms to a normal probability curve. But one cannot ignore, according to Burt (1963), that exceptional deviations in intelligence at both ends of the continuum may be determined by single genes. A distribution of IQs of 4665 children tested on Stanford-Binet showed that more than 10% had IQs below 80 and 7.7% above IQ 120. Burt (1963) argues that these figures provide an empirical basis for doubting that intelligence is normally distributed and hence, single genes and mutations do not contribute substantially to individual differences in IQ (Burt, 1963).

Whenever one makes a strong statement that intelligence is predetermined by genes, the question is asked, Is it immutable? Partly, the answer will depend on the proportion of genetic contribution, which now stands at 68–70%. Variations in intelligence, then, can be large or small depending on the contributions of nongenetic components—life's experience, education, and opportunity for growth are some of these. But even when one is considering only the genetic component, phenotypic variations are expected. "A given genetic endowment is compatible with a whole range of developmental reactions and consequently of acquired attainments [Burt, 1972, p. 188]." This observation is not new, but it needs to be stated in order to realize that genetic determination of intelligence does not preclude improvement in educational attainment through compensatory education or other forms of environmental intervention.

Reading Burt, one is also amazed at the flexibility of attainment permitted even when an individual is performing within the limits of his genetically given "capacity." It seems as though genes do not matter in practice within the normal range of intelligence, once we exclude the dull and the gifted among us. For instance, in a paper on intelligence and social mobility, Burt (1961) reports that very few of those individuals who had low motivation rose above the occupational class into which they were born. And, in fact, anyone who had risen above the class of his birth had good intelligence and high motivation. A good grammar school education was not enough to guarantee upward mobility; on the other hand, many individuals without any formal education beyond elementary school worked their way up. Burt remarks that motivation, and "qualities of personality and character" are the major factor behind social mobility apart from intelligence.

Burt is also flexible in assessment of an individual's intellectual "capacity." He advocates the use of Binet's *méthode clinique* in his last paper (Burt, 1972), but he had held this view all along. As a psychologist in the schools of London County Council, Burt could not ignore the extra-intellectual factors which produce variations in IQ test performance. The cold, standardized approach to testing had not then set in, perhaps partly because the testing movement was new, and partly because the testers were full-blooded psychologists rather than psychometric technicians. IQ scores must be adjusted (Burt, 1943), and a great deal of the data reported in kinship studies by Burt are based on adjusted assessment which raises problems with an objective interpretation of his findings (Jensen, 1974b). The adjustments are made on the basis of the tester's own observation, and taking into consideration whether the test was fair for the child.

We shall conclude our examination of the flexible relation between genetic endowment and attainment by considering Burt's (1943) paper on ability and income. As anyone knows, cognitive ability is not reflected either in one's output or in income. Whereas intelligence is more or less normally distributed, the distribution of output or income is far from normal. Income to a certain extent depends on the level of education. A university education almost guaranteed a better-than-average income in Britain in the late 1930s and 1940s. Burt mentions the inequality in opportunity for obtaining a university education: Some 40% of students who have the adequate IQ cannot get into the university whereas 40% of students receiving university educations do not have the required intelligence. We believe that the inequalities in society far outweigh in significance the inequalities in hereditary endowment so far as output is concerned. Burt may not have disagreed with it.

Finally, was Burt an inaccurate scientist? It seems that he was, at least in his old age. Jensen (1974) has prepared a comprehensive paper, reporting errors in Burt's kinship correlations and claims that no new errors have been discovered by other recent critiques of Burt such as Leon Kamin's (1974). This claim is made in a 1976 general refutation of "fraud" and "fakery" charges against Burt (Jensen, 1977b). The charges of fakery and inaccurate reporting of data concern two aspects of Cyril Burt: the validity of his research and Burt as a person. The latter has a less serious implication for science. We may consider the first one. We start with a quotation from Jensen (1974, p. 25): "It is almost as if Burt regarded the actual data as merely an incidental backdrop for the illustration of the theoretical issues in quantitative genetics, which, to him, seemed always to hold the center of the stage." If one disregarded Burt's data from the heritability of IQ literature would it matter? One suggestion is that the heritability will drop to 60% (Wade, 1976). Already a 68% figure has been accepted even without disregarding Burt's data. Thus there would not be any great change in the heritability literature if Burt's empirical work were entirely discarded on the ground of unreliability. His other findings not related to kinship correlations may not be summarily rejected. For instance, the 1961 paper on social mobility was also written in his old age. Burt does not accurately report the sample size in this paper. But that does not make the results invalid. For, in spite of such sloppiness in reporting, the essence of his findings on social mobility is confirmed by a study in America (Waller, 1971).

As a person, Burt's integrity in old age is certainly questioned. Burt was a very bright and creative individual, and like many in that category was passionate and predatory. People around him felt that Burt was not always honest in academic matters. It was alleged that he wrote critical reviews of books he did not like under pseudonyms and published these in the *British Journal of Statistical Psychology,* which he edited. Whether these instances are faults in character or aberrations due to senility cannot be established clearly. But there are lessons to be drawn for the scientific community from the failing of Burt. As Jensen points out, genetic data should be preserved in the archives after obtaining as complete information as possible on the individuals in the sample. The other lesson is that psychological data should be somehow made more public, and more easily verifiable at the source. Faking is perhaps harder to detect with psychological data than it is with physical. But now and then fakery is reported in the hard sciences, and one wonders how many instances are not caught. The need to fake should be eliminated by professionals and those who evaluate their performance. But one doubts if one can entirely prevent "faults in character" from appearing occasionally in the literature.

Godfrey H. Thomson

In the ability versus process debate, Godfrey H. Thomson seems to be a supporter of processes although working within the framework of abilities. "Mental measurements tend to show hierarchical order, and to be susceptible of mathematical description in terms of one general factor and innumerable specifics, not because there are specific neural machines through which its energy must show itself, but just exactly because there are no fixed neural machines [Thomson, 1939, p. 280]." The mind or mental processes are flexible and plastic until education, occupational requirements, and "political beliefs of adult life have imposed a habitual structure on it."

Thomson conceives of the mind as consisting of a large number of bonds. A sample of these is required for the performance of a given task. Statistical correlations between tests are due to sampling from a common pool of bonds or elementary units. The structural basis of bonds is physiological, a notion first expressed by Thorndike. Bonds or connections as Thorndike used to call them represent neural processes, and are dynamic by nature. An appropriate sample of bonds is called for by a specific task or test; obviously such a sample is ad hoc and does not have an immutable structure.

At the same time, the sampling of bonds is not random. Thomson interprets Spearman's g factor as a measure of the whole pool of bonds, a representation of all mental functions. Specific abilities, then, may be thought of as independent subpools of bonds. This is, however, an error, according to Thomson. Mental processes cannot be so separated. We seem to infer unique abilities by deriving orthogonal factors; the factors do not represent reality. All through Thomson's brief theoretical exposition, one finds this to be a recurrent theme—the statistically derived factors do not reflect factors of the mind. Then what is the use of factor analysis in studying human ability? Although Thomson does not answer this directly, one can infer that factors are useful in looking at performance on mental tests in an orderly manner, and that they suggest the complexity of mental processes.

What they should not lead us to believe is clearly answered: Mind is not a static repertoire of abilities, different minds varying only in terms of how many of these abilities one has. Thomson adds that different minds perform any task or test by different means and the same mind does so at different times. Nothing could be further from a fixed ability approach to mental functions. Finally, why do minds differ? The structures are different. Some of these are certainly innate; the mind of an Einstein and of a severely retarded individual strongly suggest innate differences. But the structures are different largely because of the environment, education, and life's experience. Has the research on intelligence since 1939 compelled us to revise Thomson's view?

Phillip E. Vernon

Phillip E. Vernon's theory of intelligence stands at the end of a British legacy which has its roots in Spearman's (1904, 1927) classical formulations. The two-factor theory of intelligence proposed by Spearman, as described earlier, consisted of a common factor g and a series of lesser factors, each specific to particular tasks. Performance on any task, then, was seen as a combination of the effects of g and the specific ability tapped by the task, with this combination varying according to the extent that tests measured simple or higher order conceptual abilities.

Spearman's model was expanded by Burt (e.g., 1940, 1949) under the influence of McDougall to include group factors which were intermediate between g and specific factors, and error factors, which attempted to take account of fluctuations in performance from one time of measurement to the next. This structure, in turn, was developed further by Vernon (1950) to form his now well-known hierarchical structure of human abilities. The four-tiered model used by Vernon to describe abilities has g at the peak of the hierarchy. Below this general factor are two major group factors which are unique to Vernon's model, and are designated as v:ed and k:m. The former is a verbal–educational factor, and the latter is a spatial–mechanical factor. These two factors, in turn, are built up from minor group factors below them. Minor factors which contribute to v:ed, for example, are creative abilities, and reading, spelling, and linguistic abilities (Vernon, 1969). The k:m factor has as minor factors, for instance, psychomotor and physical abilities and mechanical information; also, some minor factors are shared between v:ed and k:m, such as mathematical abilities. Finally, at the lowest level below the minor group factors are the specific factors representing performance on discrete tasks with little general psychological meaning applicable to other tasks. The structure of the hierarchy, then, from top to bottom, is a distinction of general to specific. A particular test may contain elements of all four levels, but will share elements across a level only with those other tests within its superordinate category.

The principal technique employed by Vernon to develop and apply his theory of intelligence is factor analysis. In contrast to some other researchers in his field, however (e.g., Cattell, 1971), Vernon does not adopt the position that the factors yielded by this technique must necessarily always have psychological meaning. Rather, he views factors as a convenient form of classification and frequently notes the many limitations of the technique (Vernon, 1969). His view of the existence of factors in a particular population may be termed ecological, in the sense that environmental and social demands are proposed as the mainsprings for the development of a particular ability. This view is buttressed by his famous studies in cross-cultural psychology which have allowed the breadth of empiricism evidenced in his work (Vernon, 1965a, 1965b, 1966, cf. 1969).

Vernon's extensive cross-cultural research has also led him to form a distinction between three types of intelligence. Beginning with Hebb's

(1949) concepts of Intelligence A and B, Vernon added Intelligence C as a third type. Intelligence A refers to innate capacity and is primarily genetically based. Intelligence B designates behavior that is often societally recognized as intelligent, such as quick-wittedness and cleverness. Finally, Intelligence C refers to ability as measured on an intelligence test, and is indicated in terms of IQ or mental age. These types of intelligence are interrelated; Intelligence A sets limits to potential, and corresponds roughly to the concept of mental capacity. As such, it is not possible to measure Intelligence A, and no operational techniques of measurement are likely to be developed which will accomplish this. Intelligence B is dependent in part upon Intelligence A and also upon the environmental history of the individual. In turn, Intelligence C is a test sampling of the range of skills represented in Intelligence B, often with a particular emphasis on those skills necessary for school success. Returning to Vernon's cross-cultural work, these distinctions are used frequently to emphasize the point that a test of Intelligence C may reveal little regarding Intelligence A or B if the test is not appropriate for use in a given culture.

Vernon's distinctions between the three types of intelligence have also formed some of the basis for describing the differences between his hierarchical theory of intelligence and other competing theories. He suggests, for example, that there is some similarity between his hierarchical model and Cattell's (1971) fluid and crystallized abilities (Vernon, 1969). Fluid ability appears to correspond to g with a slight mixture of spatial ability, and crystallized intelligence is suggested by Vernon to correspond to g with a mixture of v:ed. A point of major difference between the two theories, however, is that Cattell appears to be referring to Intelligence A in his description of fluid intelligence as the result of biological factors. Cattell is suggesting, therefore, that Intelligence A can be measured, which clearly differs from Vernon's views (Tyler, 1974). No resolution of this issue has been reached, but it is clear that Cattell's position, if taken to the extreme, is untenable. Psychological tests will always be limited in their ability to represent physiological make-up, for well-known reasons including measurement error.

Vernon's discussion of Cattell is exemplary of his general approach to competing theories of intelligence. He has identified and discussed the essential differences between his model and others at some length over the last quarter of a century, including in his discussions Thurstone and Guilford. He notes that many of the differences can be defined in terms of three sources: factor-analysis techniques, population sampling, and test sampling (see Butcher, 1968). The factor-analysis techniques adopted by Vernon differ from those used by Thurstone and Guilford in that a general factor g is extracted first, followed by subsidiary analyses. Thurstone and Guilford proceed directly to the analysis of specific factors. Population-sampling differences between the investigations are due to the highly heterogeneous populations that have been represented in Vernon's studies, whereas Guilford and Thurstone have tended to use samples of selected populations such as Army recruits. Finally, Vernon has used a wide range of tests, some of which are not purely cognitive, and he suggests that this has resulted in a broader theoretical framework than those proposed by Thurstone or Guilford. Differences between the Vernon research and the Thurstone–Guilford tradition, then, are based partly on factor-analytic philosophy and partly on matters of pragmatics in conducting research, such as obtaining subjects.

Viewed in its entirety, the research contributed by Vernon over the past three decades is substantial, and his work clearly stands as one of the major contributions to our understanding of human intelligence. Despite the obvious significance of this contribution, however, his studies have never wandered into overly abstract and tenuous theorizing. Rather, his writing is characterized by a remarkable clarity of style, and one finds constant reference to the limitations of the work and the need to retain practical purpose. In these latter aspects particularly, Vernon's contributions to research on intelligence may be incomparable.

Raymond B. Cattell

Raymond B. Cattell's contributions can be found in three areas—factor analysis, personality, and intelligence. His work on intelligence, specifically, the notions of fluid and crystallized intelligence, is of interest here. Since the publication of his most important paper on fluid (g_f) and crystallized (g_c) intelligence (Cattell, 1963), a great deal of research has been carried out, some of which advances the two concepts, and some of which goes against his theory. Horn (1968) is probably the best advocate of Cattell's theory. Among his detractors are Humphreys (1967) and Eysenck (1973).

According to Horn (1968), the two kinds of general intelligence, g_f and g_c, have brought the factor-analytic work into the context of process theories. The two factors reflect processes. If they do, Cattell's theory may contribute to the understanding of the processes underlying general intellectual abilities. But first, a description of g_f and g_c is in order.

Cattell describes g_f or fluid ability as that which is displayed in the perception of complex relationships. In contrast, g_c, or crystallized ability, is expressed in an individual's judgments which have been taught to him systematically; g_c is similar to many traditional tests of IQ, such as verbal ability, reasoning, and number ability. However, some of these are also related to g_f when factor loadings are considered. Tests which load more on g_f than g_c are accepted as measures of g_f. The same principle applies for tests of g_c. This sort of double loading is only to be expected since g_f and g_c themselves correlate between .4 and .5.

Fluid intelligence is measured by tests similar to Raven's Coloured Progressive Matrices and tests of classification. It operates "whenever the sheer perception of complex relations is involved [Cattell, 1971, p. 98]." According to Cattell's own description, g_f is similar to the capacity required for problem solving (one that he attributes to Spearman), the capacity to perceive relationships and to educe correlations. It is essentially a logical ability.

At the same time, Cattell does not think that the tests which make up g_f are in the category of culture-free tests. Is g_f innate and g_c acquired? The answer is, not quite, although Cattell thinks that research on the hereditary basis of intelligence will show g_f to be more innate than g_c (Cattell, 1971, p. 102). And certainly, g_f and g_c are not to be confused with Vernon's $k{:}m$ and $v{:}ed$. $k{:}m$ or spatial–mechanical may partly correlate with g_c because of its mechanical component—Cattell views mechanical ability as a product of learning.

Cattell uses Thurstone's tests and through oblique rotation comes up with g_f and g_c. The weakness inherent in oblique rotation of factors derived by Thurstone has been discussed earlier. The same criticism is made by Humphreys (1967) of Cattell's procedure: g_f and g_c form a general factor by using "hyperplane" analysis, but this hyperplane stuff cashes in on random relationships existing between tests. The other point made by Humphreys casts serious doubt on the existence of g_f and g_c: Apparently parallel forms of the tests used to measure g_f or g_c have zero correlations and sometimes load on separate factors.

Besides, one may question the use of postulating two new abilities if these could be subsumed under Thurstone's "primary mental abilities" (PMA). Cattell's tests show an r of .30 with the primary mental abilities; the r is increased to .44 by excluding the spatial relations test from PMA. Fluid intelligence can be easily confused with Jensen's Level II ability (see the section on Jensen in this chapter), and crystallized with school achievement, since the factors are correlated up to .5, which is not too far from the correlation between Level II and school achievement. Further dependence of school achievement (as g_c) on Level II (as g_f) is underscored when Cattell mentions that the acquisition of a crystallized ability, such as how to calculate the area of a circle, depends partly on the level of what he called "insightful and fluid ability."

Fluid is not any more innate than crystallized intelligence, contrary to Cattell's assumptions (Eysenck, 1973). In a study of monozygotic twins cited by Eysenck, Shields (1962) could not support Cattell's claim; and Jinks and Fulker (1970), using Shield's data, concluded that the broad heritability of a major test of g_f was 71% and of a major test of g_c was 73%. If g_f were innate and g_c were acquired, a serious genetic study offered no support for such a notion.

How can one defend g_f and g_c? The basic assumption for g_f is that the "fluid" form of intelligent behavior, which is logical ability, is culture-free, an assumption that is hard to defend. Consider the views of Thorndike, Vernon, and Luria, whose work and backgrounds are quite different. None of them can support the assumption that expressions of logic are independent of an individual's academic and cultural experience. Thorndike (1926) maintains that one cannot ignore the differences in opportunities for training while comparing individuals on their intelligence scores. Vernon (1960) attributes intelligence to the cumulative experiences of a lifetime, and does not wish to distinguish it from attainment, which is obviously a product of learning. For Luria (1971), expression of intelligence is a social rather than a biological phenomenon. Following his earlier research on the peasants from Uzbekistan, he concluded that not only the content of thinking and reasoning but also their structure were products of an individual's experience, academic as well as social.

Cattell seems to be continuing on the same line of work which led him to make a culture-free test in 1940 (Cattell, 1973). A perceptual intelligence test was made up by him which was to be a precursor of g_f. The culture-free perceptual test was narrow according to Cattell, and at best measured spatial ability. Nevertheless, Cattell recommended it as a good test for Western school children and for aboriginal unschooled children. However, he recognized that the aboriginal children might need a lot of practice, appropriate incentives, de-emphasis on speed, and one-to-one trustful testing conditions. As a student of Burt, Cattell may not have significantly advanced one's understanding of intelligence beyond his teacher. Perhaps history will judge the usefulness of g_f and g_c as concepts. They are difficult to assess at present.

J. P. Guilford

Research on intelligence in North America, and on human abilities specifically, had its first major impetus supplied by Thurstone's influential studies. As noted earlier, Thurstone fostered the concept of simple structure, which was a principle based on both orthogonal factors and organization of zero factor loadings. At a later point, this scheme was modified from orthogonal to oblique factors, resulting in the now-familiar system of primary mental abilities (e.g., Thurstone, 1938).

Thurstone's model of seven primary abilities attracted the attention of J. P. Guilford early in his research career. Guilford agreed with the need to define mental abilities rigorously and operationally, but he differed with Thurstone on at least two essential points. First, Guilford suggested that mental abilities should be defined in orthogonal terms, and that, therefore, Thurstone's later work on oblique factors required revision. Second, Guilford believed that the seven primary abilities found by Thurstone in his factor analyses were neither exhaustive of the domain of human abilities, nor were they sufficiently differentiated to account for the many possible cognitive tasks used in the assessment of ability.

Guilford's first step in developing an alternative theory to Thurstone's was to devise a schematic model of human abilities which was to serve as a framework for the development and validation of tests. This procedure differentiated Guilford from other psychologists of his era because the predominant method used to that point had been the development of a theory through factor analyses. Typically, in other research, large batteries of tests were given to subjects and the results of factor analyses were used to define the structure of human abilities.

The model developed by Guilford is in the shape of a cube, with three principal dimensions (Guilford, 1956, 1959). These dimensions allow the classification of possible kinds of abilities according to (1) the psychological operations involved, (2) the kind of material or content, and (3) the forms that information takes as a product. Each of these three major dimensions has, in turn, a number of sub-classifications. The operations dimension consists of cognition, memory, divergent production, convergent production, and evaluation. The contents dimension includes figural, symbolic, semantic, and behavioral distinctions. Finally, the products may be units, classes, relations, systems, transformations, and implications. The result of these many sub-classifications on each dimension, and the orthogonal structure of the schematic cube, is that 120 possible different abilities are defined by the model.

The basic structure outlined initially by Guilford served the purpose in subsequent years of guiding what was possibly the most ambitious research program in the history of human abilities. Guilford's next step in the development of his theory was to select and develop tests to represent the individual cells in the model, and then to collect data using the tests in order to validate his classifications. This process has resulted in an extensive series of empirical studies and several major treatises of his theory (Guilford, 1967, Guilford & Hoepfner, 1971). To date, the majority of the cells in Guilford's model have been defined operationally by one or more cognitive tests.

Criticisms of Guilford's model have been common since its inception. As expected, the British psychologists have suggested that Guilford's insistence on orthogonality in the model and its supporting factor analyses are inconsistent with the hierarchical nature of human abilities (Butcher, 1968). From a less partisan viewpoint, Cronbach (1970) notes that Guilford's procedure of fitting data to hypotheses will never yield information on the validity of the model itself. Cronbach notes also that data contrary to Guilford's exist in the literature, and these data most often contradict the orthogonal structure of the model. These criticisms are magnified by Carroll (1968, 1972), Horn (1970), and Horn and Knapp (1973), who simply state that the model has little or no theoretical basis, and is not empirically supported. Further, it has been observed that Guilford's operations and contents are not innovative notions, they only indicate how g (reasoning and memory) gets to work on different kinds of cognitive materials such as perceptual, verbal, and numerical.

Despite these criticisms, however, one should not overlook the contribution made by Guilford's theory of human abilities. There are specific areas in which the model has facilitated other useful and independent research on, for example, divergent and convergent thinking. The root of divergent thinking as an operation can be traced to Spearman who recognized, in addition to g, verbal ability and fluency as basic abilities. Fluency has emerged as divergence in Guilford's scheme. Also, the three dimensions of operations, products, and contents have served as an exemplar for psychologists analyzing the basic demands of tasks that they use in factor analyses, in that results be made more psychologically interpretable (see Merrifield, 1970). Thus, the scheme may be seen as an important step in research on intelligence, even if the details of the theory itself are questionable. It may be that Guilford's model, as suggested by Tyler (1974), is more of a contribution to psychologists than practitioners by virtue of the questions that it raises rather than the answers that it supplies.

Hans J. Eysenck

Trained by Cyril Burt and emerging from the British school, Hans J. Eysenck offers a panoramic view of tradition and change in the field of intelligence. We shall describe the essence of his theory; details are best obtained by referring to Part V of his book, *The Measurement of Intelligence* (Eysenck, 1973).

According to Eysenck, intelligence scores are global, without any indication of the constituent processes that make up the scores. Units of analysis should be the individual test items, not IQs. Broadly, the solution of test items is dependent on speed, accuracy, and persistence as Furneaux (1956) originally suggested. Speed, in the guise of mental speed as measured by reaction time tests, had attracted the attention of early workers in intelligence. So also "cautiousness" was thought to be an important determinant of performance scores. But persistence had not been recognized as a crucial element in intellectual behavior. In any case, Eysenck uses Furneaux's model in order to demonstrate the relative contribution of cognitive and personality factors to intellectual performance. Following Furneaux, Owen White (1973) has been working on a mathematical model of intelligence in order to conceptualize the role of these three elements in determining individual differences.

Speed may be a relatively pure measure of intelligence whereas accuracy and persistence are measures of personality. The cause of a high or low score on an intelligence test must be analyzed in terms of these three categories. If these three attributes are present in any kind of intellectual performance, then we have a common base for comparison. However, before comparing performance on different intellectual tasks, two basic aspects of the task must be considered. These are the type of problem and the difficulty level of the problem (Furneaux, 1960). A problem can be of one of two types, verbal or spatial; it may need perceptual or memorial processes. These are illustrations of "type" differences. Likewise, one visual–spatial problem can be easier or more difficult than another. Scaling for difficulty is recommended. Once these two aspects are controlled for, intelligent behavior has the three common attributes.

When proper instructions have been shown to improve IQ, usually it is not speed that has improved. Accuracy or error-checking can be favorably influenced through instructions. Horn (1968) would probably call this carefulness or unwillingness to give incorrect answers. Thorndike had a similar concept, namely, inhibition of impulses. Instructions and incentives can also influence persistence or, as Eysenck now calls it, continuance—to continue with a problem when it is difficult to solve.

Mental speed is a fascinating concept which may tax our ingenuity for measurement. Many a researcher has wasted his life in pursuit of a "speed" measure of intelligence. Ertle is the most recent example. But the current advances in electrophysiology may hold hope; Eysenck is now engaged in looking at event-related potentials. There are two problems with this line of research. Event-related potentials are typically responses to simple sensory stimuli: Could they reflect one's efficiency of processing complex information? The other problem is sensitivity to mental speed at widely different levels of IQ. Perhaps this type of measurement has some promise for separating the dull from the bright, the subnormal from the normally intelligent. But within the range of normal IQ, will it be a sensitive discriminator?

Eysenck's views on intelligence can be summarized as follows:

1. The cause of high or low IQ scores of individuals must be analyzed in terms of speed, error-checking, and continuance. The last two components relate to personality.
2. Instructions can improve IQ by influencing the personality components.
3. A genetic basis for each of these components should be a topic of investigation, since such a basis cannot be ruled out.
4. Speed of intellectual response or cognitive speed may be displayed in terms of the speed of evoked potentials.
5. All in all, a return to the methods of experimental psychology is recommended for prospectors in the field of intelligence.

Eysenck has brought the study of intelligence back to the laboratory. Perhaps it is there, as in the airless chamber of Newton, that the laws of intelligence can be perfected. But Eysenck does not call them laws as yet; the three aspects of intelligence have a heuristic value in that they will lead to an organized examination of the concept through the methods of experimental psychology.

Arthur R. Jensen

Among the many investigators in the history of research on intelligence Arthur R. Jensen has become one of the most controversial in recent years. His views of mental ability reflect the hereditarian position strongly, and are founded on independent research as were Cyril Burt's studies in England, as well as his own numerous projects.

There are actually two sides to Jensen's research on intelligence, although these are related. The first of these is his theory of cognitive abilities known as Level I and Level II (Jensen, 1970). This theory of abilities, as noted earlier, is a hierarchical model in the Spearman tradition. Jensen posits that an individual's intellectual competence can be conceived of as a combination of the two abilities. Level I is simple associative learning ability and memory, and is measured by tasks such as serial learning and memory for paired associates. Level II ability, in contrast, is higher order conceptual learning and problem solving. Level II abilities are measured by tasks such as Raven's Coloured Progressive Matrices and Figure Copying. Jensen (1969, 1970) proposes that the hierarchical arrangement of these two abilities is that Level I is necessary but not sufficient for Level II. Thus, memory is necessary for reasoning, but not the converse. This assumption of hierarchical dependency has been reviewed by Horn (1976), and found to be empirically unsubstantiated. The lack of evidence for a hierarchical arrangement is one source of dispute, then, in acceptance of Jensen's theory of Level I and Level II abilities. In all fairness, however, it must be mentioned that the issue is a complicated one. If Level II partly depends on Level I, is the difference between the two a qualitative or a quantitative one? The question had plagued Thorndike. In 1926, he wrote "The essential element of our hypothesis is that it offers a purely quantitative fact, the number of C's (connections), as the cause of qualitative differences either in the kind of operation (association vs. reasoning) or in the quality of the results (truth vs. error, wisdom vs. folly) so far as these qualitative differences are caused by ordinary nature [Thorndike et al., 1926, p. 417]." Jensen refers to the amount of transformation necessary as the key to distinguishing between Level I (small) and Level II (extensive transformation of information) abilities.

The other side of Jensen's theory of cognitive ability is concerned with the heritability of intelligence. The theory of Level I and Level II abilities is brought into the genetic domain by Jensen's proposing that Level I ability has largely a normal distribution, with relatively equivalent representation throughout different socioeconomic status and racial groups. Level II ability, however, shows different distributions for these groups, and Jensen proposes that inheritance is largely responsible for these differences.

The notion of the inheritance of cognitive ability is certainly not new. Why, then, did Jensen's research cause such a furor? The reasons lie in part in the tenuous relations between scientific research and social policy. Jensen began his career in the area of verbal learning in the early 1960s and his research during that period was of interest only to the academic community. During this period a number of changes were taking place in the United States, many of them centering around increasing concern for individual rights, equality of opportunity, and social responsibility. As a consequence of these concerns, and mounting evidence for the importance of early experience (Bloom, 1964), the largest educational special program in U.S. history, Project Head Start, began in the summer of 1965 (Akers, 1972). The main purpose of this project was early intervention for disadvantaged children. From this period on, Jensen concentrated his research on children of low socioeconomic status and, as a consequence, on different racial groups. Jensen was known at that time as an academic liberal, and he published with other social-minded academics such as Deutsch.

The clear point of change in Jensen's position occurred in the late 1960s with the publication of his monograph *How Much Can We Boost IQ and Scholastic Achievement?* (Jensen, 1969). In this lengthy work Jensen reviewed the evidence from Project Head Start on the results of early intervention, proposed the Level I–Level II theory, and tentatively suggested a genetic basis to some racial differences in IQ.

The negative responses to Jensen's views were immediate and have continued only slightly abated to now. Jensen was immediately thrust into the arena of social policy by virtue of the educational implications of his proposals. Interestingly, almost all of the debate, both public and academic, focused on the technical validity of his genetic work, or the social-policy implications of the theory (Cronbach, 1975a). Remarkably little has been said about the adequacy of the theory of Level I and Level II abilities in comparison to other theories in the history of research on intelligence. In response, Jensen's later research was mainly in behavioral genetics, with less attention given to the Level I–II theory from the perspective of cognitive abilities (e.g., Jensen & Frederiksen, 1973).

Jensen's theory of Level I and Level II, then, appears to have had little impact outside of its genetic aspects. This is regrettable in some regards, for Jensen has made a substantial attempt to place his theory in perspective regarding others (Jensen, 1970), in contrast to some other investigators. Perhaps the major contribution of Jensen's theory lies in his insistence that the quantity of processing in a task, which is the discriminating feature between Level I and Level II, is an essential consideration in theory construction. In this sense, Jensen appears to be a process theorist. But as a process theory, it is at a rudimentary stage because no quantitative index of processing is available. In other regards, however, his work reflects a classical abilities approach, and appears to be little different from the early faculty school of thought. Perhaps, above all, Jensen has shown that it is unrealistic to expect that genetically based differences in intelligence can be discussed dispassionately in the public domain.

Jean Piaget

The work of Jean Piaget in many areas of psychology is so voluminous and well-known as to be referred to as a topic of study in its own right. This is particularly true in the area of cognitive development, where, in the last two decades, Piaget's research has attracted wide attention. Prior to this period, Piaget's studies in Switzerland were little known in the mainstream of psychology. The period immediately following the turn of the century was characterized largely by the debates between the hereditarian and behaviorist schools of thought, with cognitive psychology emerging as a major influence in recent decades (Hebb, 1960). It was only with the emergence of the cognitive position that attention turned to Piaget's research.

Contemporary views of Piaget's contribution to our knowledge of intelligence and cognitive development have consistently stressed the uniqueness of his theory. This feature is so notable as to create distinct varieties of research that aim to test, extend, and elaborate on Piaget's initial studies, and tend not to serve an integrative function related to other theories and research paradigms. Some exceptions to his insularity have begun to emerge recently, however, particularly in investigations of children's memory (Brown, 1975).

The differences between Piaget's position and other research is quite apparent in the contrast with psychometric views of intelligence. This contrast has led Elkind (1969, 1974) and others to suggest that the Piagetian and psychometric literature form two distinct views of the concept of intelligence and that neither of these views is likely to replace the other. Instead, the Piagetian perspective may be seen as complementary to the premises of psychometrics. Elkind (1974) elucidates these two views by identifying some of their areas of similarity and differences. Regarding similarities, Elkind notes that both the Piagetian and psychometric views of intelligence recognize the contribution of genetics to cognitive ability. For Piaget, with his historical antecedents in biology, the role of genetics in cognitive development is a natural factor to be taken into account. The psychometric view, with its roots in the tradition of Sir Francis Galton and G. Stanley Hall, has attempted to quantify the role of genetics, with this effect most prominent in the debates following Arthur Jensen's research (*Harvard Educational Review*, 1972). A second area of similarity is the fact that neither the Piagetian research nor the psychometric research is truly experimental. Piaget employed his famous clinical method in his studies, which is a technique of probing and questioning in problem-solving situations, but which is not fully standardized and lacks controls. Psychometric research typically involves examining correlational patterns between different mental measurements or between mental measurements and other variables, but does not manipulate variables in order to assess the consequences of these manipulations. Finally, the Piagetian and psychometric views appear to share a good deal of common ground in their conceptual definitions of intelligence. Both of these views place a strong emphasis on reasoning and abstraction and therefore stress the rationality of intellectual ability.

These three areas of similarity must be tempered, however, with three distinct points of difference, and indeed, these points of difference are what have precipitated the distinctiveness of the research in the Piagetian tradition. A major point of difference is in the role of genetics in the determination of cognitive development. While both the psychometric and Piagetian traditions emphasize this factor, as noted previously, the function of genetics is different in the two views. The role of genetics in Piaget's theory of cognitive development is formed predominantly by his emphasis on biological organization over time. Piaget emphasizes the gradual emergence within individuals of increasing complex cognitive structures, with this emergence facilitated in part by genetic influences. The psychometric view contrasts this by emphasizing individual differences, and specifically, by attempting to quantify the extent to which genetic factors account for measured differences in levels of intelligence. A second area of contrast is found in the chronology of cognitive development. Piaget's well-known stage theory is based on the principle that qualitatively different cognitive functions emerge with the development of the individual. The psychometric tradition, in contrast, has incorporated research on the predictability of intelligence; this emphasis on prediction is inconsistent generally with a view of cognitive functions changing over time. Finally, Piaget's research reflects a different orientation toward the nature–nurture controversy than that found in the psychometric literature. Piaget views assimilation and accommodation as the two basic processes responsible for cognitive growth, and suggests that the role of these processes is dynamic and changing. Thus, nature and nurture cannot be balanced against one another because cognitive development is an ongoing process of adaptation based on prior development. Psychometrics, on the other hand, has viewed the nature–nurture issue as a statistical problem, where nurture contributions to cognitive development are basically the balance of unaccounted variance in studies of heritability, or nature.

It is difficult to overemphasize these distinctions between Piaget's theory and research in the psychometric tradition. The fact that Piaget's theory has been contrasted with the collective work of many researchers, and found so distinctive, attests to the creativity of its originator. It is particularly interesting to note the trend of recent years toward attempts to translate Piaget's theory to psychometric definitions (Tyler, 1976). Suggestions for the future advantages of this endeavor have been made by Tuddenham (1969), although at present many technical difficulties still characterize these efforts. Perhaps, as suggested by Elkind (1974), Piaget's theory will remain as a separate model of cognitive development with its own unique advantages and limitations.

Jerome Kagan

A well-known developmental psychologist who has conducted research on many topics in child development is Jerome Kagan. Kagan's research indicates a continuing interest in the application of basic research to educational and social problems, particularly those which are most directly identified with U.S. education.

The early research on intelligence conducted by Kagan through the Fels Institute served to complement the results of the Bayley (1968) studies in knowledge of long-term change processes involved in intellectual growth (Kagan, Sontag, Baker, & Nelson, 1958). In this period, Kagan was particularly interested in the longitudinal aspects of various personality traits, such as aggressiveness, independence, initiative, and competitiveness, through their effects on intellectual development. Kagan noted that there appeared to be a functional relationship between these traits and IQ, such that children high in aggressiveness, initiative, and competitiveness are more likely to gain in IQ as they develop, whereas children highly dependent and passive tend to be characterized by decreasing IQ scores as they grow older.

This interest in personality variables as they relate to intellectual development led Kagan into research on a dimension that subsequently became known as reflectivity–impulsivity (Kagan, Moss, & Sigel, 1963; Kagan, Rosman, Day, Albert, & Phillips, 1964). Kagan noted in his earlier research that children tend to differ markedly in the time they take to respond to a problem, such that they can be classified in terms of being reflective or impulsive. This characteristic was found to affect the accuracy of responses. Later independent research revealed that the amount of attention paid to tasks constitutes a part of this dimension (Reppuci, 1969), and as more research on reflectivity–impulsivity was conducted, other interesting findings emerged. Use of different measures revealed that this tendency was quite stable across many task situations, and longitudinal research suggested a general developmental trend toward reflectiveness with increasing age. It was also found that reflective children tend to have higher IQs and experience more success in school. The extent to which reflectivity–impulsivity is causative of school success, as opposed to the converse, however, has not been settled, although several studies have used experimental designs in an attempt to clarify this (e.g., Schwebel & Bernstein, 1970).

In recent years, Kagan has become best known for his cross-cultural research (e.g., Kagan & Klein, 1973; Kagan, Klein, Haith, & Morrison, 1973). In particular, Kagan's studies of children from primitive environments in Guatemala have suggested new lines of research on the nature of cultural deprivation and retardation. In these studies, Kagan was surprised to find that apparently unstimulating environments had no long-term effects on basic abilities such as perceptual analysis and memory. Rather, children appeared to develop in response to strong maturational factors, and tended to develop adaptive skills for the environment as required. This finding was contrary to popular belief at the time, including opinions held by Kagan, for the essence of his findings was that early environment and performance were not predictive of later cognitive development. The *zeitgeist* of that period in American psychology was the contrary, based upon many major reviews (e.g., Bloom, 1964).

Kagan suggests that the implications of his cross-cultural research for the educational problems of the U.S. include a need to distinguish between culture-specific skills, which are primarily educational, and basic skills. It is often found that American culturally disadvantaged children are behind their middle-class counterparts in educational skills, and Kagan cautions that this finding should not be used to infer that the children lack basic skills, or that these basic skills will not emerge. In this sense then, Kagan's cross-cultural studies in very different milieus than the North American education system have potential contribution to the education of minority children. The future possibilities based on Kagan's research have not been identified to this point, but his studies have already served the purpose of questioning assumptions that are inherent in some approaches to the education of culturally disadvantaged children.

1.4 THE LEARNING THEORY POINT OF VIEW

It is obvious that performance in intelligence tests must be learned by the individual; the information required to answer a test item or the skill necessary to solve a problem in an intelligence test must be picked up somehow. Acquisition of skill is another name for learning. Some individuals have acquired the specific skill for answering the test items and some have not. Quite a different problem is the use of the skills; we shall not go into it here. Skills need time to be acquired, and are to be built upon subskills. Time is usually conceived of as chronological age. Given a period of 9 years from birth, a child should have acquired a certain number of cognitive skills. This indicates the level of his competence, his mental age. There are individual differences in the rate at which a child reaches the particular level. A "bright" child reaches the level common for his age earlier than an "average" child, who in turn is relatively faster than a retarded child of the same age.

Why do these individual differences exist? Does the child have the capacity, but merely cannot perform at the level required by his age? Capacity indicates something that is given, and perhaps cannot be altered. Individual differences are determined to a great extent by the experience of the individual, the history of his life. They must also depend on the biological structure, the brain with its physiological and biochemical attributes. Cognitive deficit found in the mentally retarded is certainly a structural deficit. But within the normal range of intelligence differences in "ability" reflect differences in learning and thinking.

It seems to us that assuming that "ability" differences underlie differences in performance lands us in trouble. We have advocated a "process" approach which is consistent with the view that an analysis of learning processes underlying an ability is much more useful, a view persuasively argued by Estes (1974). It is impossible to know what kinds of processes are involved in solving the test items of an intelligence test from the score on the test of the item. A relatively simple task such as digit–symbol substitution is found to involve learning skills that have not been identified fully. Estes takes this test as his example, and concludes that it could involve two types of information processing, and possibly it is mostly a verbal task.

The point that Estes makes is that an understanding of the processes underlying such "abilities" as digit–symbol substitution and vocabulary is a prerequisite for understanding intelligence. We may add that it is essential for designing any remediation program. Probably most existing programs are ad hoc in nature and are not based on a sound theoretical rationale; consequently such programs do not work efficiently.

According to Estes (1976b), learning theory and cognitive development are likely to provide the basis for understanding intelligence. Correlational studies do not explain how intelligence can be determined by learning and the individual's history of cognitive experience. Probably the role of short-term memory and long-term memory is not as important as it is made out to be by those who approach intelligence through computer simulation. How does one study intelligent behavior? One of the obvious methods has been through problem solving. But, even there, one must not limit oneself to studying this behavior as a reactive phenomenon, as a response to a problem set by the experimenter. Such an approach would be narrow, and restrict the variety which is present in intellectual behavior. According to Estes, some of the higher forms of intellectual activity are displayed in a person's capacity for producing novel organizations of information.

In thinking about the future, Estes observes a decline in the construction of refined measures of ability and an increment in the sort of research that will advance one's understanding of intellectual behavior. This trend is reflected in the work of Hunt and Carroll, which will be considered next.

Earl Hunt

Earl Hunt and his colleagues have taken his "distributed memory model" (Hunt, 1971, 1973) and applied it to the study of individual differences in intellectual abilities. They have studied the performance of university students, for whom general indices of verbal and quantitative ability were available, in a variety of laboratory tasks related to components of the memory model (Hunt, Frost, & Lunneborg, 1973; Hunt & Lansman, 1975; Hunt, Lunneborg; & Lewis, 1975).

The distributed memory model is typical of information-processing models: Incoming information is briefly stored in a series of sensory and iconic buffers, from which it can be transferred to short-, intermediate-, and long-term memories. The only slightly unusual feature of this model is the inclusion of intermediate-term memory, which is said to contain semantic codes, the current informational context, and perhaps some plan of processing action.

Hunt's research plan has been relatively simple: He has selected subjects on the basis of being in the first and fourth quartiles of verbal ability and quantitative ability, thus forming four groups of high–high, high–low, low–high, and low–low ability. Subjects from these groups are then invited to participate in laboratory experiments. Groups are then compared on the performance indices in the various experiments. Several examples might clarify his approach.

One of the tasks administered to the groups was the free recall of organized lists of words. In one condition the word lists were presented in a *blocked* fashion, that is, organized by categories, while in the other word lists were in an essentially random order. No differences were found among the four ability groups in number of words recalled, nor were there any group differences in performance in the blocked condition, when clustering should have been obvious. However, and perhaps contrary to expectations, it was found that the low-verbal subjects employed significantly more clustering than the high-verbal subjects. Whatever verbal ability as measured by Hunt is, it is inversely related to the spontaneous use by subjects of clustering strategies.

A second example from Hunt's work makes use of the Sternberg memory scanning paradigm. In this experiment, subjects are presented with a series of from one to five digits, called the *memory set*. The memory set is then removed and the subject shown a further digit, called the *probe digit*. The subject then has to respond yes or no to whether the probe digit was in the memory set. Errors are generally very low, and reaction times are used as the index of performance.

Hunt, Frost, and Lunneborg (1973) showed that there were differences between high- and low-verbal subjects in this task, particularly as the number of items in the memory set increased. High-verbal subjects were able to search the larger memory sets more quickly than low-verbal subjects.

Across a large number of tasks, Hunt and his colleagues have found two general patterns to occur. High verbal ability is associated with the speed of accessing verbal codes for letters and words, the ability to retain order information in short-term memory, and the speed with which information can be scanned or manipulated in short-term memory. The second general pattern, though less well documented, is that quantitative ability is related to the ability to resist interfering information in short-term memory tasks.

Hunt's research has been limited both by the nature of the samples tested (university students, representing a narrow range of the population) and by the nature of the ability variables studied (verbal and quantitative abilities being quite broad). His results are valuable, however, for having applied a model of cognition to individual differences phenomena.

John Carroll

John Carroll (1976) has recently taken Hunt's distributed memory model and used it to analyze subjectively tests which represent a number of more specific ability factors. His intention was to create a new structure of intellect model to replace Guilford's famous contents × operations × products cube. Carroll's hope has been to describe the traditional primary mental abilities in terms of the cognitive processes and memory stores that underlie them.

For each ability factor, Carroll noted the principal memory store involved, any cognitive processes required (such as addressing buffers or memories, or manipulation in short-term memory), and whether or not the selection of a strategy by the subject was important. Throughout the exercise his interest was not in determining which components were involved, as virtually all would be involved in all tasks, but rather the components that could be seen as responsible for producing individual differences. The result was a complex description of each factor, in which individual differences could seldom be ascribed to a single component.

Again, a couple of examples might help to clarify matters. In Carroll's system, what is normally called *spatial ability* or *spatial orientation* is dependent upon the mental rotation (an executive manipulation) of short-term memory contents (the spatial configuration). Strategies are not seen as important. Memory span tasks are also seen to involve the short-term memory store, but the executive manipulation in this case consists only of storing and retrieving items. Unlike the spatial tasks, strategies involving chunking or grouping are involved in memory span.

Associative memory tasks, generally involving paired-associate learning, require intermediate-term memory and, again, storage and retrieval operations. Strategies involving mediation or rehearsal are also important.

Factors that are generally considered of a higher level, such as verbal comprehension, induction, and reasoning, are seen by Carroll to rely extensively upon the retrieval from long-term memory of hypotheses and word meanings.

Though Carroll's efforts have been very useful and provide a new approach, there remain a number of limitations. One of these, which he mentions, is that his results do not match Hunt's findings concerning verbal and quantitative ability. While some of the mismatch may be due to Hunt's use of broader factors, Carroll would still insist that Hunt's verbal ability was primarily long-term memory dependent, instead of short-term memory related as Hunt demonstrated. This discrepancy could be explained if Hunt's results are taken to show how verbal ability was acquired, while Carroll's present how verbal ability tasks are performed at a particular time.

1.5 CONCLUDING REMARKS

The fundamental premise of this book is that intelligence and other (cognitive) individual-difference variables can and should be examined in the light of the complex cognitive constructs advanced by modern experimental psychology. Ferguson (1954) and Cronbach (1957), among others, have commented upon the need for more integration of individual-difference psychology with experimental psychology. We support this need for integration, and expect that from it will flow better, more comprehensive models of cognition, and better, more realistic theories of human abilities or intelligence.

There is no good reason why intelligence should not be seen as a cognitive construct. As was discussed in the previous sections, the early theorists in intelligence (e.g., Spearman, 1923) saw it as such. Because their theories were unsuccessful (perhaps due to poor supply of cognitive constructs from the experimentalists), attempts at theory construction were either abandoned or attenuated. As Carroll (1976) has observed, individual-difference psychology became increasingly empirical at the time when experimental psychology was realizing the need for congitive constructs. Eysenck (1967b) describes the study of intelligence as having evolved into a "testing movement," a technology divorced from psychological theory and experimentation. It is certainly not feasible to have a theory of intelligence that is separate from psychological theory, and we would suggest that even a technology of testing must be well-founded in adequate theory.

There are a variety of sources from which to draw information relevant to a theory of intelligence. The most obvious of these is the individual-differences tradition. While this tradition has not provided an adequate theory, it certainly has developed what would be considered to be a list or taxonomy of intelligent behaviors. Most of the list consists of school-related skills. In Chapter 5 the relation of simultaneous–successive processing to school achievement will be examined in some detail.

Another area which has been considered as a source for a theory of intelligence is cognitive development. The developing child is growing in mental ability, and studies that indicate what is changing during the course of cognitive development should be relevant to a theory of intelligence. We have considered the work of Piaget, Elkind, and Kagan in this context.

A contemporary theory of intelligence must also make extensive use of the constructs of modern cognitive learning psychology. Developed originally to describe memory phenomena (e.g., Atkinson & Schiffrin, 1968), these constructs include short- and long-term memory, control processes, coding and rehearsal, and can be extended to describe cognition in general. Individual differences in these components or processes should be the basis of observed individual differences in intellectual abilities. We have considered briefly the contributions of Estes, Hunt, and Carroll in this chapter.

Last, an important source for a theory of intelligence would be clinical neuropsychology. This field, which studies the functions of the various areas of the brain, is obviously relevant because it is describing the nature of the organism which is producing the intelligent actions. Those studies which concentrate on the molar brain–behavior relations, as opposed to those dealing with more molecular or neuronal analyses, are particularly useful. The model that we are proposing is derived from the work of Luria (e.g., 1973a) and will be discussed throughout the remainder of this book.

2

The Workings of the Brain

It is not always apparent that intellectual functions are firmly based on cortical and subcortical structures. Some factor analysts, such as Thurstone and Guilford, do not find it necessary to refer to the brain. Others, such as Thomson and lately Eysenck, consider intelligence in terms of its physical basis in the brain. There were good reasons for disregarding the value of information on brain functions in the earlier part of the twentieth century. Localization of functions in the brain were derived from observing a lesion in a certain part of the brain and correlating it with behavioral abnormalities, as it is done today. But there is one basic difference in the new approach. Contemporary work on localization looks for a system of functions rather than for a single function. To give an analogy in terms of a nonintellectual function, consider digestion. It is a system that depends on the orderly interaction among several physical units such as the lower end of the alimentary canal, the stomach, and the pancreas. A defect in any one of these results in the malfunction of the digestive system. One cannot study the effect on digestion of only one of these components to the exclusion of others. Thus, if a "localizer" attempts to localize digestion in only one of these components, it will result in confusion; a "mass-action theory" about digestion could be offered as a plausible alternative, but in the process the specific importance of pancreas, etc. would not be discovered. A good example of such obsessional localization is Exner's attempt to locate a functional center by minutely partitioning the cortex (Clarke &

Dewhurst, 1972, p. 117). Psychologists like Lashley rejected much of the information on brain localization and opted for a mass-action theory.

Pavlov replied to Lashley and reiterated the basic usefulness of studying localization of functions in the brain in order to understand intellectual behavior. His article (Pavlov, 1941) originally appeared in *Psychological Review* of 1932 as a reply to Guthrie and Lashley. He recognized that "it is not possible to carry out at once any far-reaching correlation between dynamic phenomena and the details of structure; but this correlation is by all means admissible . . . [Pavlov, 1941, p. 132]." There is a basic objection to the mass-action theory of brain functions—how can the highest organ of the body act in an undifferentiated manner? Pavlov takes issue with Spearman for assuming that intelligence is a function of some undifferentiated energy. He points out the absurdity of Spearman's notion by giving "an analogy to the tissue of sponges or hybroids, which being crushed and sifted through blotting cloth, afterwards when settled out or centrifuged down, forms itself anew into a mature specimen with characteristic structure [Pavlov, 1941, p. 125]."

In recent years, much understanding of intellectual functions in terms of the workings of the brain has been achieved through the collaboration of Soviet and American scientists (e.g., Pribram and Luria, 1973). The structural analysis of psychological processes has been advanced by the recognition of the dynamic nature of interaction at different depths of the cortex as well as between the depths and spread of a system of functions over a wide surface of the cortex. Luria (1973a, d) has studied the coding functions of the occipital–parietal areas and the frontotemporal areas of the brain, which are respectively related to simultaneous and successive processing. Along with this, he has delineated the functions of the frontal lobes (Luria, Chapter 1 in Pribram & Luria, 1973). We shall discuss the coding and planning functions at length in this chapter and in the following one. We have assumed that it is necessary to refer to the brain structure to understand mental functions, even though our behavioral research is not directly related to neuropsychology. But, through such an assumption, we can understand why "apparently identical psychological processes can be distinguished and apparently different forms of mental activity can be reconciled [Luria, 1973d, p. 41]." First, let us consider some basic features of Soviet research, specifically in neuropsychology.

2.1   SOVIET PSYCHOLOGY

Sokolov was invited to write a chapter on brain functions for the *Annual Review of Psychology*, 1977. His chapter, in a sense, is indicative of the acceptance of Soviet physiological psychology by American psychology. An increasing amount of collaborative work by Soviet and American psychologists has appeared in recent years, giving the impression that psychological science is one, in spite of national differences in emphasis (Das, 1976). Sokolov demonstrates his mastery of the literature published in the West, as a contributor to the *Annual Review of Psychology* should. The same comprehensive grasp of Western psychological work is evidenced by Luria (1973d) in the book *The Working Brain*. In spite of the similarity of current Soviet psychology to that of the West, one should be aware of some of its basic characteristics. The work of Luria, the central focus in this chapter, will be better understood if we know the peculiarities of Soviet psychology.

Preoccupation with physiology is evident in most of Soviet psychology. A commitment to neural interpretations of the most complex behaviors (e.g., consciousness) is undoubtedly present. But as Razran (1965) points out, this is not a feature unique to Soviet psychology. Hebb and Neal Miller demonstrate a similar commitment: Miller's research on interoceptive conditioning, the conditioning of visceral organs, could be considered as an extension of Pavlov's work. More recently, Pribram (1971) has shown a strong bias toward neural interpretation; his book *Languages of the Brain* is an instance of this.

The behavior in question is human behavior, the activity of higher nervous processes. The object of the Soviet research is to understand the mental rather than the neural phenomena. The Soviets are well aware of the dangers inherent in devoting too much emphasis to the neural aspects. This would result in the formulation of crude connections between the neural and mental events and thus would severely limit the value of neural interpretations. Such an emphasis would also restrict the range of mental events studied: Only very simple events would be selected for neurophysiological investigation. Luria's work is a good example of the breadth of psychological functions that are studied by the Soviets.

> It is evident that man lives in a world of objects which he perceives and that he receives information regarding the experience of generations of other individuals; he is capable of conscious, willed activity which distinguishes him from animals. Man sets himself goals, formulates plans and programmes for his behavior, regulates his actions, controls them as they proceed and corrects his mistakes [Luria, 1973d, p. 72].

These are the "higher nervous activities," legitimate topics of concern to the psychologist. These are also typically human.

What is unique about human mental processes is the use of language. The verbal, or second, signalling system is regarded as a characteristic evolutionary development that separates man from animals. Whereas animals are mainly guided by primary signals, or direct perceptions, man functions largely in a world of second signals, of words and other symbols that are signals of the primary signals. These ideas are attributed to Pavlov, who wrote:

> The developing animal world on reaching the phase of man acquired an exceptional supplement to the mechanism of nervous activity . . . words have built up a second system of signalling reality, which is only peculiar to us, being a signal of the primary signals. The numerous stimulations by words have . . . removed us from reality. . . . On the other hand, it was nothing other than words which has made us human . . . [Pavlov, 1941, p. 179].

An example of how the Pavlovian notion of a second signal system has been carried forward in contemporary Soviet psychology is to be found in Voronin (1973). He makes a distinction between those "conditioned connections," or as we would say, learned behaviors, that are mediated by language, and those that are not. Conditioned responses in animals are obviously not verbally mediated. These are unstable conditioned responses, subject to the laws of reinforcement and practice. Above these (see Figure 2.1) are the "stable conditioned connections," which are verbally mediated. The mediation may be covert, the type which Spence was studying in his later years and which has led to the work on semantic conditioning.

At a higher level are the "combined conditioned connections." Because of verbal mediation, discrete habits can be combined in a set. When the need arises, transfer of learning takes place. Of course, animals demonstrate transfer of learning, but theirs cannot be as versatile as man's. Man uses previous learning in a new situation so competently only with the aid of verbal mediation.

The highest form of activity according to Voronin (and any other psychologist) is abstract–logical association or thinking. "These associations, in the form of specific rules, laws, and logarithms, are formed as a result of directly acquired personal and general experience transmitted to individual from generation to generation . . . usually referred to as conscious activity [Voronin, 1973, p. 107]." Much of Luria's research, to be discussed in this and the next chapter, is in the area of intellectual functions (which Voronin calls *abstract logical association*). Thus, in the evolution of higher mental processes, language has an important role. It separates animal from human behavior. This is schematically presented in Figure 2.1. The shadowed areas indicate verbally mediated responses.

Besides the two major characteristics of Soviet psychology just described, preoccupation with physiology and emphasis on language, we can think of two additional features: a historical rather than a purely biological

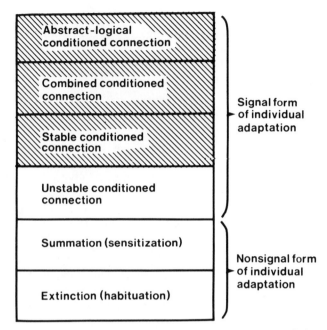

Figure 2.1. Voronin's conditioned response model of higher mental functions. (After Voronin, 1973.)

view of mental functions, and the importance given to the practical implications of any scientific work.

Vygotsky is largely responsible for the view that man's higher mental functions have a social rather than a biological origin. In agreement with Marxist thinking, Luria and other contemporary psychologists have assumed this as a major premise. Developmental changes in childhood certainly have a biological basis. But as the child gets to be an adolescent, and the adolescent an adult, his experience in the context of his social milieu assumes an increasing importance, influencing not only the content of his thinking but also the structure of his thought. Luria paraphrases Vygotsky's views on this as follows: "In order to understand the substance of higher psychological processes in man, it is necessary to go beyond the limits of the organism and to search for the roots of these complex processes in the historically formed environment, in the communication of the child with the adults, in the objective relations among objects, tools and language which have been laid down in the course of social history [Luria, 1971, p. 260]." Language and modes of thinking, when acquired "spontaneously," reflect the interactions that the child had with adults and the experiences that occurred during the course of his development. Herein lies the significance for education; it should be deliberate, and designed to facilitate learning. If the child happens to have a cognitive deficit, one has to give him the opportunity to interact with adults and to be taught through deliberate instruction. At the end of this, his improvement must be checked. Indeed this is the method adopted for separating the truly retarded from the "temporarily backward" children. Inherent in such an orientation is the assumption that cognitive competence can be improved, while recognizing the existence of biological limitations. The extent of biological versus social influence may vary according to the stage of development. Lomov (1971) outlines the relationship between the two in a position paper on the official policy of Soviet psychology as follows: "Obviously the correlation between biological and social factors should not be viewed abstractly, but only in the context of the different mental levels and different stages of human development. There is most likely no simple solution to the question; it admits of different solutions for different levels of development [Lomov, 1971, p. 357]." This orientation is certainly a flexible one, and not many Western psychologists would quarrel with it.

Last, Soviet psychology like other Soviet sciences, is not divorced from society. Psychology in particular is one of the sciences which has direct applications: Research into cognitive functions is constantly applied to problems of intellectual efficiency (creativity, talent searches) and deficiency (mental retardation, neurological impairment). The need for practical application determines the choice of the research topics. Brain–behavior relations have to be understood because of their myriad applications or potential for application. Practice also improves theory—practical problems compel the psychologist to take a rigorous approach toward the construction of psychological theory about mental functions (Lomov, 1971).

In conclusion, it is perhaps necessary to point out how the first three major concerns of Soviet psychology just described have aided in the application of psychological knowledge about mental function to the encouragement of cognitive competence and the remediation of deficits (the fourth major concern). First, a neural base for higher mental functions is assumed; this has led to a search for structural defects. Such defects are not always discovered, but the root of the defect is assumed to lie in the structure. Second, the importance given to language is justified because the functional properties of neural structures can be controlled or influenced by verbal instructions. A restitutive program for lost function can be established by training which has a strong verbal component; even visceral functions can be verbally conditioned. The third concern, for the historical determinants of behavior, is due to the recognition of the role of experience and training in the modification of even biologically predisposed functions, and often suggests predagogical intervention. Neither the presence of an ability nor its loss or absence is immune to change. A number of complex activities are needed to fulfill a certain function, such as the simultaneous coding of incoming information, but these functions can be fulfilled in a variety of ways, some acquired through past experience and others developed through rehabilitative training.

2.2 THE THREE BLOCKS OF THE BRAIN

Luria has described in some detail the three functional units of the brain. The earlier descriptions (1966a, 1966b) were given along with copious case histories of dysfunctions brought about by lesions in the brain. His later accounts (1969, 1970, 1973d), however, are relatively theoretical. The three blocks of the brain are concerned, respectively, with arousal, coding, and planful behavior (see Figure 2.2). The blocks are functional systems, scattered throughout large parts of the brain, and their location is determined by observing the complex interactions among the various cortical zones.

A word about functional systems: Any complex activity is undertaken to fulfill a certain function, by whatever means possible. Until the function is fulfilled (for example, the recall of a list of words), the activity continues. The task for the neuropsychologist, then, is to identify the processes which are characteristic of certain zones in the brain and determine their interactions. Since the interactions are extremely complex and the same function may be fulfilled in many ways, the task of locating the functions precisely is a difficult one. With this introduction, we shall summarize the salient features of the three functional units. For a readable account of the blocks, see Luria (1970).

Mental activity depends upon the participation of the three functional units described by Luria (1973d) as "a unit for regulating tone or waking, a unit for obtaining, processing and storing information . . . and a unit for programming, regulating and verifying mental activity [p. 43]." Furthermore, each unit is hierarchical in structure. At least three cortical zones, one upon the other, are assumed to control the functions of the unit. These are the primary, or projection areas; the secondary, or projection–association areas (where incoming information is processed); and finally, the tertiary areas, or as Luria has called them, the zones of overlapping (responsible in man for the most complex forms of mental activity). The tertiary areas require the concerted participation of many cortical areas.

Block 1 or Unit 1 is concerned with regulating the tone and maintaining

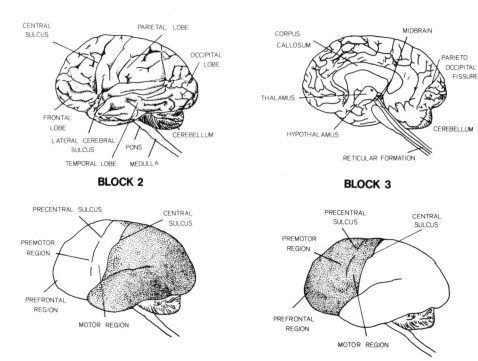

Figure 2.2. The three blocks of the brain. (From The functional organization of the brain by A. F. Luria. Copyright 1970 by Scientific American, Inc. All rights reserved.)

the waking state of the cortex, a function that is necessary for optimal cortical activity. This unit includes the upper and lower brain stem, the reticular formation, and the hippocampus. Any damage to this unit will produce marked changes in behavior such as disturbances in arousal levels. The optimal level of cortical tone is maintained through the mediation of the reticular formation. Luria describes the ascending and descending reticular systems, respectively, as concerned with activating the cortex and subordinating the lower structures in the brain to the control of the program arising in the cortex. He relates the functions of Unit 1 to the Pavlovian ideas of excitation and inhibition. Pavlov suggested that the nervous processes have three main characteristics: their strength, balance, and lability. Strength refers to the strength of either excitation or inhibition; the nervous system may be strong or weak. Similarly if it is dominated either by excitation or by inhibition it is characterized as unbalanced. Furthermore, the ease with which inhibition is replaced by excitation, and vice versa, is an indication of the lability or mobility of nervous processes (Pavlov, 1928). Pavlov also concluded that sleep is a spreading of inhibition and hypnosis a special state of inhibition. Luria refers to all of these and locates the source of excitation and inhibition in the reticular system.

Associated with excitation or inhibition is the orienting response, a response often indexed electrophysiologically to the disparity between the model of a stimulus which the brain has and the stimulus itself. If there is no mismatch then the orienting response is not evoked.

Activation or arousal appears to be one of the prime functions of the lower part of the brain, and it is by no means unimportant. Luria points out that the frontal lobes, which are concerned with programming and planning behavior, depend a great deal on the reticular formation. In its turn excitation or inhibition is controlled verbally during man's conscious activity. In sum, Unit 1 supplies the energy for all sorts of conscious and unconscious mental activities, and in turn is guided by complex cognitive processes such as intentions, plans, and programs. To quote Luria, "the *systems of the first functional unit not only maintain cortical tone but also themselves experience the differentiating influence of the cortex, and the first functional unit of the brain works in close cooperation with the higher levels of the cortex* [Luria, 1973d, p. 67; emphasis in original]."

The second functional unit is involved in the obtaining, processing, and storing of information. It is situated in the posterior regions of the neocortex, which include the occipital, temporal, and parietal lobes. As in all units, a hierarchical arrangement of cortical areas exists in this unit. The primary projection zones receive information and analyze it into elementary components. The secondary or projective association zones further organize the material and code it. The tertiary zones where information from various sources overlaps are essentially amodal. They are organized to form the basis of complex behavior.

We shall describe the tertiary zones in some detail. Within these zones the cortical ends of various sensory receptors overlap. These zones are responsible for the integration of sensory material which has already been coded. They lie on the boundary between the occipital, temporal, and post-central cortex. Their greater part is formed by the inferior parietal regions, which, in man, have developed to a considerable size occupying just about one-quarter of the total mass of the functional system which is the second unit, and can be considered as uniquely human. Obviously the occipito–parietal zones analyze information spatially, transforming successively arriving stimuli into simultaneously processed groups. Luria assigns substantial importance to the tertiary zones. He holds them responsible for the comprehension of logical-grammatical sentence structure and for the converting of concrete perception into abstract thinking. As mentioned before, the tertiary zones are not modality specific. In fact, according to what Luria calls the "law of diminishing specificity," the lower zones have maximum specificity in terms of modality. As we go up on the hierarchy, the last or the tertiary zones are more or less free of information tagged on the basis of modality. By the very nature of these zones of overlapping, the tertiary zones have to be supramodal. They are principally concerned with the coding of simultaneous and successive information.

To summarize, the second functional system is hierarchical (subdivided into primary, secondary, and tertiary zones). It works according to the principle of diminishing modal specificity, and lastly, it demonstrates increasing functional lateralization. The last point is that progressive lateralization of functions occurs as one progresses from the primary cortical areas through the secondary to the tertiary area. Luria has observed that higher functions such as speech illustrate the degree of lateralization of functions. The functions of the secondary and tertiary zones of the left hemisphere start to differ radically from those of the right hemisphere in right-handed people.

Later in this book we will touch on the relationship between simultaneous–successive processing and hemisphere dominance. It should be pointed out here that Luria is quite aware of the differences in function between the two hemispheres; in fact, it is impossible to ignore this difference when working with patients who have lesions in both hemispheres. For instance, Luria mentions that if the lesions are in the primary zone, the left–right difference is not seen. However, when these are in the secondary and tertiary zones, the differences in functions become quite apparent.

The third block of the brain, or Unit 3, is responsible for the planning and programming of behavior. It is located in the frontal lobes, or more specifically, in the anterior regions, anterior to the precentral gyrus. The outlet channel for this unit is the motor cortex, and Luria describes at length how the three zones of this unit—primary, secondary, and tertiary—are differentially related to the control and regulation of motor programs. As in the other units, the primary zone is modality specific whereas the second and third zones are not. The most important part of the third unit, according to Luria, is the prefrontal division of the brain. "It is these portions of the brain belonging to the third zone of the cortex that play a decisive role in the formation of intentions and program and in the regulation and vertification of the most complex forms of human behavior [Luria, 1973d, p. 84]." The pre-frontal region, by its anatomical nature, is in a favorable position, both for the reception and integration of the complex system of afferent impulses arising from all parts of the brain and for the organization of efferent impulses so that they can regulate all these structures. As mentioned before, the frontal lobes are also connected with the ascending and descending tracts of the reticular formation; they regulate conscious action, maintain vigilance, and realize programmed actions. They are also deeply engaged in constructing plans and strategies. Damage to the frontal lobes is immediately apparent in the random pattern of visual search in which the subject engages while scanning for information in a search task. The frontal lobes are closely related to a person's ability to carry out instructions, especially of the verbal kind. It is only natural that the frontal lobes are deeply involved in the control of behavior through speech, because plans and programs of action are verbally mediated. Luria attributes to the frontal lobes the highest function of the brain, the supervision of all conscious activity. To summarize in Luria's words, *"the frontal lobes not only perform the function of synthesis of external stimuli, preparation for action, and formation of programs, but also the function of allowing for the effect of the action carried out and verification that it has taken the proper course* [Luria, 1973d, p. 93; emphasis in original]." The functions of the frontal lobe are described in much greater detail in the book edited by Pribram and Luria (1973).

This brings us to the conclusion of a summary treatment of Luria's three units of the brain. It is perhaps in order to speculate here about the relationship between intelligence and these three units. The first unit is really associated with motivation. The important role motivation plays in any performance including intellectual performance need not be emphasized here. What must be mentioned, however, is that motivation or, specifically, arousal level should be appropriate to the task at hand. The old Yerkes–Dodson law neatly describes for us the interaction between arousal level and the level of difficulty of a task. It provides a rudimentary example of the interaction that must exist between arousal and cognitive performance. Concepts that are relevant to intellectual behavior are attention, drive, reflection–impulsivity, all of which are in some way primarily related to the first unit of the brain. The second unit is essentially concerned with coding. Coding behavior features prominently in all intelligence tests. The coding is of two kinds, simultaneous and successive, which we will discuss in detail in the next chapter.

Adult intelligence tests, however, are mostly concerned with verbal efficiency, what Vernon calls the "verbal educational factor." We would like to suggest that the third unit of the brain is as much responsible for the so-called verbal–educational efficiency as the coding unit. However, we are aware that intelligence tests only tangentially measure the functions of the third unit of the brain; planning behavior and the ability to carry out a program of action that has been formulated. Insofar as standard intelligence tests do not measure these important functions, they are unlikely to measure the intellectual potential of the brain. The frontal lobes are the most important part of man's brain; they occupy one-third of the area, were last to evolve, and have unique anatomical structures that are found only among human beings. Their functions should be measured by a comprehensive test of cognitive competence.

2.3   RELATION TO INTELLIGENCE

Luria's neuropsychological view of brain function does not give any simple answers about where intelligence would lie in such a model, or about what would be a good test of intelligence. In fact, in the Marxist tradition, Luria might even deny the reality of such a concept.

If pressed for an answer, Luria would be likely to reply that the overall functioning of the brain is dependent upon all of the brain and all of the functioning systems of the brain. His clinical methods, therefore, are aimed at determining possible functional weaknesses (perhaps due to brain damage) in specific systems that might manifest themselves in more general performance deficits. As a result, he administers a variety of tests to each individual to determine the pattern of success and failure in that subject. This is in contrast to Western psychologists who administer a number of tests to a large number of subjects to discover the average pattern of results (i.e., factor structure). Luria refers to his method as *syndrome analysis*.

The patterns of response that Luria observes in his data can thus correspond to the factors found in a Western factor analysis. They have the added benefit, however, of being directly relatable to neurophysiological structures. In this case, questions about the reality of the constructs represented by the factors seldom occur. The occurrence of a clinically observed pattern in a large number of subjects (factor analysis) argues for the generality of such patterns; the finding of a clinical pattern that resembles the results of a factor analysis aids in validating the reality of the constructs represented in that factor analysis.

It should be noted, however, that it is in principle unlikely that large-scale studies of normal individuals will always resemble in-depth studies of brain-damaged individuals. Tests which discriminate among the brain damaged may often be too simple to discriminate among even normal children. Even more importantly, there is no simple way of knowing that the causes of a brain-damaged person's failure to perform a task are the same as those which prevent a normal person from completing the task.

With these qualifications, it can be said that in general form Luria's conception of intelligence would be like the multifactorial conceptions of recent psychometricians: Some actions may be dependent upon relatively specific functional systems (factors), but a view of the entire functioning brain (i.e., all factors, including higher-order ones) is necessary to obtain an understanding of general performance (intelligence).

In substance, however, Luria's view is radically different in that it is process-oriented. Luria would see most responses as the result of a set or sequence of processes: Behavior would depend upon the action of all of these processes. The neurophysiologist can become very aware of this feature of brain function, because he can observe the damaging effects upon behavior of any break in the sequence. Messick (1973) has supported a similar view of the determinants of behavior (i.e., behavior is produced by a sequence of processes), and has noted that such sequences of processes are unlikely to emerge from a factor analysis.

Perhaps a better way of relating Luria's model to intelligence is to investigate the damaging effects on performance which are caused by weaknesses in the various components and processes that he identifies. While such weaknesses are most obvious in the brain damaged, they may also exist as individual differences in normals. These are most easily classified in relation to the three functional blocks of the brain.

Block 1. An appropriate level of arousal is required for any task, and deviations from this optimal level in either direction decrease performance (the Yerkes–Dodson law). Inappropriate arousal (whether it be habitual or situation-specific) intereferes with attentional processes, affects the processing which occurs in Block 2, and can produce a deterioration in the planning function of Block 3. The impact of different levels of arousal upon behavior is being increasingly studied in psychology, with particular emphasis on the mediating concept of attention. For instance, it has been suggested that children with "learning disabilities" may largely be suffering from difficulties with selective attention (Ross, 1976) which in turn is related to arousal level. Perhaps the most studied behavioral dimension of arousal is impulsivity–reflectivity. Impulsives are more likely to be diagnosed as hyperactive, to have less ability to attend, to use poorer scanning and problem-solving strategies, to use self-guiding private speech less often, and to do worse in school than those with a lower level of behavioral arousal (reflectives) (see Messer, 1976, for a recent review of this area). Thus many of the components of current concepts of intelligence are susceptible to the influences of arousal, as is that which intelligence is intended to predict (school achievement). These issues will be discussed more fully with particular reference to school achievement in Chapter 4, and to the learning disabled and mentally retarded in Chapter 6.

Block 2. The individual's responses are based upon information that has been processed and stored (in either a long- or short-term fashion) in this system. The two forms of processing, simultaneous and successive, that take place in this second functional block are required in different degrees to perform all tasks. Should an individual not be competent at one form of processing (a Block 2 problem) or not employ the more efficient form of processing (a Block 3 problem), performance will suffer. Later chapters will provide a number of examples of tasks that suffer from deficits in either form of processing, and examples of ways to circumvent these deficits.

Block 3.   The planning and decision-making function of Block 3 is most obviously related to the Western concept of intelligence as "adaptive functioning," but it is also the function that is least well represented in Western tests of intelligence. This third functional system is important because it coordinates the sequence of operations upon which intellectual responses are based. Performance will deteriorate if an inefficient sequence of operations (i.e., an inefficient strategy) is chosen, or if a particular plan is too rigid or insensitive to environmental changes.

3

A Model of Simultaneous and Successive Processing

3.1 ROOTS OF THE MODEL

Simultaneous and successive integration are not new concepts. These were distinctly present in Sechenov's writings, prominently in *The Elements of Thought,* which was published in 1878. We trace here their history.

We shall start with Sechenov, then refer to Kant's categories of space and time. Finally, a somewhat detailed description of simultaneous and successive processes based on Luria's research will be presented.

Sechenov begins with sensation and attempts to show that it not only provides a basis for thinking as sensory psychologists would advocate, but it is itself organized by the psychological structure of the individual. Both nativism and empiricism are implied in sensory processing. Consider visual sensation as an example. Helmholtz, who had deeply influenced the physiology of vision and hearing in Sechenov's time, tended to support an empiricist rather than a nativist view of visual perception. He minimized, if not denied, the role of experience. For Sechenov, it was impossible to separate the inborn from the acquired features of any perception or, for that matter, behavior. An innate scheme or organization is a form without the content of experience; at the same time, the sensory experience has to be coded and organized into some form. Because of an interaction between form and content, perception undergoes ontogenetic changes. An evolutionary process underlies such changes; and here Sechenov borrows the idea of Herbert Spencer. But is the organization present at the first sensation which, according to the empiricists, falls on the clean slate, the mind? According to Sechenov, it is impossible to treat the mind as a tabula rasa. There would already exist some organization or structure in the mind, even if it were possible to tag the arrival of the first visual sensation.

The nativist, Herbert Spencer, had argued that the visual apparatus at birth came complete with a full-blown organ for spatial vision. Sechenov's point was that such a capacity must unfold itself through visual experience. Auditory experience follows a similar course. The auditory receptor and its cortical projection area develop the capacity for temporal perception gradually. The potential for spatial and temporal organizations are present at birth, although there is little sense in speculating on the form in which it is present; form without content cannot be understood.

Perception of simultaneity and succession are specific to distinct receptors and their projection areas, together called *analyzers* in Soviet physiology. Of all the external receptors, the eye occupies the largest projection space in the cortex; it is, along with touch (and kinesthesis), responsible for spatial organization of sense data. Similarly, the auditory and motor regions, later called the *frontotemporal zone,* are responsible for temporal organization—of not only sound but of movements. One is reminded by Sechenov that all stimuli have to be decomposed and then synthesized into spatial or temporal form; they do not arrive in an already organized manner. Thus, when a person is asked to copy a figure, he/she must analyze it, and then recognize the spatial organization that represents the figure. Although the figure is presented in the spatial dimension, first analysis then synthesis have to be performed. Similarly, when one is asked to reproduce a string of digits in the order of its presentation, there is no straight copying of the order. The digits are discrete events which must be put together in a successive order. We wish to emphasize this elementary fact about simultaneous and successive synthesis, because, as will be shown in subsequent sections of the book, false inferences are often drawn by ignoring this. For instance, it could be wrongly argued that successive synthesis is easier than simultaneous because it needs little or no transformation of the stimulus material.

Sechenov was much more concerned with spatial than temporal ordering because, as he has mentioned in *The Elements of Thought,* so little was known about auditory perception. Subsequently, temporal or successive processing has become quite important; its relation to language and speech has compelled later investigators to understand it better. In this connection, we would like to mention Lashley's (1951) concern with serial order.

Lashley rejects the associative chain theory which states that individual responses in any serially ordered behavior are under the control of proprioceptive feedback from the immediately preceding responses. Instead, he suggests that serial ordering is determined by a generalized, central, integrative process which is largely independent of the events which are to be ordered. He writes that sequential learning may be a prerequisite to the development of symbolic representations, because of its close connection with verbal behavior. Anticipating Luria's conclusions from clinical research and the amodality of tertiary zones, he describes how it is difficult to distinguish between spatial and temporal functions in visual perception. The following quotation from Lashley highlights the flexibility of what the Soviet psychologists call zones of overlapping connections. "Spatial and temporal order thus appear to be almost completely interchangeable in cerebral action. The translation from the spatial distribution of memory traces to temporal sequence seems to be a fundamental aspect of the problem of serial order [Lashley, 1951, p. 114]."

The other point Lashley makes is that it is difficult to ascertain whether spatial or temporal ordering is the primary one. Much of memory is spatially organized and yet for even simple reproduction to occur it is essential to translate the images of memory into a serial order for their recall. For our discussion in regard to the hierarchy of simultaneous and successive processing, which is to be presented later, Lashley's observation is an important one to remember. It shows again, as Sechenov had done, that serial (or successive) ordering is no less complex than spatial (or simultaneous) organization.

Immanuel Kant (Smith, 1933) conceived of spatial and temporal organizations as extrinsic to sensory data, as something the mind imposes on stimuli. The outer world supplies the stimuli, but our own mental structure orders them in space and time. Kant, like Sechenov, admits the relevance of sense experience. Without sense experience we cannot perceive color, taste, smell, sound, or touch. But we cannot "think" about them unless they are ordered spatially or temporally. One of Kant's quotable quotes is that thoughts without content are empty and intuitions without concepts are blind. In Kant's view, simultaneous ordering is present in understanding figures and their relations. Successive ordering is apparent when we order events or objects one after another. It has only one dimension, unlike simultaneous organization in which one can think of several dimensions at the same time. According to Kant, successive ordering is critical for understanding motion. Sechenov, the physiologist, has the same view—the frontotemporal zone is concerned with movements and sound perception.

Simultaneous and successive processing are forms of coding behavior; they are "understanding" in Kant's system. They are beyond sensory experience, and thus do not inhere in the object. Luria and Sechenov would agree with Kant in this respect. Beyond coding are planning and decision making. We have discussed the possible localization of these cognitive functions in Unit 3 of the brain (Chapter 2). In Kant's writing, "judgment" comes closest to planning functions. He recognized three *cognitive* as opposed to *perceptual* functions. These are understanding, judgment, and reasoning. Of these, judgment is the highest, a faculty in itself. Its task is to explain analytically, without reference to sense experience, the form of knowledge which is found in concepts and syllogisms. Judgment is mainly concerned with the application of rules that the individual has in his repertoire. A specialist such as a physician may have a great deal of knowledge about pathological conditions. This knowledge may exist only in abstraction. When it comes to the application of the knowledge or rule to a specific case, the physician may show good judgment or may commit an error.

It is interesting to note that Kant equates stupidity with defective judgment. Though understanding can be improved through remedial instruction, judgment cannot be taught. We would like to quote the following paragraph from Kant before passing on to a further elaboration of judgment and its relation to Luria's Unit 3 of the brain.

> Deficiency in the faculty of judgement is what we call stupidity, and there is no remedy for that. An obtuse and narrow mind, deficient in nothing but a proper degree of understanding and correct concepts, may be improved by study, so far as to become even learned. But as even then there is often a deficiency in judgement we often meet with very learned men, who in handling their learning betray that original deficiency which can never be mended [Max-Muller, 1966, p. 119n.].

Contemporary teaching technology has made it possible to teach the retarded a great number of vocational skills and, to a lesser extent, academic skills which until recently were beyond the grasp of the retarded individual. But the mentally retarded remain retarded and often are inferior to their mental-age-matched normal counterparts. Could the difference be due to judgment differences that cannot be removed through instruction?

To return to the possible location of judgment, the frontal lobes are probably a logical place to consider. Frontal lobes express their function through the motor cortex; in Chapter 2 we discussed this. Thus, decisions and plans, and the ability to carry out activities already programmed by the individual are certainly related to action and the evaluation of the feedback from the response after its execution. Judgment is also closely associated with action and the evaluation of the effect of activity. A parallel between the functions of the frontal lobe and judgment is suggested. It is an intriguing suggestion.

3.2 THE MODEL

We have proposed a model of information integration based on Luria's simultaneous and successive processes. Luria has derived these notions from Sechenov, as mentioned earlier. In the early conceptualization of the two processes, the simultaneous process was very closely associated with vision and touch (kinesthesia), and the successive process with hearing and movement. Sechenov did mention that the region where the occipital and parietal lobes overlap can cope with much more complex information than the information which is processed by the respective lobes. Similarly, the overlapping temporal and frontal regions can handle complex information. The lobes themselves—occipital, parietal, and temporal—process information obtained from visual, tactile, and auditory perception, respectively.

Luria has certainly moved away from this simple conceptualization. With the delineation of a hierarchy of functions within each cortical region—the primary, secondary, and tertiary zones—Luria considers that the information processed at the secondary, and certainly at the tertiary, level is amodal. As an example, arithmetic problem-solving is regarded as simultaneous processing because lesions in the occipital–parietal lobe result in acalculia. Similarly, problem-solving, which requires discursive thinking—putting the thoughts in a coherent verbal frame—is processed in the fronto–temporal lobe. The first, as an example of simultaneous and the second of successive, cannot be identified with specific modalities of visual, auditory, or tactile perception.

What follows is a description of the essential features of a model of cognitive processes that we first proposed in a comprehensive manner in 1975. It is best to quote a portion of what we wrote at that time.

> Simultaneous integration refers to the synthesis of separate elements into groups, these groups often taking on spatial overtones. The essential nature of this sort of processing is that any portion of the result is at once surveyable without dependence upon its position in the whole. It is hypothesized by Luria that simultaneous syntheses are of the following three varieties. (a) Direct perception: The process of perception is such that the organism is selectively attentive to the stimulus input in the brain. According to Luria, this type of formation is primarily spatial, even in the case of the acoustic analyzer. (b) Mnestic processes: This refers to the organization of stimulus traces from earlier experience. Examples of this type of integration are the construction of the gestalt of a visual image by the subject when portions of the image are shown consecutively, and the organization of consecutively presented words into a group on the basis of a criterion. The stimulus traces or, as we should refer to them, memory traces, can be either short-term or long-term, and the integration of the traces is performed on the basis of criteria which can be specified either by the organism or an external source. (c) The last variety of synthesis is found in complex intellectual processes. In order for the human organism to grasp systems of relationships, it is necessary that the components of the systems be represented simultaneously. In this fashion, the relationships among components can be explored and

determined. Luria notes that the use of spatial presentation of the components is an aid in this process, for when a unitary representation of components is formed, the system is readily surveyable. . . .

Successive information processing refers to processing of information in a serial order. The important distinction between this type of information processing and simultaneous processing is that in successive processing the system is not totally surveyable at any point in time. Rather, a system of cues consecutively activates the components. As in simultaneous processing, successive synthesis has three varieties: perceptual, mnestic, and complex intellectual. According to Luria, the most obvious example of the last variety of successive processing is human speech. The structure of grammar is such that the processing of syntactical components is dependent upon their sequential relationships within sentence structure. Thus, grammatical structures which have to be understood in terms of their relationships are affected by disturbance of simultaneous synthesis, whereas sequential structures are affected by successive synthesis.

In computing terms, the sensory register is a buffer. [See Figure 3.1.] Any time information is transmitted, one could consider the question of serial or parallel transmission. One could speculate about this in terms of information from the sensory register to the central processor. The relationship between the sensory register and the central processing unit can be conceptualized in two ways. The central processor interrogates the buffer to see if anything is there, and if so allows a transmission to be made. Alternatively, the buffer interrupts the processor and forces it to accept information. The latter would occur more frequently, perhaps, because sensory information cannot be delayed.

The central processing unit has three major components: that which processes separate information into simultaneous groups, that which processes discrete information into temporally organized successive series, and the decision-making and planning component which uses the information so integrated by the other components. The processing in these components is not affected by the form of the sensory input—visual information can be processed successively and auditory information can be processed simultaneously.

The model assumes that the two modes of processing information are available to the individual. The selection of either or both modes depends on two conditions: (1) the individual's habitual mode of processing information as determined by social–cultural and genetic factors, and (2) the demands of the task.

The third component, which could be labeled thinking, uses coded information and determines the best possible plan for action. Perhaps it is also crucial for the emergence of causal thinking, which Hess (1967) describes as "an integrative activity which brings simultaneous and successive patterns of nervous excitation into a subjectively meaningful frame of reference [p. 1283]."

Both simultaneous and successive processing can be involved in all forms of responding. This is the case irrespective of the method of input presentation. Perhaps Lashley's (1951) work is relevant to the decoding or behavioral part in serial tasks. Serial ordering of behavior may not depend on either the manner in which information was coded or the motor aspects of the behavior itself. The output unit, then, determines and organizes performance in accordance with the requirements of the task. For example, in memory tasks a subject may be required to recall serially or recall the items in categories supplied by the experimenter; thus, appropriate output organization is necessary.[1]

---

[1]From J. P. Das, J. Kirby, and R. F. Jarman. Simultaneous and successive synthesis: An alternative model for cognitive abilities. *Psychological Bulletin*, 1975, *82*. Copyright 1975 by the American Psychological Association. Reprinted by permission.

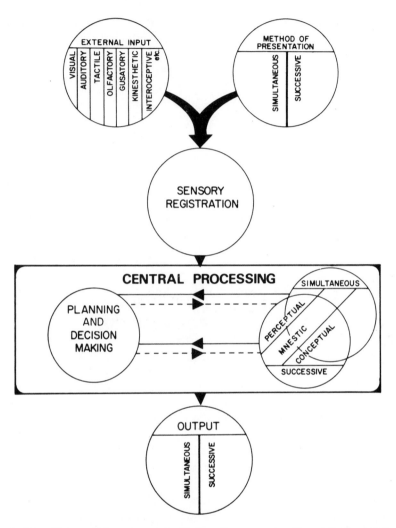

Figure 3.1. Diagram of the components of information processing. (From J. P. Das, J. Kirby, & R. F. Jarman. Simultaneous and successive synthesis: An alternative model for cognitive abilities. *Psychological Bulletin*, 1975, *82*. Copyright 1975 by the American Psychological Association. Reprinted by permission.)

3.3 MEASURES OF THE TWO PROCESSES

Subsequent chapters will consider a number of studies that have involved operationalizations of the concepts just described. Because we are not dealing with brain-damaged subjects, it will be important to realize that we are talking about these constructs as dimensions of individual variation.

Successive processing, for instance, does not either exist or not exist in some particular individual: It is a process in which individuals will vary in adeptness, though intra-individual differences should be small.

Before describing the tests that have been used to measure simultaneous and successive processing, it is important to note that these are construed as tests of those processes, not as tests of the ability to employ those processes optimally. This latter skill, involved in what are referred to as strategies, plans, or programs, is more accurately a function of the third unit of the brain.

In the studies conducted so far with non-brain-damaged individuals, the most commonly used tests of simultaneous processing have been: Raven's Coloured Progressive Matrices (Raven, 1956), Figure Copying (Ilg & Ames, 1964), and Memory-for-Designs (Graham & Kendall, 1960). While Raven's Matrices were originally intended as a culture-free measure of reasoning ability, and are still sometimes used as such (e.g., Cattell, 1971), they fulfill the requirements for a test of simultaneous processing in that their solution requires the construction of a spatial pattern or scheme. Only after such a scheme has been formed can the option which correctly completes the pattern be chosen. Our research (Kirby & Das, 1978a, 1978b) has shown this test to be more related to spatial ability than reasoning, a relationship that is maintained when Raven's Matrices are broken down into several subscales.

In Figure Copying, the subject is required to copy a geometric figure which is pictured on the same page (see Appendix, pp. 210–211). While a variety of strategies are possible with this test, the most successful appears to involve inspecting the figure to be copied, coding it as a particular pattern (e.g., "square," "diamond," "British flag," "cube"), and then drawing it. This clearly involves simultaneous processing. The other common strategy, copying the figure line-by-line, is far less successful with the more difficult figures and may be seen to involve excessive reliance upon successive processing.

The Memory-for-Designs test is similar, but adds a memory component, requiring subjects to draw more complex figures from memory. As in Figure Copying, however, successful performance is dependent upon the maintenance of geometric relations, a simultaneous function (see Appendix, p. 210).

Among them, these three tests measure simultaneous processing quite well, ranging from the relatively simple and perceptual (Figure Copying) to the far more complex (Raven's). Importantly, one of these tests (Memory-for-Designs) involves memory.

A number of other tests have been used less often or less consistently to measure simultaneous processing. Among these have been tests of visualization (Cummins, 1973), Paradigmatic Verbal Clustering (Kirby, Jarman, & Das, 1975), and Concrete Paired Associates (Cummins, 1973; Kirby, 1976). It has further been shown (Kirby & Das, 1977) that traditional tests of spatial ability are highly correlated with simultaneous processing.

Successive processing has typically been measured with a variety of tests that require the maintenance of a temporal order for input items: Digit Span, Visual Short-Term Memory, and Serial or Free Recall. Digit Span is clearly the simplest of successive tests: A series of items input in a particular order are immediately output in the same order (verbally). In Visual Short-Term Memory, however, digits are presented visually in positions on a grid. Either immediately or after a brief filler task subjects are required to reproduce the digits in correct position on a blank grid (see Appendix, pp. 215–216). Again a variety of strategies are possible, but the most successful seems to involve choosing a particular order (such as top-to-bottom, left-to-right; or, clockwise and then the center item), and then following this order in reading and in reproducing the digits. As opposed to Digit Span, the input in this task is visual, and the response is in writing.

The third common test of successive processing is Serial (or sometimes Free) Recall. In this task, 24 four-item lists of words are presented, auditorily, to the subject, who then has to repeat the words, in the same order (responses can also be in writing). Responses may be scored for correct serial recall, or for correct free recall without affecting the loading of this test. Different sorts of words have also been used—unrelated words, acoustically similar words, and semantically similar words—without affecting the loading of the test. As with all three of the tests described, there is no difficulty in seeing Serial Recall as a test of successive processing. Again, other tests such as Abstract Paired Associates (Cummins 1973) have infrequently been used to measure successive processing.

While all of the tests of successive processing are essentially memory tests, it should be clear that the factor they define is not, in essence, a memory factor, because other memory tests (e.g., Memory-for-Designs, Concrete Paired Associates, and Paradigmatic Verbal Clustering) load far more upon the simultaneous factor. Their most important common aspect is the requirement of maintaining a temporal sequence. In fact, when this successive factor is related to a factor defined by traditional paired-associate tests, which do not require the maintenance of any temporal order, the resultant correlation is no higher than that between the successive factor and reasoning ability (Kirby & Das, 1978a).

Several other constructs will also appear in the research we will describe. One of these will be that of "speed," which is measured by several tests which require subjects to read a number of words, or name a number of presented colors, as quickly as they can (the tests are taken from Stroop,

1935). The speed factor is generally unrelated to the simultaneous–successive tests.

Two other constructs (arousal level and planning ability) are of relevance to our theoretical model, but have not yet received much attention in our research. Arousal has been studied by Williams (1976), and his research will be reported in Chapter 6. Planning ability has recently been measured by Ashman (1978); his planning factor is defined by the Trail Making test, a test of visual search and organization in written composition. Thus, research related to coding will be presented in the following chapters; work on arousal, and more importantly, on the planning and decision-making functions is in progress.

Simultaneous and Successive Processing in Children

The cognitive tests that we described in the previous chapter have been employed in much of the research to be discussed in the remainder of this book. These tests have been drawn from a variety of sources including Luria's clinical investigations, as well as human-abilities research of North American origin. Our use of tests that have been employed by Luria, however, varies substantially from his application of them in a clinical setting. A clear point of difference is that we have administered these tests to moderately large samples of children, in contrast to the small numbers of subjects that have been studied in depth by Luria. Further, the populations from which our subjects have been drawn constitute a range from normal to different types of atypical children, the latter including mentally retarded and learning disabled subjects. Finally different age levels have also been represented in our samples, as have different cultures and ethnic groups.

In the next four chapters we will describe the results of our research and that of colleagues involving these various groups. Prior to beginning our description of these studies, some of the similarities and differences in methodology between Luria's research and our own investigations are noted, in order to place our respective lines of research in context.

4.1 CLINICAL METHODS AND FACTOR ANALYSIS

Luria's clinical studies have mainly used a procedure known as "syndrome analysis" (Luria & Artem'eva, 1970). The guiding principle of this procedure is the progressive compilation of information on a single subject drawn from a variety of sources. In brain-injured patients, this method typically takes the form of careful identification and mapping of the location and degree of the injury, and then the construction of a behavioral profile of the patient. In the latter case, it is essential to identify normal areas of functioning as well as disturbed or deficit areas, in order to determine the specific types of behavior that are affected by the lesions.

The areas of behavior studied by Luria in order to assess the effects of brain lesions have typically covered a very broad spectrum (see Luria, 1973a, b, c). Ability to orient oneself while walking, the extent to which a musical melody can be detected or reproduced, and the comprehension and generation of language are examples of this range. In his use of cognitive tests, Luria has guided his investigations according to the same principles. A variation of tests are given to a subject, and those for which atypical responses are recorded are used to define the syndrome. This process proceeds by progressive convergence; that is, the investigator varies and adds more tests until a composite picture of the subject's cognitive processing is formed. An analysis of the tests for which deficit behavior is shown is then conducted, in order to identify the common task characteristics of these tests. It is interesting to note that this task analysis process is similar to its recent use in the entirely different area of learning hierarchies and instructional development (e.g., Gagné, 1973, 1974; Resnick, 1976; White & Gagné, 1974). The final step in this process is the collation of the types of brain injury with the behavior patterns, particularly the cognitive test results. Inferences are then drawn concerning the areas of the brain responsible for the generation and control of different types of behavior.

A contrast is evident between Luria's technique of syndrome analysis and the methods of investigation that we have employed. Our research has been conducted using almost exclusively multivariate statistical methods, and in particular factor analysis. The use of factor analysis in investigations of cognitive ability has a long history, often marked by controversies on particular procedures. Advocates of different techniques within factor analysis have adopted clearly defined positions, and debates over the relative merits of the positions have occupied a good deal of space in technical journals and books.

It now appears essential in the use of factor analysis to address at least four issues in a given investigation. Two of these relate to the philosophy of science rationale reflected in the use of the technique, and the last two are operational decisions based in part on this rationale.

The first consideration in the use of factor analysis is the question of the epistemological status of factors. Some researchers, such as Sir Cyril Burt, have suggested that factors have little psychological meaning, and should be viewed only as a convenient taxonomic system (see Coan, 1964; Eysenck, 1972). The opposite point of view is that factors carry psychological meaning, dependent upon the choice of variables involved in the analysis, and may even be regarded as causal agents in explanations of behavior (see Coan, 1964; Maxwell, 1972).

In practice, these epistemological positions form the poles of a continuum, on which many of the factor-analytic views of intelligence discussed in Chapter 1 can be placed. Cattell and Guilford, for example, have clearly adopted an explanatory view of factors, while Vernon and Eysenck tend to use factor analysis in a partially taxonomic and partially explanatory role.

Within each of the distinctions of taxonomic and explanatory, one may further ask whether the purpose of the analysis is exploratory or confirmatory (Mulaik, 1972). This second issue in factor analysis concerns the expectations of the investigator regarding outcomes. Exploratory analyses are conducted with no a priori constraints on the outcome of the analysis, and generally nonsubjective or "blind" statistical procedures determine the results. In contrast, confirmatory analyses represent patterning the outcome of the analysis to estimate or conform to an expected factor structure.

The manifestation of the choices that must be made on the two preceding issues is in the selection of a model for the analysis, and a procedure for rotating factors, or as it is sometimes known, factor transformation. Models for factor analysis fall into essentially two varieties: component analysis and common-factor analysis. Component analysis analyzes all of the variance in a set of tests into a linearly independent set of variables. Common-factor analysis, on the other hand, divides test variance into common and unique varieties, and attempts to determine the unique variance of each variable. Principal-components solutions are such that the model is determinate, that is, estimation procedures are not required. For common-factor analysis, however, because of the difficulty in defining unique variance, the model is indeterminate and many possible mathematical solutions exist for a given set of data.

Once analyzed, a factor matrix is generally rotated, or transformed. This second step also has several alternatives, mainly orthogonal and oblique varieties. Orthogonal rotations transform derived factors into positions independent of one another, and oblique rotations allow the factors to retain some intercorrelations with one another (Gorsuch, 1974).

The direct implication of the variations that have been noted here, and other subvariations not described, is that many possible alternatives exist for the factor analysis of cognitive test data. This variety of techniques has contributed to both the strength and the weakness of the procedure. The variations open many options to the researcher in discovering patterns in data, but also, if so many options are available, how can one claim with any certainty that a given set of results represents the true state of phenomena under investigation?

Our approach to these problems has been to adopt a view of factor analysis that appears quite comparable to that of some British researchers. On the taxonomic versus explanatory issue, we find it both necessary and compelling to give psychological meaning, and therefore explanatory power, to our factors. We do so on the basis of multiple forms of independent evidence, the nature of which will be developed in the course of our later discussion. We also view our analyses as confirmatory, even though we do not use statistical procedures to fit our factors to a preconceived solution. Rather, this confirmatory view is based largely on Luria's original clinical investigations, in that relationships among tests suggested by Luria are confirmed in the factor-analysis procedure.

The analysis techniques that we have used have varied considerably, from common-factor solutions to principal-components solutions, and from orthogonal to oblique rotations on these factors. In general, we have found comparable results in cross-comparisons of these procedures, and therefore have often returned to the most heavily used solution in factor analysis, which is the principal-components model with an orthogonal rotation conducted on the factors.

With reference to the use of this model, we note with interest the current debate among factor analysts, regarding the indeterminacy of the common-factor model. Recently strong cases have been made that the principal-components model is the only technique that is logically defensible and does not involve a host of arbitrary decisions (Schonemann & Steiger, 1976). Finally, we also rely on the fact that our use of orthogonal rotations for factors is consistent with the theoretical independence of the two cognitive processes that we suggest are represented by the factors. The independence of simultaneous and successive syntheses has been confirmed by using oblique procedures however, and noting that our assumption of orthogonality appears warranted.

Viewed in a broader perspective then, the factor-analytic techniques that have been employed in our investigations form a direct complement to Luria's method of syndrome analysis. The unique contributions of Luria's investigations lie in the indentification of physiological structures which are responsible for various cognitive processes. A unique contribution of our investigations is the study of these processes in many different populations of subjects, including normal children, which allows us to use our results to shed some light on current issues in human-abilities research, and cognitive psychology generally. Finally, we find an area of similarity between the two lines of investigation. The clinical method derives a set of tests which appears, to define a syndrome, and common task demands in these tests, are then used to define the cognitive process which is deficient. Factor analysis also defines cognitive processes common to a set of tests, with the difference that a range of individual differences is used to facilitate this definition. Thus the two methods are highly complementary, each with its unique contribution, but also with some shared features.

4.2   SIMULTANEOUS AND SUCCESSIVE FACTORS: A REPRESENTATIVE STUDY

The purpose of this section is to introduce our line of investigation by discussing a single exemplary study. The discussion of this study will state some of the reasons for our interpretation of our factor analyses as representing simultaneous and successive cognitive processes, as opposed to alternative interpretations. The balance of the rationale for this interpretation will then be developed progressively in the subsequent chapters.

The study of interest here was completed by Kirby (1976). Kirby included 104 fourth-grade boys and 98 fourth-grade girls in his sample, and administered to all subjects a battery of tests drawn from those discussed at the end of Chapter 3. These tests were administered both in groups and individually. Raven's Coloured Progressive Matrices and Figure Copying were given to classroom-size groups because reliability of data from these tests is sufficiently high under this procedure. The Memory-for-Designs test requires individual viewing of the figures, and was administered in small group sessions with 4 to 6 children in each. Each child viewed a figure and then drew the response while the figure was being viewed by other subjects in the group. Serial Recall and Digit Span were administered individually in the usual format for tests of this type. The Visual Short-Term Memory test was given to groups of 2, in order for the color-naming interference part of the test to be monitored closely by the tester. Finally, two speed tests were included, Word Reading and Color Naming, and these were administered individually with the use of a stopwatch. The data were intercorrelated and analyzed by the principal-components model, with a Varimax rotation performed on the factor matrix. The results of this analysis are found in Table 4.1. The factors presented in Table 4.1 show some interesting trends, which have encouraged us to label them as designated in the table, and which appear to rule out several alternative explanations. To begin, let us consider the first two factors. One interpretation of these factors that may be considered is that they represent reasoning and memory, respectively. This view would be based on Jensen's (e.g., 1970) model

Table 4.1
Rotated Factors for Grade 4[a]

	Factors		
Test	Simultaneous	Successive	Speed
Raven's Coloured Progressive Matrices	.796	.132	−.201
Figure Copying	.705	.182	.039
Memory-for-Designs	.786	.014	.098
Serial Recall	.395	.624	−.240
Visual Short-Term Memory	.164	.812	−.176
Digit Span Forward	−.108	.807	−.039
Word Reading	−.053	−.273	.795
Color Naming	−.140	−.039	.865
Percentage of total variance	23.89	22.84	19.01

[a] $N = 202$.

of Level I and Level II abilities. Jensen uses Raven's Coloured Progressive Matrices and Figure Copying to measure Level II, or reasoning, and these two tests have high loadings on the first factor. The second factor, following this interpretation, would be Level I, or memory. This factor is formed predominately from the Serial Recall, Visual Short-Term Memory, and Digit Span tests. Jensen uses Digit Span as a measure of Level I, and also the other two tests to measure memory; the interpretation of the second factor as Level I, therefore, appears reasonable on first inspection.

A Level I–Level II interpretation of these two factors is made quite tenuous, however, by the data for the Memory-for-Designs test, which loads on the first factor. If this factor is designated as reasoning, as suggested by Jensen's model, then the reasoning–memory distinction is contradicted by the test. This contradiction, we may note here, is consistent through all of our analyses, and it has formed some of the basis for a reinterpretation of the Level I–Level II model in terms of simultaneous–successive processing (Jarman, 1978a).

A better example of the complex relationship between memory on the one hand and simultaneous–successive processing on the other is given in Table 4.2 which comes from Lawson, 1976. The factor analysis, based on the scores of 70 Grade 4 children, yielded three factors which can be clearly labeled as simultaneous, successive, and speed. Here three tests that were not in Kirby's analysis are crucial to our argument that successive processing is not merely associative learning or rote memory. Consider the substantial loading on the simultaneous factor of Concrete Paired Associate learning scores and, to a lesser extent, the loading of Abstract Paired Associates. Recognition memory for words, however, loads on the successive factor. All three are "memory" tests, but obviously the pro-

Table 4.2
Factor Analysis (Varimax Rotation) for Grade 4 Recognition Group: Expanded Battery[a,b]

Test	I	II	III
Raven's Coloured Progressive Matrices	.763	.151	−.138
Figure Copying	.653	.345	.040
Memory-for-Designs	.726	.065	.147
Serial Recall	.354	.721	−.013
Visual Short-Term Memory	.167	.710	−.294
Digit Span Forward	−.054	.821	.029
Word Reading	.073	−.335	.811
Color Naming	−.194	−.036	.852
Concrete Paired Associates	.615	−.123	−.261
Abstract Paired Associates	.458	.283	−.142
Recognition Memory	.116	.476	−.214
Percentage of total variance	21.25	20.71	14.97

[a] From Lawson, 1976.
[b] $N = 77$.

cesses they require are different, which may explain their disparate loadings.

If the data reported by Kirby and Lawson do not fit the Jensen model of human abilities, one may wish to consider a sensory modality interpretation. Referring to Kirby's analysis specifically, the three tests that load on the first factor are visual in content and it is tempting to label this factor accordingly. The second factor, however, has both visual and auditory tests loading on it, the latter of which are Digit Span and Serial Recall. Thus, a possible visual–auditory interpretation of the first two factors is also contradicted.

In order to derive an adequate explanation of the factors, let us return to Factor 1 in the analysis. We observe that some common task characteristics of Raven's Coloured Progressive Matrices, Figure Copying, and Memory-for-Designs tests appear to be spatial synthesis. Each of these tests, whether it includes memory task demands or not, requires the subject to organize information in a form where elements are positioned in a pattern relative to others. Raven's Coloured Matrices test involves a strong component of matching spatial information, as well as some verbal syllogistic elements (Bock, 1973); the latter elements will be of interest to us at a later point in demonstrating that simultaneous synthesis is not solely spatial. The Figure Copying test requires successive pencil movements in drawing the figures, but the important aspect of this task for successful completion is the ability to draw the elements in correct position relative to one another. The Figure Copying test, then, even though it involves a succession of physical movements, has its main task demands in an integration of these movements. Finally, the Memory-for-Designs test has similar integrative demands as the Figure Copying test, but these demands are tested in memory. In short, then, all three tests require an integration of information such that elements are surveyable relative to one another, which is the general definition of simultaneous synthesis.

Turning to the second factor, we also find a common theme in the Serial Recall, Visual Short-Term Memory, and Digit Span tests. Despite the fact that these memory tests are both auditory and visual, the retention of serial order in recall is a shared feature among them. The content of these tests also varies between words and digits, but these variations are not of importance in defining the factor. The dimension of individual differences in these tests is the sequential ordering of information, which is designated as successive synthesis.

We may now turn to the third factor in Kirby's (1976) analysis, which we have designated as speed. The two tests that load on this factor are Word Reading and Color Naming; these are variations of the Stroop (1935) tasks. Both of these tests are timed, and the subject is required to complete the task as quickly as possible. In the Word Reading test, the names of four primary colors are read as rapidly as possible, and in the Color Naming task, the names for color bars are to be given by the subject as quickly as possible. This factor is defined by speed of verbal output then, and as may be seen, the simultaneous–successive tests do not load appreciably on this factor.

The three factors presented in Table 4.1 have been remarkably consistent among many analyses. This generalizability is particularly encouraging when we examine the factors in light of Luria's original definitions of simultaneous and successive processes. We have seen that the properties of the factors themselves are consistent with his definitions, but it is also noteworthy that these processes are defined in factor analyses independent of one another. Luria did not conceptualize these processes as hierarchical, that is for one to be functionally dependent upon the other, and our analyses are consistent with his view.

We also find some consistency between our results for the speed factor, and other research on human information-processing speed. Horn (1968) has emphasized the need to include speed in theories of human abilities, and Cronbach (1971) specifically suggests that tests such as the one test we have used here could be employed for this purpose. Cronbach notes that speed often forms a separate factor, similar to the factor we have found in our analyses.

In summary we suggest that the factors reported here operationally define three qualitative aspects of cognitive processing. These are simultaneous and successive forms of integration, and rate of processing. We now turn our attention to studies of variation and nonvariation of these processes in different groups.

4.3   COMPARISON OF CHILDREN IN GRADES 1 AND 4

A fundamental question asked in our line of research on simultaneous and successive cognitive processes is whether or not changes in types of processing take place with increasing chronological age. It should be noted that this question has not been addressed by Luria, by virtue of the emphasis in his clinical studies on brain-injured subjects. And yet for our purposes here (we deal in large part with the education of children in North American school systems) this question is basic. Any program of research on cognitive abilities that intends to derive implications for school learning must differentiate these implications according to age, if developmental changes are indicated in groups of subjects at different age levels.

It will be seen from the discussion of our research and that of colleagues that nearly all of our studies incorporate subjects from the early grades in school. We have concentrated on this age range of children for several reasons. First, our research interests were motivated historically, in part, by the results of other investigations on cognitive abilities. For example, Jensen's (1969, 1970) research on Level I and Level II abilities, White's (1965) analysis of hierarchical arrangements of learning processes, and Farnham-Diggory's (1970) research on cognitive synthesis have all served as motivation for us to concentrate on this age range. We have not necessarily agreed with the conclusions drawn in some of these studies, of course, but we do share their view that children in the early years of school should receive concentrated research attention.

A second reason that we have focused on children in the early school grades is suggested by our discussion in Chapter 6. Our research on simultaneous and successive cognitive processes has not been concerned only with general theoretical issues in cognitive psychology and instructional implications for normal children. We have also been engaged in a good deal of comparative research on atypical children, particularly those who are mentally retarded or learning disabled. It is our premise that research with these latter groups should be oriented such that early intervention and programming may become a reality and be based on both strong theory and sound empirical information. This, once again, necessitates a concentration on the early years of school in the design of research.

In the light of these considerations, we may return now to our fundamental question on developmental changes in simultaneous and successive cognitive processes. Research on this question was done by Das and

Molloy (1975) who studied Grade 1 and Grade 4 subjects, and compared the results for those two groups. Das and Molloy administered a set of cognitive tests to 60 boys at each of the two grade levels. Only boys were included in the study because an additional variable to age under study was socioeconomic status, and Vernon (1969) had suggested that cause–effect relationships were more straightforward for this variable in the case of males.

The battery of tests administered included Raven's Coloured Progressive Matrices, Figure Copying, and Memory-for-Designs as measures of simultaneous synthesis. Measures of successive synthesis included Visual Short-Term Memory and Serial Recall. The Serial Recall test was also scored on a free recall basis, creating a second score for this task. Color Naming and Word Reading were given as speed tasks, as described earlier in a discussion of Kirby's study. Finally, a test of cross-modal coding was administered. This test involves listening to an auditory sequence of taps, and then finding a dot pattern among a series of alternatives on a card which corresponds to the sequence. Birch and Belmont (1964) were some of the early researchers in the use of this test, and it has been used heavily for many purposes since their study (Freides, 1974). Das and Molloy, however, were not able to give this test to the Grade 1 children because it was too difficult. Color Naming was also not given to both groups, and only the Grade 1 children performed this task. The results of the Color Naming task for children at the Grade 4 level may be inferred from the study by Kirby, discussed previously.

Das and Molloy intercorrelated the test results for the grades separately and performed a principal-components analysis with a varimax rotation on factors. The results of this analysis are presented in Table 4.3, where the factors are labeled as successive, simultaneous, and speed. The Grade 4 and Grade 1 results for each of these factors are positioned side-by-side for comparison purposes.

In general, the results for the two grades show a marked similarity, but with some variations in the case of several tests. The successive factor shows some of this variation. In the Grade 4 children, this factor is defined by the Visual Short-Term Memory, Serial Recall, and Free Recall tests, similar to the Kirby (1976) study. For the Grade 1 children, however, Visual Short-Term Memory was associated more heavily with speed, and the successive factor was defined mainly by the Serial and Free Recall tests.

The simultaneous factor demonstrated much more consistency in a comparison of the two grades. Raven's Coloured Progressive Matrices, Figure Copying, and Memory-for-Designs all loaded heavily on the simultaneous factor in both of the analyses. In the Grade 4 analysis, the cross-modal matching task also loaded heavily on the simultaneous factor.

Table 4.3
Rotated Factors (Varimax) for Grade 4 ($N = 60$) and Grade 1 ($N = 60$) Children[a]

Test	Successive		Simultaneous		Speed	
	Grade 4	Grade 1	Grade 4	Grade 1	Grade 4	Grade 1
Raven's Coloured Progressive Matrices	-.042	-.146	.873	.784	.013	.088
Figure Copying	-.031	.290	.757	.762	.147	-.108
Memory-for-Designs (errors)	.162	-.119	-.706	-.713	.190	.394
Cross-modal Coding	.267	*	.665	*	.087	*
Visual Short-Term Memory	.710	.060	.021	.163	-.192	-.557
Word Reading	-.112	-.287	.035	.046	.973	.766
Serial Recall	.934	.951	-.045	.101	-.009	-.166
Free Recall	.927	.955	.003	.051	.011	-.108
Color Naming	*	-.161	*	-.067	*	.801
Percentage of total variance	29.4	25.6	28.5	21.9	13.1	21.9

[a] Asterisk indicates test omitted.

65

Finally, the speed factor is similar in the two analyses. Word Reading and Color Naming define this factor in the Grade 1 sample, in addition to a moderate negative loading from Visual Short-Term Memory. Word Reading alone is the major determinant of the factor in the Grade 4 sample.

What general conclusions may be drawn from these data with respect to developmental trends in simultaneous and successive processes? Certainly one of the striking features of the data is that there is a good deal of similarity between children at the Grade 1 and Grade 4 level in the cognitive processes required by these tests.

The areas of difference between the two age levels appear to be confined mainly to speed of information processing in successive synthesis. The Visual Short-Term Memory test, it will be recalled, involves viewing a grid of digits for 5 seconds, engaging in a rehearsal interference task for 2 seconds, and then attempting to recall the digits in the grid by writing them on a response sheet. Because the task is timed, speed of rehearsal likely determines final performance in part. The data appear to indicate that for Grade 1 children where spontaneous rehearsal (Flavell, 1970) would be slower, individual differences in speed determined performance in the memory task more directly. To return to Table 4.2, this is shown by the reverse signs of Visual Short-Term Memory in comparison to Word Reading and Color Naming. Thus, as latency scores went up across subjects, indicating a slower rate of response, Visual Short-Term Memory scores went down, reflecting this lower rate of processing in effectiveness of rehearsal.

The interpretations above primarily reflect variations in the cognitive abilities of the children at the two grade levels, and are based mainly on limitations in cognitive processing. We may go beyond these interpretations to add an additional dimension dealing with strategic behavior. In the latter case, we are not concerned as much with the processing limitations of the child, but rather, we are interested in habitual methods of completing various types of cognitive tasks. By so doing, we do not preclude the possibility that if an habitual method of task completion is modified, levels of performance may change accordingly. It is this latter issue which brings us closer to educational implications.

If we return again to Table 4.3, we may now look at the results for the Figure Copying test as a case in point. In most populations, this test predominantly measures simultaneous synthesis, but it is notable that in the Grade 1 results, a small loading is found for this test on the successive factor. In the course of testing the children in this study, Molloy observed that some of the Grade 1 children tended to approach the Figure Copying task as a series of unrelated pencil movements, rather than as a total composite to be produced. We may speculate from this observation and data for the test that the Grade 1 children tended to use a strategy of reproducing desired elements of the figures in succession, rather than concentrating on coordination of their drawing to produce elements of correct proportions and in correct positions relative to one another. The latter strategy, of course, would mainly engage simultaneous processes. This speculation is admittedly quite rudimentary, using only the present results, but it will be seen in other analyses that it is possible to infer strategic behavior from these comparative results.

We may summarize the results of the study, then, in terms of three points. First, simultaneous and successive cognitive processes were identified at the Grade 1 and Grade 4 level, by very similar factor-analytic results for subjects in these two grades. Second, some of the variations in the factor-analysis comparisons were likely due to developmental changes in the limitations of information processing, primarily in the area of speed of processing. Finally, strategic differences between the age groups were also suggested by the results, although conclusions on these differences are more tentative, and they account for much less of the variation between the groups.

Beyond these three points, the study also relates these variables to school achievement. The results of the achievement data will be presented in the next chapter in the context of several other studies which have this focus.

5

Relationship of Simultaneous and Successive Coding to School Achievement

5.1 THE PREDICTION OF SCHOOL ACHIEVEMENT

The prediction of school achievement has long been the goal of intelligence testers. Beginning with Binet's original attempts, the argument regarding how best to predict success in school has continued. Some have favored the concept of general ability as the best predictor (e.g., McNemar, 1964), whereas others have supported multifactorial predictors (e.g., Vandenberg, 1973). In fact this debate has paralleled that concerning the unitary nature of general intelligence (see Chapter 1).

Although measures of intelligence can be shown to predict school achievement successfully, a number of difficulties remain. The primary difficulty, to which the others can be related, is the lack of a theory relating the intelligence measures to the achievement measures. Because a theory of the nature of intelligence has been lacking, it has not been possible to specify exactly how this general ability manifests itself in school performance. We do not know why intelligence predicts achievement, hence we do not know what to do when low achievement is predicted. Often the assumption is made that little can be done because intelligence is interpreted as fundamentally immutable, and the correlation between intelligence and achievement is interpreted as inferring causation (i.e., intelligence causes achievement). The immutability of intelligence, if such is the case, may well be unimportant if this inference of causality is incorrect. Supporting evidence for a causal relationship is lacking, and evidence that

69

is available (Crano, Kenny, & Campbell, 1972; Dyer & Miller, 1974) indicates that a causal relationship is at best uncertain, and that causation may occur in the opposite direction (i.e., early achievement causing later intelligence) for some groups. Furthermore, the fact that intelligence *normally* correlates with achievement need not imply that it will always correlate with achievement in all individuals. Remedial programs may be able to lessen this presumed dependence of school achievement upon intelligence.

New approaches for the prediction of school achievement seem to be more fruitful. One approach, proposed by McClelland (1973), for instance, has proposed that more criterion-referenced measures be developed as predictors. Rather than blindly devising tests that predict school achievement without delineating why they should predict, McClelland suggests that one should first identify the competencies actually involved in what we seek to predict. Prediction of achievement that is based on competency will require a more complete knowledge of the skills actually needed in school and, by the same token, produce a rational basis for remediation of low achievement.

Cronbach (1957, 1975b) has proposed and developed another approach to school achievement. It considers those individual difference variables which may interact with school programs (treatments) to produce school achievement. In this model, there is no simple relationship between a set of predictors (abilities, intelligence, personality characteristics) and school achievement, because the former interact with the educational treatments. Thus, a particular skill (for example, rote memory) may be the major determiner of school achievement in one educational environment (a strict authoritarian one), but may be unrelated to achievement in a different educational program (perhaps one based more upon discovery learning). This Aptitude × Treatment Interaction (ATI) model has several implications for studying the determinants of school achievement. It stresses that students may be able to follow a variety of routes to the same absolute level of achievement—those lacking an ability which is normally associated with high achievement may be able to circumvent this problem by the application of a different ability, perhaps within the context of a different educational environment. One of the implications of the ATI model is that low levels of achievement are not necessarily problems within the student that are immune to remediation; rather, these problems necessitate the investigation of the student's strengths. The ATI model encompasses two remedial strategies: If the skills that the individual is lacking can be improved, then improving them is the easier route to take; if, on the other hand, these skills or abilities are relatively immutable, then alternative educational environments must be designed to make use of the strengths of the individual. It will not always be possible, of course, for all individuals to reach the same level of achievement.

Yet another perspective upon the determinants of school achievement is supplied by a number of theorists who have considered the impact of transfer and learning upon the development of abilities (e.g., Ferguson, 1954, 1956; Buss, 1973a, 1973b). They suggest that the cluster of tests which form an ability factor result from the application of an overlearned skill to the tasks represented in the different tests. It cannot be assumed that all individuals possess the same overlearned skills, nor that the skills themselves have been overlearned to the same extent. Furthermore, different individuals may apply different skills to the same task, perhaps as a function of developmental level or cultural background (Scribner & Cole, 1973). Then, what is in general a good predictor of school achievement? Any predictor can be a good one if most individuals (within our dominant culture) apply the same skills both to the predictor and the tasks which measure school achievement.

5.2 SIMULTANEOUS–SUCCESSIVE PROCESSING AND ACHIEVEMENT

The simultaneous–successive information-processing model of cognition that has been described in the preceding chapters is an example of a new approach to achievement that attempts to meet the criticisms discussed in the last section. The greatest advantage of such a model is that it is theory-based. Relations that appear between its constructs and achievement should be explicable in terms of the model and need not fall back upon "blind prediction." Because the model is process-oriented, it also is capable of making constructive suggestions about remediation of low achievement. Furthermore, because the model's constructs (simultaneous and successive processing) can be seen as stable individual-difference variables, the model can be applied in an ATI fashion. The existence of these processing factors at various developmental stages allows the investigation of changes in the relationship between them and achievement.

The model does not predict a simple relationship between simultaneous and successive processing and school achievement. School achievement itself is a complex combination of many different things, many of which would be dependent upon both simultaneous and successive processing. Those areas of achievement which involve interpretation of spatial information (e.g., mathematics) should be more related to simultaneous processing, while any subject in which retention of essentially unrelated information were required (e.g., spelling) would relate more highly to successive pro-

cessing. Most importantly, the complex language subjects (reading, comprehension, etc.) would be dependent upon both forms of processing. As
has been suggested in Chapter 2, these latter areas, particularly when
expression is involved, may also be highly related to planning ability.

It should be noted that there is no reason to expect that simultaneous
and successive processing will correlate more highly than traditional intelligence tests with achievement: As McClelland (1973) has suggested, those
traditional IQ–achievement correlations may be as high as is possible. The
simultaneous–successive processing model offers two other advantages, an
understanding of the correlations that result, and a rational basis for the
remediation of low achievement.

The remainder of this chapter will examine a number of recent studies
that have sought to relate school achievement to simultaneous and successive processing. Mainly, the studies indicate that school achievement is
related to both simultaneous and successive processing. Achievement measures correlate with factor scores representing simultaneous and successive
processing. But the correlation is not apparent if those measures are factor
analyzed together with the simultaneous–successive battery of tests; then
an orthogonal "achievement" factor is consistently obtained.

The Four-Factor Structure

When the simultaneous–successive battery is factor analyzed with
achievement variables included, the simultaneous, successive, and speed
factors emerge separate from a fourth factor which is defined by the
achievement measures (Das, 1973b; Sprecht 1976). As we have previously
commented with reference to the earlier Das (1973b) study, this fourth
factor apparently resembles Vernon's well-known verbal-educational factor. While that study was with 10-year-olds, a similar result was obtained by Sprecht (1976) with 65 low-achieving high school students
(Table 5.1). The first factor is defined clearly by the Mathematics, Vocabulary, and Reading comprehension tests. The second, third, and fourth
factors conform closely to, respectively, successive processing, simultaneous processing, and speed. It should be noted, as anticipated above and in
Luria's clinical work, that mathematics achievement has a moderate loading on simultaneous processing.

The emergence of a separate school achievement factor is not surprising.
The school achievement measures have more in common with one another
than they have with the simultaneous–successive tests: For instance they
shared a similar multiple-choice format, and, more importantly, required
skills and knowledge learned in school. This separate school achievement
factor, whether it is called verbal-educational (Vernon, 1969) or crystal-

Table 5.1
Principal-Components Analysis (Varimax Rotation) of Eight Simultaneous–Successive
Tests and Three Achievement Tests[a]

Test	Factors			
	School achievement	Successive	Simultaneous	Speed
Raven's Coloured Progressive Matrices	−.157	.210	.796	.024
Figure Copying	.187	−.081	.793	−.032
Memory-for-Designs (errors)	.064	−.100	−.579	−.299
Serial Recall	.223	.697	−.015	−.309
Visual Short-Term Memory	.087	.759	.120	.206
Digit Span Forward	.128	.779	.087	−.233
Word Reading	−.165	−.239	.102	.836
Color Naming	−.084	−.009	.063	.879
Mathematics Achievement	.705	−.093	.446	−.208
Vocabulary Achievement	.872	.266	−.059	−.192
Comprehension Achievement	.872	.263	−.161	.008
Percentage of total variance	19.90	17.60	16.94	16.94

[a] $N = 65$ low-achieving high school students.

lized intelligence (Cattell, 1971), does not explain how school achievement is related to underlying cognitive processes.

Regression Analyses

A better means of relating school achievement to cognitive variables is multiple regression. Two step-wise regression analyses were performed in the study by Sprecht referred to above, with mathematics achievement and reading achievement (sum of vocabulary and comprehension scores) as the criteria (Table 5.2). Mathematics achievement was best predicted by Figure Copying ($r = .36$), followed by Color Naming and Serial Recall. The fact that the Progressive Matrices was only the fourth best predictor ($r = .22$) came as a surprise to the local school psychologist: That test had previously been used to assess potential for mathematics achievement in the school!

Somewhat more of the variance of the reading scores was predicted by the simultaneous–successive battery, Serial Recall ($r = .40$) and Word Reading ($r = .34$) being the best predictors. Both of these tests (and Digit Span, $r = .35$) are verbal in nature.

These results were somewhat comparable to those of a previous study (Das, Manos, & Kanungo, 1975) with fourth-grade children of high ($N = 60$) and low ($N = 60$) socioeconomic status, in which Word Reading,

Table 5.2
Stepwise Regression Analyses, Predicting Mathematics and Reading Achievement from the Eight Simultaneous–Successive Tests[a,b]

Criterion			
Mathematics		Reading	
Predictor	Percentage of variance	Predictor	Percentage of variance
Figure Copying	13.01	Serial Recall	15.6
Color Naming	17.6	Word Reading	20.5
Serial Recall	18.8	Progressive Matrices	22.4
Progressive Matrices	19.7	Visual STM	24.8
		Figure Copying	27.0
		Digit Span	28.1

[a] $N = 65$.
[b] Predictors added if percentage of variance added was 1%. All p values $< .01$.

Color Naming, and Digit Span were not included (Table 5.3). Mathematics is well predicted by Figure Copying in both groups, but in the low-SES group it is surpassed by Serial Recall. This suggests that simultaneous processing, as represented by Figure Copying, is the optimal form of processing in a mathematics task and that the low SES employ it less often than successive processing. The low-SES group also appears to be more reliant upon successive processing than the high-SES group in reading achievement. Das, Manos, and Kanungo (1975) concluded that both forms of processing are important, particularly in reading achievement, but that the low-SES group demonstrated a preference for the successive mode. Although the regression analyses only accounted for a relatively small percentage of the variance, they do confirm the importance of both forms of processing, and stress the complexity of the relationship between the information-processing dimensions and school achievement. One analysis further suggested that different groups might employ different processes in achievement tasks.

Differences between High and Low Achievers

Krywaniuk (1974) studied processing differences in greater detail, choosing for his study high and low achievers in the third grade. He defined high and low achievers, respectively, as those students who fell in the upper and lower thirds of the distribution of measures of school work and teachers' ratings. The 56 high achievers also exceeded the 56 low achievers on WISC verbal (108.9 versus 93.8) and performance (109.9 versus 98.9) IQs,

Table 5.3

Stepwise Regression Analyses, Predicting Mathematics and Reading Achievement from Five Simultaneous–Successive Tests, for High ($N = 60$) and Low ($N = 60$) Socioeconomic Groups

Criterion: Mathematics				Criterion: Reading			
High SES		Low SES		High SES		Low SES	
Predictor	Percentage of variance	Predictor	Percentage of variance	Predictor	Percentage of variance	Predictor	Percentage of variance
Figure Copying	17.0*	Serial Recall	20.7**	Figure Copying	21.6**	Serial Recall	24.2**
Cross-modal Coding	22.9*	Figure Copying	24.6*	Visual Short-Term Memory	27.5*	Visual Short-Term Memory	29.8**
		Cross-modal Coding	26.6*			Figure Copying	33.7***
						Cross-modal Coding	35.7*

* $p < .05$.
** $p < .01$.

both differences being significant beyond the .01 level. Krywaniuk sought to determine whether the low achievers would score lower than the high on the simultaneous–successive tests, and also whether similar factor structures would emerge in the two groups, particularly with reference to a set of achievement tests administered to the children. As it turned out, the high achievement group was superior to the low on *all* of the simultaneous–successive tests, particularly those of simultaneous processing (Table 5.4).

When the battery was factor analyzed within both groups separately, factors recognizable as successive processing, simultaneous processing, and speed emerged (Table 5.5). The structure within the low group conformed quite closely to the typical results, but that of the high group showed two unexplicable deviations: Both speed tests split their loadings between successive and speed, and Visual Short-Term Memory split its loading between simultaneous and speed, rather than helping define successive processing. In general, however, it may be said that both groups evidenced similar factor structures, in spite of their difference in absolute level of performance (Table 5.4). We shall refer to a study on high- and low-IQ groups in Chapter 6 and discuss further the similarity between achievement and IQ levels in relation to simultaneous and successive processing.

Krywaniuk also conducted exploratory factor analyses, including a battery of achievement tests with the simultaneous–successive battery. His achievement tests were the Gates–MacGinitie Reading Test (vocabulary and comprehension scores), the Stanford Achievement Tests (word meaning, paragraph meaning, and word study skills scores), locally standardized

Table 5.4

Comparison of Means of High- and Low-Achieving Groups (Scheffe Procedure) on Simultaneous–Successive Tests[a]

Variable	High achievers		Low achievers		
	$\bar{X}$	SD	$\bar{X}$	SD	p
Raven's Matrices	29.98	3.97	23.84	6.43	<.01
Figure Copying	14.09	6.41	11.89	6.93	<.01
Memory-for-Designs (error)	3.52	3.67	5.52	4.29	<.02
Cross-modal Coding	18.14	2.60	15.32	4.41	<.01
Serial Recall	145.45	26.40	130.43	32.78	<.05
Visual Short-Term Memory	33.93	9.30	28.09	10.26	.02
Word Reading (time in seconds)	22.14	4.29	25.52	5.30	<.05
Color Naming (time in seconds)	72.73	19.72	79.54	19.13	<.05

[a] $N = 56$ for both groups.

Table 5.5
Principal-Components Analyses of Nine Simultaneous–Successive Tests in High (N=56)
and Low (N=56) Achievement Groups

	Factors					
	High achievers			Low achievers		
Test	Succes-sive	Simulta-neous	Speed	Succes-sive	Simulta-neous	Speed
Raven's Coloured						
Progressive Matrices	.128	.745	.296	.189	.792	.097
Figure Copying	−.054	.654	−.083	.070	.685	−.067
Memory-for-Designs						
(errors)	−.233	−.583	.041	−.140	−.764	.125
Cross-modal Coding	.248	.603	−.261	.521	.429	.008
Serial Recall	.913	.244	−.093	.917	.111	−.107
Free Recall	.892	.193	−.050	.905	.155	−.069
Visual Short-Term						
Memory	−.244	.407	−.623	.601	.077	.055
Word Reading	−.571	.058	.532	.004	.128	.893
Color Naming	−.359	.099	.765	−.063	−.239	.855
Percentage of						
total variance	25.31	21.80	15.90	26.19	22.01	17.52

tests of spelling and arithmetic, and the Schonell Reading Vocabulary Test. The results of these analyses (Table 5.6) are complex, but are yet another step toward understanding the relationships among the information- processing dimension and school achievement.

The first factor in each analysis can be seen as a verbal-educational factor, even though it is lacking some expected loadings (e.g., Word Meaning). Simultaneous processing (Factor III of the high, Factor II of the low) also emerges; in the low achievers it is moderately related to Arithmetic and the Schonell Reading test. The relationship to Arithmetic confirms the findings of Sprecht's regression analysis. The negative loading of the Schonell test suggests that low-achieving children pay attention to details in this task, adopting an analytic approach rather than the global one required by the simultaneous tasks.

Successive factors are identifiable in both groups: The Serial and Free Recall tests define Factor II in the high achievers and Factor III in the low. In the high-achieving groups, vocabulary, comprehension, and paragraph meaning also load moderately on this factor. It should be noted, however, that the third test of successive processing, Visual Short-Term Memory, does not load upon the factors identified as successive processing. In both analyses it helps form other factors (as it had done for the high achievers in Table 5.5), Factor V for the high achievers and Factor IV for the low.

Table 5.6
Principal-Components Analysis (Varimax Rotation) of Eight Achievement Tests and Eight Simultaneous–Successive Tests for High (N=56) and Low (N=56) Achievement Groups

Test	High achievers					Low achievers				
	I	II	III	IV	V	I	II	III	IV	V
Gates–MacGinitie (Vocabulary)	.650	.405	.279	.140	.307	.767	.166	-.052	-.063	.315
Gates–MacGinitie (Comprehension)	.727	.320	.183	.192	.209	.735	.007	.116	.272	.393
Stanford (Word Meaning)	.328	-.001	.279	.003	.676	.097	.148	-.209	.057	.768
Stanford (Paragraph Meaning)	.602	.346	.128	.377	.355	.654	.087	-.009	.221	.373
Stanford (Word Study Skills)	.462	-.064	.008	.652	.184	.772	.248	.257	.093	-.209
Spelling	.846	.139	-.110	.106	.181	.768	-.066	.181	.121	-.026
Arithmetic	.123	.249	.097	.814	.048	.036	.480	.019	.708	-.072
Schonell Reading Vocabulary	.843	.147	.096	.010	-.071	.639	-.462	.143	-.068	.229
Raven's Coloured Progressive Matrices	-.055	.033	.862	.130	.080	.130	.716	.094	.298	-.080
Figure Copying	-.093	.092	.418	.201	-.573	.457	.597	.130	-.204	-.010
Memory-for-Designs	-.351	-.101	-.638	.150	.082	.132	-.801	-.187	-.124	-.177
Cross-modal Coding	.036	.267	.525	.437	-.187	.334	.311	.177	.614	-.165
Serial Recall	.318	.909	.150	.134	-.004	.160	.132	.942	.169	-.034
Free Recall	.271	.915	.064	.139	-.040	.178	.183	.908	.202	-.046
Visual Short-Term Memory	.343	-.049	.184	-.227	-.604	.054	-.091	.267	.768	.103
Word Reading	-.527	-.201	-.023	-.275	-.146	-.247	.162	-.140	.146	-.778
Percentage of total variance	23.63	14.35	11.86	10.83	9.74	22.74	14.12	12.96	11.63	11.06

In brief, these last analyses were very complex. While verbal-educational, simultaneous, and successive factors could be identified, the nature of the fourth and fifth factors was not clear. For the high achievers, some achievement tests cluster with the successive factor, which is verbal in nature. Within the low achievement group, some achievement tests cluster instead with the simultaneous factor. Again it appears that the two groups process information differently; the success of the high achievement group suggests that they are able to employ their processes appropriately. It is difficult to make any more precise conclusion about the relationship between the information-processing factors and achievement from Krywaniuk's research. A more detailed picture should be available from the next study that we will consider.

The Prediction of Reading Achievement

When achievement scores are factor analyzed with the information-processing battery, it is possible for them to form a separate factor, and thus tell us little of the relationship between information processing and achievement. As was mentioned earlier, this is not surprising, as the achievement tests have more in common with each other than with the simultaneous–successive tests. What variance does load upon the information-processing factors may not be that which is central to the achievement tests. Furthermore, even if the achievement tests do load upon factors with the simultaneous–successive tests, these factors may no longer be recognizable as those of the simultaneous–successive model; interpretation is thus made difficult.

Kirby and Das (1977) adopted a different approach to this problem. They administered the simultaneous–successive battery to 104 fourth-grade boys for whom achievement data were also available. The simultaneous–successive battery produced the familiar three-factor structure, from which factor scores were then generated. Thus it was possible (a) to correlate the factor scores with the achievement data, and (b) to perform a double-median split upon the simultaneous and successive factor scores and do a series of 2 × 2 analyses of variance, with the achievement measures as the dependent variables. The four achievement variables were: Gates–MacGinitie Vocabulary and Reading scores (grade equivalents) and Lorge-Thorndike Verbal and Nonverbal IQs. The latter two IQ scores were considered as achievement variables because of their relatively high relationship to school achievement. Further details concerning this study may be found elsewhere (Kirby & Das, 1977).

This analysis permits further exploration of the relationships among general ability, school achievement, and simultaneous–successive processing. Table 5.7 contains the correlations among the achievement measures

Table 5.7
Correlations between Factor Scores and Achievement Variables

	Unrotated factors			Varimax factors		
Achievement	I	II	III	Successive	Simultaneous	Speed
Reading Vocabulary	.564	−.148	.023	.422	.316	−.212
Reading Comprehension	.654	.057	.115	.507	.420	−.114
Verbal IQ	.608	.136	.006	.407	.414	−.188
Nonverbal IQ	.612	.055	−.062	.360	.451	−.225

and the unrotated and rotated factors. It can be seen that all four achievement scores are related to the first unrotated principal component: This can be taken simply as a demonstration that general ability (the achievement scores) is related to general ability (the combination of the information-processing scores). If our only interest were to *predict* school achievement, the first principal component would serve as a good, reliable predictor, but that, of course, would put us no further ahead than when we started to examine school achievement. If we want to understand the prediction of school achievement, we must relate it to more interpretable constructs; this function is performed by the Varimax rotation. It can be seen in Table 5.7 that the school achievement variables are related to both successive and simultaneous processing, a finding that emphasizes our major point, that complex performances (such as reading achievement) are dependent upon both modes of processing.

An alternative analysis of the same data would be to perform a double-median split on both the simultaneous and successive factor scores and then use the resultant high–low dimensions as independent variables in analyses of variance. The group means for these analyses may be seen in Tables 5.8, 5.9, 5.10, and 5.11. In all four cases, the main effects for simultaneous and for successive processing were significant; no interaction even approached significance. Inspection of the means for the four groups

Table 5.8
Means of Four Groups on Reading Vocabulary

	Simultaneous processing	
	Low	High
Successive processing		
High	6.00	6.53
Low	4.89	5.65

Table 5.9
Means of Four Groups on Reading Comprehension

	Simultaneous processing	
	Low	High
Successive processing		
High	5.99	7.09
Low	4.50	5.37

Table 5.10
Means of Four Groups on Verbal IQ

	Simultaneous processing	
	Low	High
Successive processing		
High	102.4	112.0
Low	94.2	100.7

Table 5.11
Means of Four Groups on Nonverbal IQ

	Simultaneous processing	
	Low	High
Successive processing		
High	109.6	118.6
Low	99.3	109.2

indicates that the high–high group performed consistently best and the low–low group consistently worst. The two "off-diagonal" groups were similar and intermediate in performance.

A number of conclusions may be drawn from these complementary analyses. A significant proportion of the variance of the achievement measures can be predicted by the information-processing factors. (Because the Varimax factors of Table 5.7 are orthogonal, their correlations with any achievement test can be squared and summed: Thus the proportion of vocabulary variance accounted for is 32.3%, for comprehension 44.6%, verbal IQ 37.2%, and nonverbal IQ 38.4%.) Second, neither one of the information-processing dimensions was more related to achievement than the other; a moderate (i.e., average in the population) level of achievement may be attained by those high in only one of the two modes of processing. Finally, high achievement would seem to be reserved for those with relatively high levels of ability in both forms of processing.

Cummins and Das (1977) followed up these findings with a study involving different criterion measures of reading achievement. Sixty Grade 3 students were involved and the analytic procedure employed by Kirby and Das was adopted. Subjects were divided into four groups on the basis of simultaneous and successive factor scores, and performance of the groups on the Decoding and Comprehension sections of the Elementary Reading Test developed by the Edmonton Public School Board was compared. The means and standard deviations of the four groups are shown in Table 5.12. These children had a slightly higher IQ than the sample in the Kirby and Das study.

Two-by-two analyses of variance showed significant main effects for simultaneous processing in both Decoding ($F = 7.20$, df 1,56, $p < .01$) and Comprehension ($F = 4.65$, df 1,56, $p < .05$) analyses. The main effect for successive processing and the interaction were nonsignificant in both analyses. The results of the analyses of variance were supported by correlations between simultaneous and successive factor scores and reading performance. Simultaneous factor scores correlated significantly with both Decoding ($r = .45$, $p < .001$) and Comprehension ($r = .40$, $p = .001$) performance. Correlations with successive factor scores were nonsignificant.

In order to investigate further the hypothesis that simultaneous processing is especially important at more advanced stages of reading we performed median splits on both comprehension and decoding distributions and carried out correlational analyses in the top and bottom halves of each distribution. Despite the reduced variance in comprehension scores, simultaneous processing correlated significantly ($r = .41$, $p < .05$) with comprehension in the top but not the bottom half of the distribution. When the decoding distribution was divided into top and bottom halves the relation-

Table 5.12
Means and Standard Deviations (in Parentheses) of Four Grade 3 Groups on Reading Scores

	Decoding	Comprehension
High simultaneous–high successive	50.27 (5.34)	56.40 (12.12)
High simultaneous–low successive	52.13 (4.61)	56.44 (9.54)
Low simultaneous–high successive	48.27 (4.70)	51.73 (10.12)
Low simultaneous–low successive	47.13 (5.50)	49.07 (10.89)

ship between decoding and simultaneous processing disappeared. From this it can be concluded that simultaneous processing may be necessary for the development of more advanced levels of comprehension skills. The fact that in the present study successive processing related less to reading performance than in the Kirby and Das study may be due either to the different criterion measures of reading or to the fact that these children had higher IQs.

Comprehension and inferencing are related to simultaneous and successive processing. McLeod (1978) explored the possibility that individual differences in simultaneous–successive processing may influence backward and forward inferencing; and attempted to reconfirm that comprehension at a higher level of reading competency is predictable by simultaneous processing. McLeod selected 40 students from Grade 4 who had reasonably good vocabulary (above 70th percentile for the grade level). However, one-half of this sample had difficulty with comprehension as judged by their teachers and the comprehension test in the Stanford Achievement Test. This "less proficient" group of 20 children had English as their first language as did the 20 "proficient" children. The two groups were comparable on a measure of nonverbal IQ (average IQ was 110), but on the comprehension test, their scores were well apart: Percentiles for mean comprehension were about 45 for the less proficient sample and 92 for the proficient sample.

The 40 children were divided into four simultaneous–successive groups (high simultaneous–high successive, etc.) on the basis of a double-median split following the procedure used in the Kirby and Das, and Cummins and Das studies. However, only Memory-for-Designs and Visual Short-Term Memory provided a basis for dividing the groups as high or low simultaneous and successive processors. The full battery of simultaneous–successive tests was not administered. Despite this limitation and the limitation of a small sample size, the following results were obtained.

1. On reading vocabulary and on comprehension, those children who were above the median on Memory-for-Designs (the high-simultaneous groups) were significantly better than those who were below the median (low-simultaneous groups). Their position on Visual Short-Term Memory test (successive) made little difference. The conclusions are based on analyses of variance which had simultaneous and successive as the two main effects as in the two previous studies. These results agree with the findings from Cummins and Das (1977) that at higher levels of reading competence it is simultaneous processing that is more important than successive processing.

2. In an inferencing test based on oral reading, the high-simultaneous–high-successive children had the highest score; the low-simultaneous–low-successive children had the lowest score. In the remaining two groups, the high-simultaneous–low-successive were better in inferencing than the low-simultaneous–high-successive groups. Competence in simultaneous processing and in inferencing (supported by the text) are closely related.

3. The next set of results are about forward- and backward-looking inferences from passages that were read by the children. A short description of these types of inferences will be given before the findings are reported. McLeod (1978) describes "forward-looking" inferences as those which went beyond the text to generate new information which elaborated the given textual information. In "backward-looking" inference, the child gave the necessary information that linked a given unit of textual information with previous information, or supplied a cause for a given action in the text. Examples of "forward-looking" and "backward-looking" inference are in italics in the narrative recalled by the subject.

Forward-looking inference:

Subject 35: ". . . Days came when the leaves on the trees changed color. *That must be fall.* Then the sounds of shots echoed through the woods from Miss Bella's farm. *Probably duck hunters, or something or animal hunters.*"

Backward-looking inference:

Subject 6: ". . . The young clerk wiped the forehead with the back of her hand. *Well, she must have been sweaty 'cause she's a young clerk.*"

Subject 1: ". . . She shuddered with each report. *Like she's sad because everybody's shooting at her animals.*"

(The inference about Miss Bella's shuddering is linked with the previous information in the text.)

Results of analyses of variance on the number of forward- and backward-looking inferences given by the simultaneous–successive groups were that the simultaneous main effect was significant for forward-looking inferences (positively related) ($p = .03$), whereas the successive main effect was significant for backward-looking inferences (negatively related). The means of inferences were examined by McLeod. Forward-looking inferences were more often given by the high-simultaneous groups, 67 as against 54 for the low-simultaneous processors. Backward-looking inference, however, was more often found among the *low*-successive processors; their mean was 64 compared to a mean of 54 for the high-successive processors. It means that children who predominantly use the successive mode of processing have difficulty with backward-looking inferences which require linking new information back to previously supplied information.

McLeod's research points out how the two modes of processing may interact with comprehension and, more importantly, with inferencing. Different types of processing are required by the demands of forward versus backward inferencing. The results point to the rich and complex relationships that remain to be investigated. McLeod mentions the interesting possibility that differences in frontal lobe functions of decision and planning should be considered when comparing the less proficient with the proficient in comprehension.

These studies, taken together, suggest a number of possible directions for future research. Insofar as the coding processes are susceptible to improvement, it may be possible to increase school achievement through training in appropriate ways to process information. An alternate possibility, if the coding processes are resistant to change, is the design of learning environments (curricula) to exploit an individual's processing strengths (the classic ATI paradigm). These possibilities will be elaborated in Section 5.3.

Summary of Existing Research

We have examined a number of studies which have explored the relationships between simultaneous–successive processing and school achievement. Their results can be seen from two complementary perspectives. The first perspective derives from the factor analyses that have found a separate school achievement or verbal-educational factor (Das, 1973b; Krywaniuk, 1974; Sprecht, 1976). These findings indicate that school achievement is to some extent separable from the information-processing battery, a result which is in common with Vernon's (1969) concept of $v{:}ed$ or Cattell's g_c. One may suggest that the school achievement cluster can be seen as a partial measure of planning and goal-setting behaviors. This suggestion will be tentative, however, until specific tests of planning and decision making (which are by no means easy to devise) have been related to the simultaneous–successive battery and to school achievement.

The second perspective is supported by the regression analyses (Krywaniuk, 1974; Sprecht, 1976), the factor score studies (Cummins & Das, 1977; Kirby & Das, 1977), and by McLeod's (1978) doctoral dissertation on inferencing. School achievement is dependent upon both simultaneous and successive processing. For the average reader, reading achievement seems to be equally dependent upon both processes, and only on the simultaneous for the better reader. Mathematics achievement may be more dependent upon simultaneous processing. These two different perspectives need not be seen as contradictory since school achievement as an indication of planning may well be dependent to a certain extent upon simultaneous and successive processing. From another point of view, school achievement may emerge as a separate factor because the tests comprising school achievement are similar, perhaps, in their input and output demands. Nevertheless, the same tests, taken individually, may correlate with simultaneous and successive factor scores. Statistically speaking, this is not unusual.

Though much more work is required to confirm these conclusions, it should be noted that the results, while complex, are reasonably consistent. Similar patterns have been found within different age groups (elementary and secondary students). Interpretable differences have been found among groups at different levels of achievement. Most importantly, the general pattern of these results is suggestive of a number of remedial and educational applications to which we turn briefly. A full account will be found in Chapter 9.

5.3   IMPLICATIONS FOR REMEDIATION AND EDUCATION

As was demonstrated earlier, school achievement is related in a meaningful fashion to simultaneous and successive processing. The importance of this relationship is not in its predictive power: The amount of school achievement variance predicted by the simultaneous–successive battery is by no means as great as that predicted by most standardized group intelligence tests. The importance lies rather in the understanding that this gives of the nature of school achievement, and in the suggestions that arise to deal with poor school achievement. We will discuss three approaches to remediation.

Improving Process.   Because both simultaneous and successive processing can be seen as cognitive *skills,* the model leads one to expect that they are subject to improvement through some form of instruction or training. Such optimism is generally not generated by cognitive constructs that are defined as *capacities*. It would seem that the most obvious application of the simultaneous–successive model would be in designing remedial programs that would encourage the development of improved processing abilities in those judged low in them.

Improving these skills, however, will not necessarily be an easy matter. In normal development they have been built up in an integrated manner over many years: In particular, the importance of the different primary, secondary, and tertiary zones should be remembered. A simple-minded remedial program that does not ensure the generalization of the skills taught over the various levels will not be successful. Transfer of training to school achievement tasks will be most likely to occur if the training involves school-related materials. Even if programs begin with simpler materials, they should eventually include tasks of the complexity of the desired behaviors. If improved reading is the ultimate goal, even a process-oriented approach must use reading and language-based materials.

The model itself does not suggest any estimate of the mutability of these processes. In some subjects, certainly those with detectable brain damage, improvement in a mode of processing may not be possible. In fact, the optimism that this model generates may be entirely misplaced: Both forms of processing may prove to be virtually unchangeable.

Design of Alternate Educational Environments. If processes are difficult to improve, a second approach to remediation would be to design educational programs that make use of whatever processing strengths the individual does have. Such programs would attempt to present materials or tasks in a form that would be congruent with an individual's more efficient form of processing, and would also provide the individual with as many "supports" as possible with regard to his less efficient mode of processing. These supports would include strategies to employ the more efficient form of processing, as well as more artificial aids (e.g., notebooks, etc.). Because these programs would have very similar educational goals for the student, they would necessarily involve materials and tasks of the desired complexity.

Teaching of Strategies. The third remedial strategy involves the teaching of strategies to individuals, so that they employ the optimal processes in a task. Unlike the first two remedial strategies, this one assumes that there is no processing deficit, but rather a strategy weakness. (It will be remembered that we have distinguished between processes and strategies. The former occur in Block 2, the latter are a Block 3 function and involve the proper deployment of a sequence of processes.) The two remedial studies conducted to date made use of this strategy; they will be more fully described in Chapter 9.

In conclusion, it might be suggested that this third strategy will prove to be the simplest to implement and the most effective. Subsequent chapters will demonstrate that both simultaneous and successive processing can be identified in a variety of ability and cultural groups. If in fact these processes do exist in most groups (with the possible exception of the brain damaged), the solution may then be seen as teaching the individual how best to use these in approaching an academic task.

6

Understanding Mental Retardation and Learning Disability

The previous discussion of school achievement has dealt with simultaneous and successive cognitive processes within the normal range of individual differences. This range is composed of children who are generally coping with the requirements of school learning, but who differ widely, nonetheless, in their degree of success.

Of particular interest to us in this chapter, however, are those groups of children whose degree of success is markedly low for reasons of problems in cognitive functioning. Our discussion here focuses on two dominant varieties of these children, namely the mentally retarded and the learning disabled. Our purpose is to discuss the results of recent research on simultaneous and successive cognitive processes in these two groups, and to suggest the implications of these studies.

6.1 GENERAL AND SPECIFIC COGNITIVE PROBLEMS

Research on simultaneous and successive syntheses suggests that this theory is both a comprehensive and valid description of cognitive activity. To the extent that the theory is accurate in this regard, as suggested by research on children within the normal range of behavior, the parameters of the model may also be used to describe children encountering problems in cognitive functioning. If we return to our basic model, we may raise several questions in advance concerning how these problems may arise.

It will be recalled that Luria's conception of the brain is that it consists of three blocks. The first of these is responsible for arousal, the second controls simultaneous and successive varieties of coding, and the third is responsible for planning and decision making. A basic, and as yet largely unresolved question that may be asked of this conception is the extent to which the blocks may be functionally independent of one another. This question is particularly important because the degree of independence will determine, in large part, whether problems in cognitive functioning will necessarily be general to the total area of cognition, or may be specific to one type of cognitive activity. If, for example, the relationship between coding in Block 2 and planning and decision making in Block 3 is highly interdependent, one would not expect to find children who are quite adequate in functioning in one of these areas, but highly deficient in the other. Furthermore, if the activity of Block 1 may interfere with the activities of the other blocks, inadequate coding or decision functions may be the result of such interference.

Beyond this question of the relationship between the blocks of the brain, we may focus on the second block and ask this question again of its functions. It will be recalled that our elaboration of Luria's model suggests that central processing in Block 2 is either simultaneous or successive, and each of these may be found in perceptual, mnestic, or conceptual tasks. To what extent are the two varieties of processing independent of one another in different populations, and to what extent is performance in the perceptual, mnestic, and conceptual areas interdependent?

The questions raised here regarding the theory are certainly substantial and difficult to research, but they should form the essential basis of any discussion of problems in cognitive functioning. Past research on children encountering many different varieties of problems, in addition to the mentally retarded and learning disabled, has often made implicit assumptions regarding these issues but without recognition of the implications of these assumptions. Some views of learning disabilities, for example, propose that modality-specific defects are responsible for the learning-disabled child's problems, while others propose a more generalized central process defect. Gaining some resolution of this issue is particularly important, because effective planning of remedial programs should flow directly from research results.

In the discussions to follow in this chapter, we attempt to keep these questions before us as we discuss the results of our studies. We will then return to them explicitly in our concluding remarks.

6.2 UNDERSTANDING MENTAL RETARDATION

Intellectual subnormality has not been adequately defined, partly because "intelligence" itself does not have a definition that is generally accepted. As we have indicated previously (cf. Chapter 1), the major reason for this lack of definition has been the lack of adequate theory. The study of intelligence had long consisted of the atheoretical measurement of intelligence; thus, "Intelligence is what intelligence tests measure."

The equating of intelligence with IQ test scores leads to a number of problems. A fundamental difficulty is that this denies the efforts of the early workers in the field (e.g., Galton Binet, Spearman) to describe the nature of higher mental functions. By reducing intelligence to IQ scores, which in turn are only designed to predict success in our culture's current schools, we lose sight of the concept of intelligence as adaptive mental functioning. A person's intellectual behavior cannot be captured in his or her performance on tasks requiring mostly school-related skills (e.g., analogical reasoning, etc.). The philosopher, the scientist, and the artist are all too different in their "mental" functions, even if they might have had the same IQ when they were school children.

The second major difficulty relates to the issue of increasing intelligence test scores. Binet originally designed his intelligence test to sort out children of different "abilities" for the purpose of school learning. This ability was thought to be basic, independent of the child's performance in reading, writing, or arithmetic, though manifested both in the school tasks and the IQ test scores. So powerful has this assumption been that educators have ever since been looking for disparities between ability and achievement, and attempting to bring the child's achievement up to the level of his or her ability. However, measures of ability (intelligence) and school achievement are separate though not independent. Unless the test score distributions are unusual, for every child whose ability exceeds his achievement, another's achievement will exceed his potential. There may be as much of a case in favor of tutoring the child so that his IQ reaches the level of his achievement scores. This is patently absurd, but tutors of intelligence have flourished lately (cf. Whimbey, 1975). Their main objective is to improve a person's score on intelligence tests or similar tests of "ability." When intelligence is defined solely by what the test measures, one can expect such reductionist approaches to improving intelligence.

Zigler (1966) sums up the need for understanding intelligence in a chapter on mental retardation as follows: "A major section of this chapter was devoted to a discussion of our critical need for a comprehensive theory of intelligence, including an adequate definition of this construct. The limitations of the psychometric approach, with its emphasis on the contents of behavior, rather than on the cognitive processes which mediate behavior was noted [p. 158]." We have presented in this book the beginnings of a theory of intelligence in terms of cognitive processes. We would like to present some data, first on mentally retarded children and later on children with learning difficulties.

Before we attempt to understand mental retardation with the help of our information integration model, let us first examine how it should be defined. Currently, both intellectual deficiency and social adjustment are considered for the purposes of categorizing the retardate. The manual of the American Association on Mental Deficiency emphasizes adaptive behavior as much as IQ as criteria for classification. The inclusion of adaptation is defensible if IQ test performance does not exhaust what we understand as intelligent behavior, and if the IQ can be supplemented by indices of social adjustment; even the two criteria together cannot be seen to encompass all of intelligent behavior. Because of problems in quantifying adaptation, classification based upon it is likely to be weak. As we do not have an entirely adequate measure of intelligence, we must tolerate some weakness in defining mental retardation.

If we define intelligence not in terms of the ability to reason or to abstract, to memorize or to code, but rather in terms of the competence in the utilization of information for goal attainment (Das, 1973a), then social adaptation need not be outside the sphere of intelligent behavior. An individual's efficiency in decision making and in carrying out activities that are programmed for attaining a goal are functions of the second and, in particular, the third blocks of our information integration model. From our point of view, the retarded child is backward in the decision-making and planning processes which determine how information is encoded and the task executed. The basic Block 3 problem is manifested in the poor control of Block 2 or even Block 1 processes, thus giving the impression of general depressed ability.

The retarded child may never reach the same level of competence as a normal child of the same age. This is in contrast to the view held by some, such as Zigler, who has argued that the cultural familial retardate is merely at a lower stage of development, there being no qualitative differences between his cognitive functions and those of a normal child. Zigler considers the cultural familial retardate to be no more developmentally different from the normal child than the latter is from the gifted child. Presumably children of equivalent mental age, whatever their chronological age, would be at a similar developmental level.

We think that it is an error to suggest that the child with superior intellect on one hand and the retarded child on the other differ from the intellectually average child only in degree, or that children of equal mental age have equivalent cognitive abilities. A bright 10-year-old does not have the same strategies in, say, problem solving as a dull 15-year-old child of equal mental age. The retarded and the normal differ not only in the level of their performance, but also in the processes they use in cognitive tasks (cf. Das, 1972). It should be emphasized, however, that the difference is not merely in the coding processes, but more importantly in those planning or strategic processes which control the coding processes. We shall discuss these points in subsequent sections in relation to a number of factor-analytic studies of simultaneous–successive processing and mental retardation.

Mental Retardation and Simultaneous and Successive Processing

The theory of simultaneous and successive cognitive syntheses has been applied several times in the study of mental retardation over the last 5 years. Indeed, encouragement to develop this theory originated in a study of nonretarded and educable mentally retarded subjects by Das (1972). Following Das's study, several other investigations have taken place which have modified his conclusions somewhat, but also have been instrumental in developing the theory. We will discuss these studies in their order of completion.

Das (1972) compared 60 retarded and 60 nonretarded subjects in cognitive test performance. The nonretarded subjects had a mean IQ of 92.06 and the group of retarded subjects had a mean IQ of 67.08. All subjects were given a series of cognitive tests consisting of some of the instruments discussed previously. These tests were Raven's Coloured Progressive Matrices, Memory-for-Designs, Cross-modal Coding, Visual Short-Term Memory, Auditory Serial Recall, and Auditory Free Recall. One should note the absence of Figure Copying and the two speed tasks (Word Reading and Color Naming).

The data from the tests for each group were intercorrelated and subjected to separate principal-components analyses with Varimax rotations. The resulting factor matrices are given in Table 6.1. It is seen that two factors emerged in each of the analyses.

The factors in the analysis for the nonretarded group show some discrepancies from some of the analyses discussed in earlier chapters. Factor I may be considered simultaneous synthesis, because of its strong loading from Raven's Progressive Matrices. This factor also has strong loadings from Cross-modal Coding and Visual Short-Term Memory. However, the loading of Visual Short-Term Memory is quite anomalous in the light of the other research we have reported. For Factor II, the high loadings are from Memory-for-Designs, Serial Recall, and Free Recall. If this factor represents

Table 6.1
Principal Components with Varimax Rotation for Samples in Das (1972) and Jarman (1978b)

Test	Das (1972) Nonretarded sample		Das (1972) Retarded sample		Jarman (1978) Retarded sample	
	Simultaneous	Successive	Simultaneous	Successive	Simultaneous	Successive
Raven's Coloured Progressive Matrices	.792	.161	.786	.007	.943	.076
Figure Copying	—	—	—	—	.865	−.159
Memory-for-Designs[a]	.269	.579	.830	−.061	−.894	.183
IQ score from school record	.492	.176	.529	.326	—	—
Cross-modal Coding	.742	−.020	.546	.482	—	—
Visual Short-Term Memory	.693	.294	.533	.481	.060	.977
Serial Recall	.154	.683	.048	.855	.198	.879
Free Recall	.023	.757	.043	.856	—	—
Digit Span Forward	—	—	—	—	.033	.809
Percentage of total variance	28.5	21.7	31.04	29.13	41.34	40.77

[a] Error score transformed to yield positive loading in Das.

successive synthesis, then the Memory-for-Designs loading is also a departure from the results of other studies.

Turning to the results for the retarded subjects, we find, curiously, a factor pattern which is actually closer in form to the results of other studies than is the pattern for the nonretarded subjects. Factor I in this matrix has high loadings from Raven's Progressive Matrices, Memory-for-Designs, and, to a lesser extent, the IQ score from school records and Cross-modal Coding. This factor is more clearly identifiable as simultaneous synthesis. Factor II of the matrix for the retarded subjects has its major loadings from Free and Serial Recall, and has moderate loadings from Cross-modal Coding and Visual Short-Term Memory. This factor more clearly represents successive synthesis.

In explaining the results of these analyses, Das first considered an interpretation based on Jensen's (1969, 1970) model of Level I–Level II abilities. It was noted, however, that Jensen's model was not consistent with the results in such respects as the loading of a memory test, Memory-for-Designs, and a reasoning test, Raven's Progressive Matrices, on a common factor. The groups differed in mean performance in all tests; major differences were not confined to the reasoning tests, as predicted by Jensen's theory. These discrepancies, in part, led Das to introduce simultaneous and successive syntheses as possible explanations of the data.

The main issue in that study was a feasible explanation of the different factor patterns obtained for the two groups. Das approached this problem by suggesting that these different patterns represented differing uses of cognitive strategies by the subjects. It was speculated that the loading of the Memory-for-Designs test on a successive factor in the nonretarded group, for instance, represented recall of the figures as a sequence of lines. The interpretation placed on the loading of this test on the simultaneous factor in the retarded group was that the retarded child recalled the figure as a whole. Thus it was generally concluded that simultaneous and successive syntheses were functional cognitive processes in the cognitive repertoire of both retarded as well as nonretarded children, but that these two groups of subjects differed in their use of these processes. This is a subtle distinction, which led in later studies to efforts to distinguish processes from strategies and also capacities. In addition to these learner variables, task variables which interacted with these were also posited, and will be discussed.

For several years following Das's (1972) study, research on simultaneous and successive syntheses swung toward cross-cultural differences, academic achievement, and theoretical development. Recently, however, the question of different patterns of cognitive processes between retarded and nonretarded children has been readdressed. Jarman and Das (1977) broadened the question to include high-IQ subjects in order to determine if a general trend in changes in processes could be detected across a wide range of intelligence. Jarman and Das selected three intelligence groups on the basis of Lorge–Thorndike IQ scores. The low-IQ group had a mean verbal IQ of 81.70 and a mean performance IQ of 86.05. The normal-IQ group had an average verbal IQ of 101.03 and the average for the performance IQ was 100.12. The third group, in the high-IQ category, had a mean verbal IQ of 119.57 and a performance IQ average of 120.02. Thus, the composition of the groups was such that the major portion of the normalized intelligence range was represented.

A set of the simultaneous–successive tests was given to all subjects, with the tests administered individually or in small groups. The instruments that were used were Raven's Progressive Matrices, Figure Copying, Memory-for-Designs, Serial Recall, Visual Short-Term Memory, Word Reading, and an Auditory–Visual Cross-modal Matching task (see Jarman, 1977a). As in previous studies, the data were intercorrelated and analyzed by principal components with a Varimax rotation, with separate analyses for each group.

Table 6.2
Principal Components with Varimax Rotation, Low-IQ Group

Test	I	II	III
Raven's Coloured Progressive Matrices	.618	−.265	−.516
Figure Copying	.744	.070	.198
Memory-for-Designs (errors)	−.811	−.010	−.121
Serial Recall	.058	−.421	.604
Visual Short-Term Memory	.199	−.637	.292
Word Reading	.186	.881	.005
Auditory–Visual Matching	.213	−.101	.820
Percentage of total variance	24.51	20.63	20.61

The factor matrix for the low-IQ group is presented in Table 6.2. Factor I has high loadings from Raven's Progressive Matrices, Figure Copying, and Memory-for-Designs. It should be noted that the Memory-for-Designs test is scored for errors, and if these are used without negative transformations, a negative loading is obtained, as is seen here. The composition of Factor I is quite clearly simultaneous synthesis.

The second factor in Table 6.2 apparently represents successive synthesis and speed. Visual Short-Term Memory and Serial Recall both demand successive recall but in this low-IQ group, speed of rehearsal in the tasks was also a determinant of performance. In subjects with higher speeds of processing, rehearsal was more effective, which increased recall performance. Factor III of Table 6.2 represents the operation of successive synthesis in the Auditory–Visual Matching task. Raven's Progressive Matrices has a negative loading on this factor, and Serial Recall has a high positive loading. Thus, the low-IQ group may have used a strategy of sequential recall of the auditory portion of the Auditory–Visual task, and then matched this information with the visual display.

The factor matrix for the normal-IQ group is presented in Table 6.3. The

Table 6.3
Principal Components with Varimax Rotation, Normal-IQ Group

Test	I	II
Raven's Coloured Progressive Matrices	.761	.001
Figure Copying	.653	−.284
Memory-for-Designs (errors)	−.716	.098
Serial Recall	.123	−.748
Visual Short-Term Memory	.250	−.690
Word Reading	.081	.789
Auditory–Visual Matching	.722	−.033
Percentage of total variance	30.33	25.00

clearest point of difference is evident in the solution of two factors, as opposed to the three factors found for the low-IQ group.

Factor I of the results for the normal-IQ group is once again simultaneous synthesis. The Raven's Progressive Matrices, Figure Copying, and Memory-for-Designs tests identify this factor quite clearly. Interestingly, however, the Auditory–Visual Matching task also loads on this factor for the normal-IQ group. Jarman and Das (1977) speculated that this latter finding was due to the use of a visualization strategy by the normal-IQ subjects. As the auditory stimuli were presented, the subject may have visualized what form these would take in space, in order to match the information with the subsequent visual comparison. This is one of the several strategies that may be used for this task as discussed by Kahn and Birch (1968).

The second factor in the analysis for the normal-IQ group apparently represents successive synthesis and speed. This factor is quite similar to the second factor found for the low-IQ group, due to a similar relationship between speed and successive synthesis.

The results for the high-IQ group are presented in Table 6.4. It is seen that a three-factor solution was obtained once again, similar to the low-IQ group.

Factor I of this analysis for the high-IQ group is simultaneous synthesis. Figure Copying has a slightly reduced loading on this factor, but the composition of the factor is quite clear despite this change.

The second factor of this analysis represents successive synthesis. It is interesting to note that the Auditory–Visual Matching task also loads on this factor, as it did for the low-IQ group.

Finally, the third factor of these results is a speed factor, and is quite comparable to that found in other analyses, such as those reported in Chapter 4.

The results of these three analyses on the IQ groups suggest some conclusions different from those derived from the first study by Das (1972).

Table 6.4
Principal Components with Varimax Rotation, High-IQ Group

Test	I	II	III
Raven's Coloured Progressive Matrices	.789	.197	.091
Figure Copying	.595	.089	.492
Memory-for-Designs (errors)	−.741	−.116	−.050
Serial Recall	−.046	.672	−.404
Visual Short-Term Memory	−.105	.722	−.078
Word Reading	−.163	−.123	.808
Auditory–Visual Matching	.176	.643	.331
Percentage of total variance	22.81	20.88	16.91

The analyses in Jarman and Das (1977) generally show more comparability between groups in the composition of the factors. One possible reason for the differences between the two studies is that the Figure Copying test and a speed test were used in the later study, and these tests aided in a clearer definition of the factors. Through the use of more tests to define factors, this study generally supports the view that similar cognitive processes are characteristic of subjects at the lower range of intelligence, in comparison to normal subjects. Further, by the use of a high-IQ group, it was possible to generalize this conclusion of similar processes to the high-IQ range, thereby making the low–normal comparison more meaningful.

One limitation of the study, however, in its implications for analyzing the patterns of simultaneous and successive syntheses as a function of mental retardation, is that the low group involved in the study was not fully comparable to the retarded group used by Das (1972). The latter group was lower in IQ, and therefore the question still may be asked whether such subjects are characterized by qualitatively different cognitive processes. Jarman (1978b) addressed this question by studying a group of 67 educable mentally retarded children with a mean IQ of 66.17 and a mean chronological age (CA) in months of 132.07. Tests of significance on IQ and CA revealed no differences between Jarman's sample and Das's (1972) subjects.

Jarman administered the full battery of simultaneous and successive tests to all subjects. The results for the principal components analysis were presented in Table 6.1. The first factor is clearly simultaneous synthesis, as defined by Raven's Progressive Matrices, Figure Copying, and Memory-for-Designs. The second factor is defined by Serial Recall, Visual Short-Term Memory, and Digit Span, and is successive synthesis. These results indicate that the pattern of simultaneous and successive syntheses in educable mentally retarded children is directly comparable to the patterns typically obtained for nonretarded children. The retarded children do have significantly lower mean levels of performance on the simultaneous–successive tests, in comparison to nonretarded children. What the comparable factor patterns demonstrate, in effect, is that similar cognitive processes are responsible for these different levels of performance.

The three studies that we have discussed here allow some general conclusions regarding the nature of simultaneous and successive cognitive processes in retarded and nonretarded children, and more generally as a function of a wide range of intelligence. Das (1972) demonstrated different factor patterns between retarded and nonretarded children. These differences were attributed to differences in strategic behavior between the groups. The replication by Jarman (1978b), however, demonstrated that methodological considerations appeared to be responsible for these variations, and, with the Jarman and Das (1977) study, indicated that comparable patterns exist across a wide range of intelligence, from low to high IQ.

If fundamentally the same cognitive processes characterize children of widely different general intelligence levels, does this imply that differences in strategic behavior, as first conjectured by Das (1972), are nonexistent? Other lines of research in mental retardation would indicate that this is not the case.

In a recent study, for example, we investigated the strategies of educable mentally retarded (EMR) adolescents in solving two-term syllogism problems. Fifty-two EMRs, aged 13–15, were administered the simultaneous–successive battery, the WISC, spelling, reading, and arithmetic achievement tests, and syllogism tasks consisting of eight two-term syllogisms and two three-term syllogisms. Mean WISC full-scale IQ was 70. Factor scores for simultaneous and successive processing were derived, and these were analyzed with the other variables by principal components, with a Varimax rotation (see Table 6.5). The three factors that emerge are identifiable respectively as reading, simultaneous processing, and successive processing.

Of particular interest in this study is the loading of the syllogisms test upon successive processing. Previous research by Cummins (see Das, Kirby, & Jarman, 1975) with normal high school students had shown syllogisms to load upon simultaneous processing. The loading of syllogisms upon successive processing for the EMRs suggests that they are using a successive strategy in these problems, perhaps concentrating upon retaining the problem information in input (sequential) order. Thus, while simultaneous and successive processes may exist in both retardates and normals,

Table 6.5
Principal-Components Analysis (Varimax Rotation) of Fifty-Two Educable Mentally Retarded Adolescents

Test	I Reading	II Simultaneous	III Successive
WISC Verbal	.190	.197	.612
WISC Performance	−.129	.835	−.171
Spelling	.906	−.172	.090
Arithmetic	.252	.680	−.012
Oral reading	.889	−.131	.213
Silent reading	.813	.290	.154
Syllogisms	−.001	−.064	.768
Successive	.201	−.175	.715
Simultaneous	−.166	.790	.109
Percentage of total variance	24.6	19.9	16.0

and while these processes may be defined by the same set of marker tests (the simultaneous–successive battery) in both groups, the two groups may employ the processes differently in solving more complex tasks.

A Note on Strategies and Processes

In the previous section, we stressed the possibility that normals and retardates employ different strategies in performing tasks. It is important to discuss how one establishes that different strategies are being employed, and also to distinguish strategies from their component processes.

Strategies are essentially plans of action, and must be inferred. In some cases the inference of a strategy is relatively easy; for instance, in the Figure Copying task, it is possible to observe the copying behavior of the child. The number of times he stops and looks at the figure and the order in which he draws the segments of the figure provide good clues about the strategy the child is using. But our inference about his strategy is still an interpretation of his behavior.

Because they are information-processing plans or programs, strategies are composed of a series of actions and/or processes. Thus processes (e.g., simultaneous or successive processing) are components of strategies; the strategy involves a decision about which form of processing to employ at a certain point in the problem solution. Complex tasks may require a complex sequence of processes in correct juxtaposition. The strategy chosen is a function of the coded information available to the individual (e.g., his past experience), his habitual way of responding in certain situations (perhaps culturally determined), the processes he is able to use, and the outcome demands of the task. As described, strategies are clearly a function of the third functional unit of the brain, the frontal lobes (cf. Chapters 2 and 3). However, it can be seen, as Luria's interdependent model would suggest, that the workings of Block 3 can be greatly influenced by the other two blocks.

We suggest that group differences in performance, reflecting relative competence in a task, can be attributed to the use of optional or suboptimal strategies. This is not to deny that different levels of competence exist, but rather that competence to some extent may be defined in terms of the ability to choose, and use, the optimal strategy. Strategy differences may be indicated by differences in factor loadings between groups, but they may even be inferred when factor structures are similar, if other data are supportive.

In the preceding section, we suggested that a major difference between retardates and normals was in the area of planning or decision making. In the next section, we shall consider a similar issue in the context of describing learning disabled children.

6.3   LEARNING DISABILITY

One could write an entire chapter on the definitions of learning disability. So varied are these that the term hardly has a denotative meaning. Probably one should disregard the term and consider the various problems of the heterogeneous community of the learning disabled as learning difficulties. "Difficulties" is not a pejorative label; it invites the specialist, be he or she educator or physician, to examine learning difficulties with a view to remediation. Learning disability, particularly when defined to include "minimal brain damage," is sometimes classified as a pathological syndrome. Although one may look upon instances of learning disabilities within the psychopathology of cognition, it is hardly a disease. The purpose of labeling children should be to identify a group to receive certain services (Hobbs, 1975); it should not attempt to elevate the difficulties of children to the status of a disease.

An information-processing approach to learning disabilities has several advantages. First of all, it makes one relate performance to cognitive processes and hence facilitates the development of remedial measures. Because it is based upon a general model of cognition, an information-processing approach to learning disabilities would tend to suggest remediation that has a firmer theoretical rationale. Much research and practice in the field of learning disabilities has suffered either from the lack of a theoretical rationale, or from the too-rigid adherence to an outmoded one. Models should be challenged, and consequently modified or superseded, but this should cause appropriate changes in the understanding and remediation of learning disabilities. The important point is that research and practice in the field of learning disabilities should not remain insular to progress in the psychology of cognition and child development.

Probably the most appropriate point to make about learning disabilities is that they are of several kinds. In the remainder of this chapter we will consider two different approaches to learning disability, which concentrate, respectively, on reading disability and hyperactivity.

A Study of Reading Disability

One of the most important considerations in labeling a child as learning disabled is reading retardation. Reading disability or specific reading deficit refers to a relatively homogeneous class of children who are at least 2 years behind their grade norms for reading, and does not include children who are emotionally disturbed, mentally retarded, or have obvious handicaps in vision and learning. While a number of writers (e.g., McCarthy & McCarthy, 1969) prefer to include disorders of listening, thinking, spelling, and arithmetic under the definition of learning disabilities, such broad catch-all categories are not useful in the experimental investigation of the characteristics of a particular group of children. It is important when describing a problem to delimit the problem in advance, as much as is possible.

Leong (1974) studied the problem of reading disability in the context of the simultaneous–successive model. His subjects were a group of 58 retarded readers (mean age of 111 months, mean Lorge–Thorndike nonverbal IQ of 102.45), who were at least 2½ grades below in their reading, and 58 control children (mean age of 111 months, mean Lorge–Thorndike nonverbal IQ of 107.57) from the same schools who were superior in reading (above the 75th percentile on the Gates–MacGinity Reading Test). All subjects were males.

Leong matched the groups on nonverbal IQ (as well as sex, age, and school) to eliminate the possibility that differences in reading could be due to differences in IQ. Matching on verbal IQ would have eliminated the verbal processes which differentiated the groups.

Comparison of reading disabled and control children was made in terms of their performance in dichotic listening as well as in the simultaneous and successive tasks. Leong was, in fact, more interested in determining if the reading retarded group was poor in processing information given through the right ear (left brain). Incomplete lateralization of hemispheric functions has been advanced as one of the antecedents of learning disability. (e.g., Orton, 1937). His other question concerned the relationship between competence in successive processing and reading achievement.

Eight tasks were used to tap simultaneous–successive processing. Six of these were from the battery used by Das, Kirby, and Jarman (1975) and the remaining two tasks were subtests from the revised Illinois Test of Psycholinguistic Abilities (Kirk, McCarthy, & Kirk, 1968). The tasks from the battery were Raven's Coloured Progressive Matrices, Figure Copying, Memory-for-Designs, Cross-modal Coding, Visual Short-Term Memory, and Serial Recall. The psycholinguistic tests were Visual Sequential Memory and Auditory Sequential Memory. The last two were chosen because of their superficial similarity with successive tasks. In addition to these, two dichotic listening tests using digits and letters of the alphabet were included. Dichotic tasks have been used to study hemispheric specialization in the perception of speech. We shall not be able to refer here to the vast literature on dichotic listening tasks as measures of hemispheric asymmetry.

However, for the purpose of relating dichotic performance to simultaneous–successive processing it was hypothesized that dichotic listening would require predominantly successive rather than simultaneous processing. One of the dichotic listening tasks required the child to report all the digits and letters which he heard in one ear first and then those he heard in the other ear, that is, to report by sides. In the other dichotic listening task the child was instructed to report either all the numbers first or all the letters first, irrespective of ears, that is, to report by types.

We shall report only the main results of Leong's study; more complete details may be found elsewhere (Leong, 1974).

Leong first set out to investigate the similarity of the factor structures of the 10-test battery in the two groups. The results of his principal-components analyses with Variax rotations can be seen in Table 6.6. Three factors were extracted in each case. The first factor of both analyses is successive processing, defined by Serial Recall, ITPA Auditory Memory, the two dichotic tasks, and partially by Auditory–Visual Coding. Unexpectedly, Visual Short-Term Meory loads upon this factor for the control group, but not for the retarded readers. The second factor for both groups is simultaneous processing, defined as is usual by Raven's Matrices, Figure Copying, Memory-for-Designs, and the split loading of Auditory–Visual Coding. The third factor for the retarded readers was largely defined by Visual Short-Term Memory and to a lesser extent by the dichotic tasks and Figure Copying. Leong labeled this factor "perceptual organization." The third factor for the control group was marked by low scores on Figure Copying and high scores on ITPA Visual Memory.

It can be seen in Table 6.6 that the first two factors, simultaneous and successive, are similar in both groups, although there is some variability in factor loadings. This suggests that both modes of processing exist in both groups, and that they approach most of the basic tasks within the battery in similar ways. The most interesting feature of Leong's results concerns Visual Short-Term Memory, which failed to load upon successive processing in the retarded reading group. There are several possible explanations of this result. The first would be that it is due to the lack of speed tests in the battery used by Leong. These speed tests (e.g., Word Reading, Color Naming) help to delineate the nature of simultaneous or successive tests which may be otherwise confounded with speed in certain samples (e.g., Grade 1 children, Das & Molloy, 1975). Thus it is possible that the separate factor defined by Visual Short-Term Memory is really a speed factor, as might have been apparent had speed tests been included.

A second explanation of the Visual Short-Term Memory result might be that normal children make use of a sequential scanning strategy (i.e., a successive strategy) that the retarded readers do not make use of in this

Table 6.6
Principal Components with Varimax Rotation of Eight Cognitive and Two Dichotic Tasks for Retarded Readers and Control Children[a]

Test	Retarded readers Factors			Control group Factors		
	I	II	III	I	II	III
Raven's Coloured Progressive Matrices	.153	.753	-.002	-.025	.828	-.115
Figure Copying	-.144	.705	.350	.197	.533	-.634
Memory-for-Designs (errors)	-.051	-.788	-.049	.124	-.749	-.229
Auditory–Visual Matching	.431	.466	.183	.373	.520	.179
Visual Short-Term Memory	.081	.115	.832	.592	.026	.331
Serial Recall	.866	.124	.024	.082	-.048	-.072
ITPA Visual Memory	.254	.508	-.162	.123	.348	.751
ITPA Auditory Memory	.774	.062	.027	.799	-.028	-.231
Dichotic Listening (SIDES)	.456	-.073	.531	.753	.088	-.025
Dichotic Listening (TYPES)	.667	.178	.311	.800	.100	.206
Percentage of total variance	23.06	22.30	12.57	31.50	18.69	12.49

[a] $N=58$ in each group.

104

task. The retarded readers might make use of a more global strategy. This explanation would make sense, in that sequential scanning strategies are probably important in reading, and might well be absent in retarded readers.

Leong also demonstrated that the retarded readers performed poorly compared to the normals on most of the tasks. (See Table 6.7.) The control group had higher scores on all tests except ITPA Visual Memory. A Hotelling T^2 (Tatsuoka, 1971) comparing the two groups on the eight variables (omitting the dichotic tasks) was significant ($T_2 = 154.19$, $F = 18.09$, $p <$ .01).

Leong's results generally indicate that although there is little difference in factor structure for simultaneous and successive processing in the two groups, they are quite different in competence in the tasks, in spite of being matched for nonverbal IQ. As we have suggested previously, this might be due to their use of inefficient strategies for approaching the tasks. It may be suggested that the deficit is not so much in reading as in strategic behavior. Such an explanation would agree with existing findings, for example, by Senf (1969) who has given bisensory memory tasks to reading disabled children. He found that they are less able to recall bisensory pairs of digits and considers it possible that the deficit is in their ability to integrate inputs from different sources. Thus, the difficulty that the reading disabled group faces with new tasks of the kind we have used is not merely a difficulty in handling temporal sequences; both kinds of information processing may be deficient.

Table 6.7

Means for Reading Retarded and Control Group on Eight Cognitive Tasks, and Hotelling T^2 Test

Variable	Means		Hotelling T^2	F(df 8/107)	p
	Retarded readers	Control			
Raven's Coloured Progressive Matrices	22.60	28.19	45.47	5.33	<.01
Figure Copying	12.21	14.55	30.30	3.55	<.01
Memory-for-Designs	8.57	4.43	19.08	2.24	<.03
Auditory–Visual Coding (Cross-modal)	6.26	8.15	29.67	3.48	<.01
Visual Short-Term Memory	60.84	82.91	74.38	8.73	<.01
Serial Recall	57.12	72.17	58.34	6.84	<.01
ITPA Visual Memory	20.55	21.98	5.28	.62	NS
ITPA Auditory Memory	27.17	34.30	25.78	3.02	<.01
Group centroid			154.186	18.090	<.01

In Chapter 5 we discussed a study by Kirby and Das (1977) that indicated that reading vocabulary and reading comprehension were both related to simultaneous and successive processing, in normal children. While the children in that study were not retarded readers, the results of that study would support Leong's conclusion that both simultaneous and successive processing are necessary for reading competence.

Reading disability needs to be understood in the context of reading "ability"—the processes involved in the acquisition and performance of reading. Leong's work suggests that appropriate strategies as well as coding are important for learning to read or failure to do so. What these strategies are and whether or not one type of coding is more relevant than the other for the various aspects of reading (e.g., comprehension, inferencing, vocabulary) are further topics for research. The studies reported in Chapter 5 and Leong's research seem to suggest that it would be worthwhile to investigate the relation between aspects of reading competence and the three components of our model—planning, simultaneous–successive coding, and arousal. This relationship would be expected to change as a function of the child's development as well as in terms of his level of incompetence in reading. A proper developmental study of reading disability is needed.

A Study of Hyperactivity

In the classroom a second group of very visible learning disabled children are the hyperactives. Hyperactivity is characterized by behavioral over-activity, and levels of hyperactivity can be assessed through teachers' ratings of classroom behavior (Davids, 1971). Hyperactivity is common among learning disabled children although a full range of activity, from hypoactivity to normal activity to hyperactivity, is found among them. Customarily only the two extreme groups have been studied (Dykman, Ackerman, Clements, & Peters, 1971).

Hyperactivity has not generally been related to differences in cognitive processes; instead, investigators have explored the relation between physiological arousal and hyperactivity (cf. Cohen & Douglas, 1972; Wender, 1971). There are many references to the poor academic performance of hyperactives, and to an improvement in academic standing if the individual child is responsive to stimulant drugs (Satterfield, 1975). In terms of our model, hyperactivity would appear to be largely a function of the Block 1 (arousal) unit, though it can interfere with the functioning of the other two units.

There are two ways in which hyperactivity can affect academic performance. First of all, the hyperactive child may not learn efficiently because his restlessness and mood changes interfere directly with acquisition as well as with performance. Poor academic performance may thus be a secondary product of excessive activity. Alternatively, or in addition to this, hyperactivity may indicate a state of low cortical arousal, an arousal deficit (Wender, 1971). Satterfield (1975) and Williams (1976) have both confirmed that hyperactive children compared to normal children show a lower level of arousal as indexed by electroencephalographic and Galvanic Skin Response measures. These indices of physiological arousal, and thus of cortical arousal, are inversely related to measures of behavioral arousal. If cortical underarousal is assumed to be an antecedent of hyperactive behavior, it may be argued that this will interfere with cognitive functions. Eysenck (1967a), for instance, suggests that a high level of cortical inhibition (thus low cortical arousal) is responsible for the relatively poor performance of extraverts in academic tasks.

In order to establish a relationship between hyperactivity and cognitive competence, the two must be shown to vary concomitantly. It is not enough to show that some learning disabled children are described as hyperactive and also perform poorly in reading. The difficulty with reading is often the reason why these children have been labeled learning disabled in the first place. Furthermore, a full range of activity levels may exist among learning disabled children; those labeled as hyperactive may simply be the most visible problem children (cf. Das, 1973c). If cognitive skills are related to activity levels, hypoactive children should be studied in addition to hyperactive ones; at the least one should demonstrate decreasing competence with increasing levels of hyperactivity as measured behaviorally by means of rating scales *and* physiologically in terms of arousal.

The study we are going to report failed to demonstrate a concomitant variation between competence in simultaneous and successive processes on the one hand and behavioral hyperactivity on the other. However, it was possible to show an inverse relationship between measures of behavioral hyperactivity and autonomic arousal.

Williams (1976) selected 60 boys from classes for the learning disabled, on the basis of teacher-rated hyperactivity on Davids' (1971) Child Rating Scale. That scale consists of six items covering hyperactivity, short attention span, variability, impulsiveness, irritability, and explosiveness, and requires the rater to assess the activity level of the child on a 6-point scale in each of the six areas. Raw scores from the 119 completed returns from teachers of learning disability classes in 15 schools were subjected to a principal-components analysis. One principal component was extracted, and factor scores calculated for each of the 119 children. Three groups were selected from this distribution: 20 children above 1 standard deviation above the mean (hyperactives), 20 children below 1 standard deviation below the mean (hypoactives), and 20 children within 1 standard deviation of the mean (normoactives). A further sample of 20 normal (i.e., not learning disabled) boys was selected from regular classrooms: The rating scale was administered to 60 boys, from which 20 within 1 standard deviation of the mean of the factor scores were chosen. The mean age and mean Lorge–Thorndike IQ of the total group of 60 learning disabled children were 128.8 months and 98.8, respectively, while the 20 control children had a mean age of 113.8 months and a mean Lorge–Thorndike IQ of 112.2. Mean IQs were not significantly different.

The test battery consisted of Raven's Coloured Progressive Matrices, Figure Copying, Serial and Free Recall, Digit Span, and Color Naming. A principal-components analysis and Varimax rotation yielded the familiar three factors of simultaneous, successive, and speed for the 60 learning disabled children. Perhaps because he included a speed test (Color Naming) in his battery, Williams' results were consistent with expectations, as opposed to Leong's. Like Leong, however, he demonstrated the same general pattern of simultaneous and successive processing, this time in an amorphous group of learning disabled children not chosen for any specific learning problem (e.g., reading).

Williams first examined whether the three learning disabled groups were different in simultaneous and successive processing. Using factor scores for simultaneous and successive processing, a three-group one-way fixed-effects multivariate analysis of variance was carried out; the resulting F was not significant ($p < .60$). The three hyperactive groups could not be distinguished on simultaneous or successive processing. Hyperactivity would appear to be independent of competence in both forms of processing.

Williams also compared the three learning disabled groups with the normal controls on the six test variables. Means and standard deviations for these four groups are presented in Table 6.8. One-way analyses of variance followed by Scheffé tests indicated that the three learning disabled groups as a whole performed significantly (at or below the .01 level) worse than their normal controls on Figure Copying, Serial, and Free Recall. Thus the learning disabled children performed poorly on half of the simultaneous and half of the successive tasks, and were not different in the speed task relative to their normal controls.

Williams' results do not show any clear relationship between hyperactivity and cognitive processing competence. That performance on some tests is affected indicates that hyperactivity does have cognitive consequences, but that these are not confined to any processing mode. Because Williams' subjects, unlike Leong's, were not selected for any particular disability, these results should not be surprising. Williams' sample represents the

Table 6.8
Means and Standard Deviations of Three Learning Disabled Groups and Normal Group

Variable	Hyperactive		Normoactive		Hypoactive		Control	
	M	SD	M	SD	M	SD	M	SD
Raven's Coloured Progressive Matrices	26.58		26.00		28.56		29.21	
		3.89		4.17		4.16		3.88
Figure Copying	12.05		11.94		12.68		14.36	
		2.70		2.81		2.33		2.36
Digit Span	5.11		4.88		5.50		5.52	
		1.21		0.67		1.21		0.96
Free Recall	82.05		82.27		85.37		90.89	
		11.11		9.22		1.21		3.54
Serial Recall	67.17		70.55		78.00		86.21	
		22.82		16.15		16.56		8.64
Color Naming	36.82		38.27		34.75		31.10	
		7.76		12.69		5.14		5.67

heterogeneous group of children found in learning disabled classrooms (IQ of at least 85, 2 years or more behind academically): These children should not be expected to demonstrate a consistent pattern of cognitive skills. Furthermore, our general three-block functional model would suggest that Block 1 problems (e.g., hyperactivity) could have diffuse effects upon Blocks 2 and 3.

6.4   THE CAUSES OF COGNITIVE PROBLEMS: DEFECT OR DEVELOPMENTAL LAG

Mental retardation as a label is useful if it helps establish a diagnosis and leads to research directed at understanding and amelioration. The clinician is more concerned with diagnosis. For him, a multiaxial definition of mental retardation is recommended (Tizard, 1972), the axes being (1) grade of intellectual functioning, (2) etiological and medical diagnosis, (3) psychiatric aspects, and (4) physical handicaps. Grade of intellectual functioning is determined by psychometric tests, and the labels for different grades such as profound, severe, and moderately retarded refer to discrete ranges of IQ. Within the moderate level, and perhaps slightly above, is sociocultural retardation, which is recognized as a separate category by the International Classification of Diseases (see Tizard, 1972). It is important to note here that although the label may point to a social–cultural rather than genetic etiology, the authorities in classification do not mean it to be so: "At the present time there is no way of disentangling the effects of genetic, biological and social factors in the causation of sociocultural retardation [Tizard, 1972, p. 27]." Tarjan and Eisenberg (1972), commenting on this category, which includes retardates classified as cultural familial, mention that it would be erroneous if we conclude that physical or organic factors do not play a role in the causation of mental retardation. Perhaps it would be best to remember this when taking sides in the defect versus developmental lag debate.

It seems to us that the debate focuses on pseudo-issues and may detract us from the main objectives of the psychological study of the mentally retarded. The objective, according to Clarke and Clarke (1974), is to study the conditions facilitating the development of intellectual attainments as well as those which retard them. We find no reason to improve upon this general statement.

Intellectual attainment is the end-product of a dynamic interplay of cognitive processes. A defective or inappropriate process may reduce the level of attainment, as a broken link in a net may reduce the net's efficiency. Differences in levels of intellectual performance may come about by the use of a defective or inappropriate cognitive process of the sort that Ellis and Zeaman suggest—attention, retention, rehearsal. O'Connor (1976) has demonstrated precisely how a specific defect may manifest itself in a general defect. He has drawn upon Hebb's (1949) work in assuming that, because learning is a successive but hierarchical process, the absence of certain learning experiences may result in developmental failure at higher levels of learning. O'Connor and Hermelin (1971, 1975) have studied processes such as coding in several diagnostic groups. Some groups, such as the deaf and the blind, are known to have specific deficits, while others, such as the retarded, demonstrate a more general deficit in cognitive processing. Deficits may be found in specific aspects of coding (e.g., spatial, temporal), or in strategies for the use of coding processes (e.g., discarding a code that has become inappropriate, and substituting for it a more appropriate one). O'Connor's strategy has paid off: His research has contributed to our understanding of the cognitive processes of various kinds of exceptional children.

When discussing differences in achievement from an information-processing point of view, a distinction in terms of general level of attainment is insufficient. For example, reading proficiency can be analyzed into its component processes, and defects located which lead to a general poor performance in reading (Doehring, 1968; Rourke, 1975). Black et al. (1976), for instance, have found that difficulties in sequential processing can be related to reading problems. His results have been confirmed by Das and Cummins (1978), who obtained positive correlations between successive processing and the oral reading and spelling scores of adolescent EMRs. Cummins and Das (1977) further showed that, among Grade 3 children proficient in reading, reading scores were more related to simultaneous processing than among the less proficient. They concluded that "among children who are likely to experience difficulty in reading, competence in successive processing is strongly related to reading achievement. However, among normal (children) readers, at more advanced levels of reading skills, simultaneous processing is equally, if not more important in the reading process [p. 250]."

Considerations such as these within the general context of the relationship between processing and attainment (cf. Chapter 5) demonstrate the value of studying the organization of processes. This organization changes with age as a result of maturation and learning, it being impossible to separate the two. Corresponding changes in the functional organization of the brain must be assumed if we accept Luria's model of simultaneous–successive coding processes and the processes associated with decisions and plans. It is quite logical to expect that the localization of these functions and their interactions may change with development. Even what is understood to be a simultaneous process in the child may not have the same meaning in adult intellectual processes; there may be a qualitative shift. This can also be understood outside the field of neuropsychology. Psychometrically, an IQ of 120 in a 6-year-old child is not measured by the same tests as the IQ of the same child at age 15 (see Thorndike, 1966). Tests measure different intellectual abilities at different ages. The same tests are not used, and even if they are, the tests would not measure the same process.

Much interest has been generated about whether cognitive problems are due to "defects" or to developmental lags. We would conclude that (a) it may be a pseudo-issue, (b) a defective or inappropriate component may result in the appearance of a general retardation, (c) close analyses of processes and their changing relationships will lead to a better understanding of differences in the level of intellectual attainments and, finally (d) these may reflect changes in the functional organization of the brain, in the pattern of interaction between the three units of the brain due to maturation and experience.

6.5   CONCLUSIONS

In this chapter we have considered both general (mental retardation) and specific (learning disability) cognitive problems in the context of our functional model of cognition. Such an approach allows for better understanding of the problems and gives a rational basis for remediation. It also provides a perspective upon a number of issues concerning the causes of cognitive problems. Several relatively specific conclusions can be reached.

General mental retardation is to be characterized as deficits in planning and coding. Whether or not the deficit in coding leads to difficulties in planning cannot be determined at present. Learning disabilities are more difficult to characterize because they appear to be of several types. The more specific kind of learning disability (e.g., reading disability) is related to particular content or process areas, and this may be seen as a Block 2 problem. Other specific coding disabilities (e.g., dyslexias, aphasias, etc.) are equally likely to have Block 2 problems as their basis. The second sort of learning disability could be characterized as an activity problem (evidenced by hyperactivity, hypoactivity, poor selective attention), and seems to be based in a Block 1 problem. This latter type of problem has diffuse effects upon the other two blocks of the brain, interfering with some tasks and not with others. As of yet, there is no way of predicting which tasks are disrupted, though those involving planning or selective attention to a large extent might be likely candidates.

Our discussion of several types of cognitive problems has highlighted a difficulty with such "deficit" research. A process orientation demands a detailed breakdown of tasks and some specification of exactly where the problem lies. Many studies, on the other hand, include amorphous groups of children who have been placed in special classes for any of a number of problems. Until the problems are delimited, there is little hope of specifying their causes in more detail.

Finally, we can return to several issues raised at the beginning of this chapter. The first concerns the interdependence of the functional units in Luria's three block model of the brain. We have observed some of the effects of this interdependence in mentally retarded and learning disabled children. The effect of specific cognitive difficulties does spread, and sometimes sensitive experimental techniques are required to tease out one effect from another. In some cases this simply cannot be done. This functional interdependence is a problem not only for the theoretician, but also for the practitioner who must find the specific difficulty which has led to a general deficit in order to begin remedial work.

A second issue which appeared at the beginning of this chapter concerned the independence of simultaneous and successive processing. We had previously demonstrated the independence of these factors in normal populations (cf. Chapters 4 and 5), and in the present chapter showed this also to be the case for mentally retarded and learning disabled children. Both forms of processing appear to exist in most groups, even those with cognitive problems.

7

Cross-Cultural Studies

Research on cognitive processes from a cross-cultural perspective has a highly eclectic history. Studies of cultural similarity and variation may be found which represent the full continuum of cognitive psychology in terms of theoretical perspectives, including Piagetian research (Dasen, 1972), British factor-analytic research (e.g., MacArthur, 1973; Vernon, 1965b, 1969), Brunerian studies (Bruner, 1971; Cole & Bruner, 1971), investigations of cognitive style (e.g., Witkin, 1967), and studies using quite specific and traditional learning paradigms (Cole & Scribner, 1975, 1977). This general reflection of the variation present in cognitive psychology from the area of cross-cultural research appears to be caused in part by the belief that cross-cultural studies may supply the means to answer questions which are generic to psychology generally. Viewed from this perspective, cross-cultural studies are an effort to study the effects of greater variation in antecedent subject variables than it is possible to obtain in a within-culture study (Berry & Dasen, 1974; Cole & Scribner, 1974; Dawson, 1971; Levine, 1970). Thus the extent of the universality of processes is of interest, where the cultural variations included in the study allow inferences regarding the conditions responsible for the development of the processes.

Beyond this general goal of cross-cultural research, however, there is a second and equally important goal. In addition to research on the universality of processes which have already been identified in the investigator's culture, the researcher may also seek out cognitive processes that may be specific to the other cultures which are to be studied. This second objective is summarized by Witkin and Berry (1975): "The purpose of cross-cultural research is not limited to checking the universality of a phenomenon which has been observed in a single culture. It has the additional aim of seeking out new phenomena, both behavioral and cultural [p. 72]."

The distinction between these two goals has received a good deal of attention recently, and is related to the distinction between *etic* and *emic* analyses (Berry, 1969; Triandis, 1964, 1972; Brislin, 1976; Brislin, Lonner, & Thorndike, 1973; Price-Williams, 1974). An etic analysis of cultures seeks generalizations across the cultures; this type of analysis focuses on theory building because it attempts to make generalizations that account for all of human behavior. The identification of the same cognitive process in a task across many cultures, for example, would be an etic analysis, with the goal of establishing the existence of that process as fundamental to all human thought. In contrast, an emic analysis attempts to identify the specifics of a culture. As implied in the quote given earlier from Witkin and Berry (1975), these specifics may be completely novel to the investigation, for phenomena may be discovered that have never been found before in studies of children from only the investigator's own culture.

In general, it may be said that the etic–emic distinction becomes increasingly important in studies involving behavior of a highly social nature. Obviously, wide cultural variation may be found, for example, in studies of social interaction, language patterns, and need for achievement (Brislin, 1976). In these areas, the separation of universals from specifics, or etics from emics, may be expected to yield some empirical differences, and therefore emic analyses gain importance in descriptions of the dynamics of a particular culture.

But what may be expected of efforts to make an etic–emic distinction in the area of cognitive processes, particularly those varieties that are fundamental to human thought such as our current line of research on simultaneous and successive syntheses? Are these processes so basic to all human cognition that they show little variation cross-culturally? If so, we would reach somewhat parallel conclusions to Kagan and Klein (1973), for example, who found the fundamental processes of cognition in Guatemalan children similar to those of U.S. children. Perhaps we could ask this question another way by attempting to identify the possible reasons why a cognitive process may be idiosyncratic to a cultural group. Goodnow (1976) suggests four possible reasons for a lack of consistency in behavior across cultural groups. The first of these is the relationship of thought to technology; different technologies may tend to guide patterns of thought, and are reflections of patterns of thought. It may be, then, that technologies available in one culture but not in another are partly responsible for the development or submergence of a particular cognitive process in one or the other culture. Second, tasks may not operationally define similar cognitive processes in different cultural groups. This may be true particularly of Piagetian tasks, where performance is quite dependent upon the subject's interpretations of the task situation. Third, even different forms of a task may measure different cognitive processes; this may be due to variations in the task content. Finally, there may be further variation due to different age groupings, because investigators tend to assume continuity of cognitive processes with age, rather than unique differentiation and integration.

These considerations in attempting to apply the etic–emic distinction to the cross-cultural study of cognitive processes, in turn, suggest some methodological issues to be addressed. Methodology has proven to be a topic of contention for some years among cross-cultural psychologists, particularly due to the need to use techniques which may reflect both the etic and emic goals of investigations (Anderson, 1967; Berry, 1969; Brislin, Lonner, & Thorndike, 1973; Gutmann, 1967; Malpass, 1977). In the study of cognitive processes there is a need for tasks that will reflect cultural similarities and differences, and for methodology that will relate these similarities and differences to the distinct environmental patterns of each culture.

In our research on simultaneous and successive cognitive processes, one type of approach to these issues is found in the manner in which we have studied culturally different groups. In the studies to be reported here, we have used tasks which are generally quite culturally fair. It will be seen that our approach and our results are quite etic in nature, that is, we have been concerned with the identification of simultaneous and successive processes across varying cultures. Nonetheless, our analyses also reveal some cultural variation in these processes, and we are led to attempt to identify patterns in these variations and some causes of these variations.

The methodology that we employ is the same as that used in our other investigations. A small selected set of cognitive tasks is administered, and the data are factor analyzed. It should be noted that we select this technique for several reasons. First, the tasks are chosen for their etic characteristics. Factor analyses of tasks where wide variations in strategic behavior are possible would make cross-cultural comparisons of factors particularly problematic, more so than is normally the case (Buss & Royce, 1975b). Thus, if tasks which are reasonably universal in the processes they measure are used, factor identification becomes more feasible. We may note further, however, that some tasks which are sensitive to strategic behavior are also necessary, in order to reveal culturally specific variations. This means that ultimately the choice of tasks to be used must represent a range of sensitivity to cognitive strategies (Jarman, 1978a).

We turn now to our studies of cognitive processes in different cultural groups. We begin with a general discussion of cultural competence and cultural disadvantage, followed by a description of a research project in the state of Orissa in India. We then discuss several projects carried out in Canada where the major variables of interest were ethnicity and SES. School children were the subjects in all of these studies, and hence cognitive processes are examined in the context of school learning.

7.1 COGNITIVE COMPETENCE AND CULTURAL DISADVANTAGE

What is cognitive competence and who is a competent child? White and Watts (1973) asked this question at the outset of their project on competence and early experience and could not find an acceptable answer. They had to observe the behavior of the obviously competent and incompetent child in order to arrive at patterns of behavior characteristic of each. Competence, simply conceived, is ability; a competent child has superior ability. It is perhaps very close to intelligence. Basically, it is manifested in academic work or school learning. In Western cultures, reasoning and verbal abilities are central to cognitive competence. The European and American schools selectively reinforce children who are good at both reasoning and language. The education system in India does the same. The environment that fosters skills for academic success is the one that is considered desirable in India, as anywhere in the West. In spite of obvious cultural differences between nations, schools everywhere seem to share the same objectives—teaching numerical and verbal skills.

A related question at this point is whether environmental stimulation and academic teaching improve abilities. If a major part of intellectual ability is inherited, a more fundamental question is: Can genetically endowed intelligence be improved?

Three kinds of intelligence have been proposed: Intelligence A, which is genotypic, cannot be directly measured. It is inferred from measured intelligence, which is B (Hebb, 1949). Cattell (1971) makes a similar distinction between genotypic "fluid" and phenotypic "crystallized" intelligence. Vernon (1969) has added to this Intelligence C, which contains the artifacts of measuring instruments and procedures. Those like Cattell who believe that Intelligence A can never be improved would still concede that B is sensitive to teaching and training, because it measures attainment rather than ability. Vernon (1969) observes that tests of so-called genotypic "fluid intelligence" devised by Cattell are essentially tests of spatial-reasoning ability and those of crystallized intelligence measure verbal-educational ability. It may be noted that the evidence favoring improvement of spatial-reasoning ability is not well established (see Das, 1973a).

Perhaps it is no longer important to know whether or not cognitive abilities can be improved. In the study of cognitive competence, there seems to be a shift in emphasis from "abilities" to an inquiry into the "processes" which determine an individual's level of performance. The shift has been influenced partly by the need for comparing the same "ability" in different cultures (Cole & Bruner, 1971) and of explaining such differences. It has been argued that the researcher should consider the lower level performance in certain cultures as a difference rather than a defect as compared to the standards of performance by groups in Western culture. The re-examination of ability differences has been further prompted by an honest evaluation of the repeatedly observed inferiority of the children from minority groups in tests measuring cognitive competence. The lower competence of disadvantaged minority groups could be attributed to any or all of the five causes: genetic, lack of stimulating early experience, poor nutrition, social motivations, and cultural values. In addition to these biological and social–personality factors, the cognitive style or strategy—a habitual mode of processing information adopted by a group—may account for the lower performance of the disadvantaged children (Das, 1973a). For example, Jensen (1971) observed that children from the middle to upper socioeconomic classes use reasoning and abstraction much more than those from the lower socioeconomic classes. The latter are quite proficient in associative learning, however. If one considers abstraction and associative learning as processes rather than abilities, one can then investigate the conditions which cause one group to prefer one, such as abstraction, to the other method of integrating information. Evidence is now available to suggest that a particular mode of information integration, such as sequential processing, may be used by certain non-white groups in tasks which usually elicit simultaneous processing in white children (Das, 1973b). Differences in cognitive style thus exist among culturally different populations and among subpopulations within any given culture.

A general orientation for comparing cognitive competencies among culturally different groups can be proposed at this point. Following Luria (1971), one may view cognitive activities as "a social phenomenon in origin, and as processes formed during the course of mastery of general human experiences [p. 262]." In other words, intellectual processes are not unchangeable and universal, nor should they have a priori characteristics as is often reflected in IQ. They are shaped by the experience through which a subgroup passes, and these experiences, or "historical developments" as Luria calls them, are not only reflected in what we think, but also in the structure or style of our thinking. Cognitive processes "are not independent and unchanging 'abilities' or 'functions' of human consciousness; they are processes occurring in concrete, practical activities and are formed within the limits of this activity [p. 266]." Cole and Bruner (1971) essentially make the same observation by reminding one "that the most important thing about any 'underlying competence' is the nature of the situations in which it expresses itself [p. 784]." Luria's (1976) book has many examples of how historical factors in a person's life influence his/her thinking.

Cultural disadvantage refers to a complex set of conditions which favors intellectual subnormality in a child. Some of these conditions are: unstimulating environment, lack of verbal commerce with adults, poor sensory experience, and other deleterious environmental factors generally associated with poverty. The impetus for work on cultural deprivation has come from the research on early experience and sensory deprivation in comparative psychology (Wood-Gush, 1963). Hebb (1949) demonstrated that animals raised in restricted environment showed defects in sensory and perceptual development. J. McV. Hunt (1961) extended the implications of this to humans and pointed out the importance of early experience in intellectual growth: Lack of proper stimulation may hinder the development of the inherited constitutional apparatus such as the eye. As Haywood and Tapp (1966) have concluded in their review, an enriched early environment increases intelligence, whereas impoverished environment may lower intelligence level.

In recent years there has been a re-examination of the animal data on restricted environment and their application or extension to humans. A good review is presented in Jensen (1969). For example, it is seen that even in animal studies, when an animal is brought up in a lighted environment in contrast to a darkened one, and with all other conditions being constant, the animal typically does not show the ill effects of sensory deprivation. Second, animals which have been reared in a restricted environment do show initial disadvantages in discrimination learning, but such disadvantages gradually disappear with exposure to a normal environment. In other words, the gap between the sensory-deprived animals and those raised normally begins to narrow as the deprived animal is increasingly exposed to a normal environment following its early exposure to a restricted one. In the case of human children, however, the opposite is known to happen. The gap between a culturally disadvantaged child and a nondisadvantaged child begins to grow with age and exposure to normal classroom learning. Specifically, tests of verbal ability reveal a wider and wider gap between,

say, the black and the middle-class white child as they progress in school
years (Jensen, 1977a).

7.2   CASTE AS A VARIABLE

The discussion up to this point has been on the ill effects of cultural
disadvantage in regard to intellectual ability. The poverty of culture among
the lower class of people has been assumed to be universal. But in India
this may not be so. One can talk about a culture of poverty among the
Brahmins, the caste of the priests. Renunciation of material prosperity is
looked upon as a virtue. Thus the absence of material goods may not have
a devastating effect on the cultural life of the Brahmin. The Brahmin's
life-style is conducive to intellectual development. In contrast, a scholastic
tradition is lacking among the Harijans, the lowest caste. The Harijans are
poor without the advantage of a scholarly culture.

Apart from sociocultural factors which might favor cognitive growth in
Brahmins, are there genetic advantages? If we believe in the legend of the
origin of the caste system, the Harijans were the slaves of the caste Hindus,
inferior in intellect, and did the most menial jobs. In contrast, the Brahmin
was the interpreter of religious texts, advisor to the king, and generally
regarded as a source of wisdom. Each of these two castes has been
inbreeding for hundreds of years. It would seem, then, that Brahmins have
the advantage of a scholastic environment and a superior genetic stock to
start with. The cumulative effect of these should apparently widen the gap
between Brahmins and Harijans; but judged from another point, it should
not.

Marriage and social mobility patterns are quite different among the two
castes. For the Brahmin caste, it is reasonable to assume that those from the
upper economic class have IQs superior to those from the lower class. In
this respect, the conditions which favor social mobility and marriage within
one's own class are similar between the Western society and the Brahmin
caste. Higher occupations are generally associated with individuals with
higher intelligence. And because of the wide range of economic prosperity
found among the Brahmins, it is possible through assortative marriage for
the rich and the educated to marry among each other. Lower-class
Brahmins have some chance for upward social mobility; thus those who
cannot take advantage of this are likely to be less competent than those
who could.

The situation is somewhat different among Harijans. Most of them are
poor. Most of them are engaged in occupations of a menial nature as

determined by tradition. It is relatively difficult for a bright Harijan child to get higher education. The reasons are several, among which are the lack of parental interest in the child's education, need to work at an early age in order to supplement the family's income, and the expense of boarding the child in schools of higher education. Thus, social mobility is severely restricted. Assortative mating is less likely to occur among the Harijans. Since there is hardly a hierarchy of occupations and education, selection of a mate cannot be easily based on the level of ability in the cognitive domain. Noncognitive criteria may thus influence choice of a partner either by the family or by the person who wishes to marry. This would result in random mating.

If random mating in a close caste, such as the Harijans, has been occurring for hundreds of years, the genetic potential for intelligence would be randomly distributed. Even if the Harijans were of an inferior stock to start with (which has not been substantiated), over several generations the genetic pool would approximate the normal distribution of the other castes. This is known to occur in breeding experiments in which an inferior stock of animals, through random mating, eventually recaptures the mean distribution of the species.

The Harijans, then, need not be genetically inferior in cognitive abilities to the Brahmins, especially within the same economic class. When compared to poor Brahmins, particularly, we do not have any reason to believe that their intellectual ability would be lower due to genetic factors. But the social–cultural environment of the poor Brahmins is still superior, and this may contribute to their superior performance in cognitive tasks when compared with the Harijans.

Let us assume that one could separate the effects of sociocultural and genetic factors and examine these one by one. Brahmins would be divided into upper and lower economic groups. The upper-class child would grow up in a social–cultural environment superior to the lower class; hence, in cognitive tests he should be better than the Brahmin child from a poor home. Compared with a Harijan child of lower economic class, the poor Brahmin child, we assume, has grown up in a sociocultural milieu which facilitates intellectual growth. One should remind oneself that this is merely a conjecture, as we do not have any studies to show how exactly the scholastic traditions which may exist in a poor Brahmin home influence the child-rearing practices and the day-to-day interactions between the child and the parents or other elders. If the poor Brahmin children are not found to be superior to poor Harijan children on cognitive tasks of the simultaneous–successive kind we have used, it would be inferred that genetically, the former is not superior and environmental advantages of the

Brahmin child do not make enough of an impact on his cognitive performance.

7.3 SIMULTANEOUS AND SUCCESSIVE PROCESSING DIFFERENCES: CASTE AND CLASS AS INDEPENDENT VARIABLES

We wish to report briefly the findings of a study on Brahmin and Harijan children and consider their implications for the simultaneous–successive model. These findings are part of a comprehensive study (Das & Singha, 1975) on personality as well as cognitive differences due to caste and class.

Four groups of school children in Classes 4 and 5 (estimated age range of 8 to 11 years) were included in the study. There were 30 children in each group. They were (1) urban Brahmin children from middle- to upper-middle-class homes, (2) urban Brahmin children from lower-class homes, (3) rural Brahmin children from orthodox but lower-class homes and, (4) urban Harijan children from lower-class homes. The first sample, urban rich Brahmins, came mostly from professional families, although a few families were in business. Parents were college educated. The second sample, urban but poor Brahmin children, came from families in which the father had a junior high school education and held a modest job in a government office or school (e.g., mailman, office boy). The third group of children lived and went to school in an orthodox Brahmin village. The father of each family worked as a temple priest besides supervising (not laboring in) his small agricultural land. It may be generally assumed that of all three Brahmin groups, the rural orthodox home was closest to the traditions of their caste. The last sample, poor and low caste children, lived in a town as the urban Brahmin children did. Their parents (both father and mother worked) were employed sweepers, cobblers, and casual farm laborers; their father's education was between 3 and 4 years in an elementary school.

What hypotheses can be formulated? As SES is a relevant variable, the urban rich Brahmin group should have the best performance. If birth in a high caste, irrespective of urban and rural residence, confers some advantages on the child's cognitive competence, then the Brahmin children from lower class should be superior to Harijan children.

Let us look at differences in performance due to caste. The Harijan children took longer to name colors (Color Naming) and read words (Word Reading) than the Brahmin children. Means for Harijan children were 59.63 and 35.37 seconds for color and word, respectively. Comparable means for Brahmin children from the lower class were 48.07 seconds (urban) and 30.0 seconds (rural). In Visual STM, the Harijans were poorer than the rural lower-class Brahmin group: Mean numbers recalled for Harijans was 83.20 whereas the two lower-class Brahmin means were 93.60 (rural orthodox) and 91.60 (urban). Thus, birth in a high-caste family was associated with superior performance in speed and successive tasks. In terms of content, the three tests had something to do with school learning, at least relatively more so than the four other tests (Progressive Matrices, Figure Copying, Memory-for-Designs, and Cross-modal Coding). And all four tests generally load on the simultaneous factor, although in the present study Progressive Matrices had a minor loading on the successive. However, in this project, between-caste comparisons are confounded with urban–rural residence. In the next study (Das & Pivato, 1976), this situation was corrected. Results of this subsequent work will be presented after we have considered within-caste comparisons.

In order to determine the manner in which the three Brahmin samples differed from one another on simultaneous, successive, and speed, a principal-components analysis was performed on the scores of the 90 Brahmin children. Following Varimax rotation the three expected factors emerged. Each child, then, was given three factor scores—a simultaneous, a successive, and a speed score. One must mention here that only one test from the successive and one from the speed battery had been used in this analysis, which is not satisfactory; but all of the simultaneous battery of tests were included in the analysis. The samples were different only in terms of simultaneous factor scores. An analysis of variance confirmed that the urban rich Brahmin children were highest and the rural poor were the lowest (see Table 7.1). Urban but poor Brahmin children were mid between the two groups. A comparison of means on individual simultaneous tests revealed that of the four tests, means for urban rich were higher than the means for rural poor. The tests were Figure Copying, Memory-for-

Table 7.1
Simultaneous Processing Factor Scores: Within-Caste Comparisons

Group		Mean	Variance	SD
Urban Brahmin poor		0.04	0.73	0.85
Rural Brahmin poor		−0.42	1.15	1.0747
Urban Brahmin rich		0.38	0.89	0.9432
Total		0.0	1.0	1.0
	MS	df	F	p
Groups	4.79	82	5.18	0.007
Error	0.92	87		

Designs, and Cross-modal Coding. In conclusion, the urban but poor Brahmin children were not significantly inferior to the urban rich children, in spite of what was expected in terms of SES differences. Perhaps living in an urban area compensates for economic disadvantage to a certain extent. In the next study, urban–rural comparisons have been examined more clearly.

The next study on caste differences was carried out to observe the effect of malnutrition, as indirectly indicated by short stature, on simultaneous–successive processing. Other independent variables were caste and urban versus rural residence. We shall consider those findings that relate to caste and rural/urban residence. A full report of the malnutrition aspect is not relevant here, and is to be found in Das and Pivato (1976). However, in passing, we would like to mention that children of short stature in contrast to the tall performed poorly in Progressive Matrices, Figure Copying, and Serial Recall.

The three samples in this study were rural low-caste, rural high-caste, and urban low-caste boys in Class 5 (age range 9–12 years). All children were from the lower-SES families. The rural children went to village schools and the urban children went to town schools. A town was defined as an area which was under a municipality with a population above 5000. There were 120 children in each sample, 60 of short stature (below 25th percentile) and 60 of tall stature (above 75th percentile). It was hypothesized that among rural samples the low-caste Harijan children would perform poorly in simultaneous and successive tasks relative to the high caste. Another prediction was that among the low-caste children, the rural sample would perform poorly compared to the urban sample. As mentioned earlier in this section, the variety of experience in an urban setting is likely to compensate for the "cultural" disadvantage of the lowest-caste home.

The Brahmins were superior to the Harijans in three successive tasks (Serial Recall, Visual STM, and Digit Span), in Cross-modal Coding, which showed a split loading on simultaneous and successive factors, and in Word Reading (speed factor). These tests, taken together, require the traditional scholastic activities, which are oral as well as written in the Brahmin home, and should facilitate successive-verbal processing.

In terms of urban–rural differences, one could not expect that urban living favors one kind of cognitive processing over the other; thus, in both kinds the rural children should be lower than the urban. The results showed that urban children, irrespective of height, were better in Figure Copying and Memory-for-Designs (simultaneous processing), and in Color Naming (speed). Further, tall urban children were superior to tall rural children in Digit Span, a successive test. The factor analyses of simultaneous–successive tasks for these groups did not show Figure Copying and Memory-for-Designs to load exclusively on the simultaneous factor. On the whole, it would be correct to say that urban–rural differences exist in all three processing categories.

7.4 COGNITIVE PROCESSES OF ABORIGINAL CHILDREN IN ORISSA: FACTOR-ANALYTIC DATA

A group of 48 school children from aboriginal tribes had been given the simultaneous–successive tests. Reported here is a factor analysis.

The aboriginal school children were residential students in Classes 4 and 5 (equivalent to Grades 3 and 4 in age). They were mainly from two tribes of Southern Orissa (Kondh and Saura) which have inhabited that region for appropriately the last 2000 years. Their parental occupation is a combination of agriculture and hunting. Family income is often supplemented by cutting firewood from the forest around the tribal village and selling it to customers in nonaboriginal villages. All children were supported in the residential school by Government of India scholarships. The schools themselves are located in remote areas of Southern Orissa, but unlike the aboriginal villages, they are relatively accessible. Students spend a major part of their time in learning academic subjects, but they are also required to work in the school's farm and produce enough vegetables and a part of the rice for their consumption. Thus, the environmental condition and life-style in the residential school are not alien to the children, except that they have to go through an academic program.

Results of a principal-components analysis are given in Table 7.2. Sev-

Table 7.2
Rotated Factors (Varimax) for Aboriginal Children in Orissa[a]

Test	Successive and speed	Simultaneous
Raven's Coloured Progressive Matrices	.548	.527
Figure Copying	.083	.682
Visual Short-Term Memory	.830	.028
Memory-for-Designs (errors)	−.452	−.523
Cross-modal Coding	.134	.577
Digit Span	.750	.088
Color Naming	−.450	.616
Word Reading	−.743	−.140
Percentage of total variance	31.69	21.96

[a] $N = 48$.

eral points about the factors are worth noting. First, two rather than three factors were obtained: The first is a composite of successive and speed, the second is a simultaneous-processing factor. An examination of the loadings for the tests leads to many interesting speculations. Progressive Matrices has a split loading, half on successive–speed and half on simultaneous, reflecting that both processes were used in solving the matrices. A similar result was obtained previously for a sample of high-caste Orissa children (Das, 1973a). Memory-for-Designs has a split loading too, although it loads predominantly on the simultaneous factor. One should infer from the split loading that this test is approached partly as a successive cum speed task. It is not a very unusual finding; in a Grade 1 sample of white children, Das and Molloy (1975) had obtained a loading for this test on the speed factor. But the children in the present sample are older. We have reason to believe that because of a processing preference in their culture, successive processing is employed by the aboriginal children for tasks which could be solved entirely by using simultaneous processing.

Lastly, a split loading for Color Naming is of great interest. Speed in naming the four primary color strips has its loading on the successive–speed factor, which is not as surprising as its loading on the simultaneous factor. Latency (slow speed) in Color Naming seems to be the result of using simultaneous processes. If we accept such an inference, it can be substantiated by the following observations of the testers during testing. The aboriginal children were not sure of the color names except for red, which all of them knew. Questioning revealed that red was the color of blood and of the soil (in that region). Blue and green were often confused—plants and grass were "blue" and blue ink was "dark" or "black." Yellow was not confused with other primary colors, but simply was not found in the common vocabulary of many of these children. Thus, before taking the Color Naming test, while practice sessions for identifying colors by names were given, the children had to be prompted; this is seldom needed for high-caste Orissa children. During the actual test session, an aboriginal child would often hesitate before naming a color strip if it was not red. Thus, it is apparent that color naming was impeded by a need to use simultaneous comparisons with other color names before responding. Incidentally, the mean color naming speed of the aboriginal children was significantly slower than that of Harijan children from rural areas; these areas were not as remote as the regions in which the aboriginals lived. Thus, if one is willing to speculate why the aboriginals differ from other groups in Orissa, a major variable will be their "rurality." A relatively preliterate and preindustrial culture of the aboriginal tribes may be the major factor which influences their cognitive processing. The extent to which preliterate and preindustrial characteristics are present in a culture can be a rough definition of "rurality" as a variable.

7.5   WHITE, BLACK, AND NATIVE CHILDREN'S PERFORMANCE

American white and black subpopulations have been found to differ in IQ—the whites are reported to be 15 IQ points higher (Jensen, 1969). We shall not attempt to review the arguments supporting or opposing a genetic basis for this difference because the issue is not a relevant one for our purpose. Canadian black children sampled in our study (Das, Manos, & Kanungo, 1975) do not share with the American black either the same genetic stock or similar environment. The black children in our study were from schools in Montreal. Their ancestry is traced to the West Indies rather than to the United States, at least for the majority of black children in Montreal. Discrimination or social disadvantage is not as apparent. In fact, the parents of Montreal black children felt so secure in their environment that they were comparable to the whites on a test of locus of control (Rotter, 1966).

A study in which both ethnicity (white and black) and SES (high and low) were varied will be discussed briefly. This will be followed by a discussion of two separate pieces of research on native children. Data relevant to simultaneous and successive processes only will be discussed; other aspects of the work dealing with personality and school achievement have been presented in Das, Manos, and Kanungo (1975), Manos (1975), and Krywaniuk (1974).

In order to examine the effect of socioeconomic status (SES) differences, 30 high- and 30 low-SES children were compared. The children were from Edmonton, a city where the black population is negligible. For purposes of white–black comparison, the children from Montreal schools were sampled: 30 high- and 30 low-SES whites, and 20 high- and 20 low-SES blacks were selected. The children were in Grade 4 classrooms.

Socioeconomic status was determined by the occupation of the chief wage earner. Where both parents were working, the higher of the two occupations was counted. An occupational class scale developed by Blishen (Blishen, Naegele, & Porter, 1965) was used. The scale positions of low SES had a range of 32 (hunters, trappers, welfare recipients) to 43.6 (barbers, truck drivers); that of high SES ranged from 48.2 (telephone operators, jewelers, and watch makers) to 81.2 (physicians). The low-SES mean was 40.2 (messengers, shoe makers), and the high-SES mean was 59.5 (farmers, transportation managers). One should understand that the high- and low-SES groups in Edmonton were not geographically separated, except for the very high SES families who might live in an exclusive neighborhood. Except for a small percentage of the children at extreme ends of the two SES, most went to the same school. These conditions also held for Montreal.

First to be considered are the results of the Edmonton study, which is reported in detail in a Ph.D. thesis (Manos, 1975). The two groups were compared on five simultaneous–successive tasks. The high-SES group was superior ($p < .04$) to the low only on Raven's Coloured Progressive Matrices. The groups did not differ in any of the remaining cognitive tasks (Figure Copying, Cross-modal Coding, Serial Recall, and Visual STM). However, the high-SES group was better than the low-SES group on Lorge–Thorndike IQ (means 107.26 and 94.86, $p < .003$), math, and reading achievement scores ($p < .01$). Thus we can conclude that in school-related tasks, the high-SES children were clearly at a higher level, and in simultaneous–successive tasks, except in the Progressive Matrices, the SES groups did not differ.

The samples of children from different SES and ethnic groups were in Grade 4. The mean Blishen scale values were approximately 55 for high-SES white and black samples and 43 for the white and black low-SES sample. Only in two out of the five simultaneous and successive tasks did the groups differ. In their mean Figure Copying scores, the high-SES white children were better than the low-SES white ($p < .02$) as well as the low-SES black ($p < .01$). Visual STM was the other test—the high-SES white children were better than low-SES black children ($p < .05$), but not better than the low-SES white children.

In conclusion, neither SES nor ethnic differences (black and white) seem to be consistently related to simultaneous–successive processing.

Next to be reported is a study by Krywaniuk (1974) in which native children from a reserve school are compared with white children. The latter are divided into groups whose academic achievements are high and low respectively on previous years' marks and teachers' assessments.

Like the white children, the native children were in Grade 3, but they lived on a Cree Indian reservation 50 miles south of Edmonton, and went to the school on the reserve. Initially, 40 low-achieving children were selected to participate in the study on the basis of previous years' work and teacher assessment. They made up approximately one-third of Grade 3 children at the school. One cannot easily find high-achieving native children who are as good as high-achieving Grade 3 white children.

Mean WISC Performance IQs for low-achieving white and native children were 98.96 ± 11.78 (SD) and 93.39 ± 12.41 (SD); the difference between them was not significant ($p < .08$). Mean IQ for the high-achieving groups was 109.96 ± 10.76. In terms of Verbal IQ, the two low achievement groups had significantly lower mean Verbal IQ than Performance IQ, which were 78.05 and 93.88, respectively, for the white and native children. IQ differences between Verbal and Performance are expected for culturally disadvantaged children and indicate verbal difficulties in school-related work. Additionally, the native children were significantly lower in Verbal IQ than low-achieving white children as may be expected. A verbal deficit is apparent in the native children. One may suggest that the "deficit" is due to their lack of knowledge in English. On the other hand, it may be ascribed to their relative deficit in successive processing to the extent to which verbal skills are contingent on successive, and not so much on simultaneous, at an early stage of their development. Reading at the early stage, for instance, is closely related to successive processing. Specifically word recognition is so related (Cummins & Das, 1977). If the latter suggestion of a successive-processing deficit is accepted, then the low-achieving white group will be superior to the native group not only in word-related successive tasks but on tasks which do not involve words.

A comparison of means for the two groups is presented in Table 7.3. It can be observed that despite a superior Verbal IQ, the white children were not better than the natives on the Schonell word recognition test. The groups were also comparable on Raven's Progressive Matrices, Figure Copying, and Memory-for-Designs. The whites were superior, however, on the successive tasks (Serial and Free Recall) and Cross-modal Coding, which has split loadings on simultaneous and successive. They did not differ on visual STM, but one is not sure that Visual STM is a pure test of successive processing for the present samples, because it has split loadings. For the native sample, it loads on simultaneous (.400) and speed (−.790); for the white sample, it loads on successive (.622) and speed (.364).

The native children were also lower in Word Reading and Color Naming speeds. Are these strictly measures of speed for them or do they also load on factors other than speed? At this point, the results of principal-components analysis for the two groups should be consulted for clarification. These are given in Table 7.4 and Table 7.5. One should be aware of the small sample size ($N = 38$) on which the analysis of native children's

Table 7.3
Comparison of Means of Low-Achieving White and Native Children on Simultaneous–Successive Battery

Tests	White	Native	p
Raven's Coloured Progressive Matrices	23.84	23.08	NS
Figure Copying	11.89	12.08	NS
Memory-for-Designs (errors)	5.52	3.82	NS
Cross-modal Coding	15.32	10.70	<.01
Free Recall	147.61	125.39	<.01
Serial Recall	130.43	92.39	<.01
Visual Short-Term Memory	28.09	24.97	NS
Word Reading (sec)	25.52	32.97	<.01
Color Naming (sec)	79.54	97.29	<.01
Schonell	28.59	27.81	NS

Table 7.4
Rotated Factors (Varimax) for Native Children[a]

Test	I Successive	II Speed	III Simultaneous
Raven's Coloured			
Progressive Matrices	.688	.072	.379
Cross-modal Coding	.585	−.126	.125
Figure Copying	.341	.036	.711
Memory-for-Designs (errors)	−.002	.080	−.831
Visual Short-Term Memory	−.067	−.624	.481
Serial Recall	.863	−.139	−.004
Free Recall	.852	−.184	−.007
Word Reading	−.126	.856	.135
Color Naming	−.243		−.069
Percentage of			
total variance	27.28	19.46	17.90

[a] N = 38.

score is based. Despite this, the results in Tables 7.4 and 7.5 show interesting disparities. Progressive Matrices has its higher loading on successive. Figure Copying has a minor loading on successive; its major loading is on simultaneous. Apart from indicating that the loadings are a departure from what is usually found with white samples, these also suggest that native children are using a predominantly successive process in solving Progressive Matrices. It will be recalled that the test had a substantial, though not its dominant, loading on the successive factor in a sample of Brahmin and aboriginal children from Orissa.

Table 7.5
Rotated Factors (Varimax) for Low-Achieving White Children[a]

Test	I Successive	II Simultaneous	III Speed
Raven's Coloured			
Progressive Matrices	.189	.792	.097
Cross-modal Coding	.521	.429	.008
Figure Copying	.070	.685	−.067
Memory-for-Designs (errors)	−.140	−.764	.125
Visual Short-Term Memory	.601	.077	.055
Serial Recall	.917	.111	−.107
Free Recall	.905	.155	−.069
Word Reading	.004	.128	.893
Color Naming	−.063	−.239	.855
Percentage of			
total variance	26.19	22.01	17.52

[a] N = 56.

How does one account for the similarity of performance in simultaneous processing but difference in successive processing between the white and native children? Further, how does one interpret the differences in factor loadings? One may argue that since the white and native children had comparable WISC Performance IQ, and since WISC-P is akin to simultaneous, they are not expected to differ on the usual simultaneous tests. However, the simultaneous tests did not behave in the usual manner in terms of factor loadings for the native data. Similarly one may argue that since one group was higher than the other on WISC Verbal IQ, these differences on successive tests would be expected. Again a simple inference such as this will be in error: Color Naming and Cross-modal Coding are not verbal in the sense of serial recall of words. Perhaps we should understand that native children have not learnt to use successive processes effectively. Teaching them how and where to use successive processes should lead to improvement in performing the successive tasks in the battery. Krywaniuk (1974) was able to effect such improvements, which will be discussed in Chapter 9 along with another study on teaching strategies. But let us accept that the native children are less prone to using successive strategies appropriately. Whether or not this is typical of their culture cannot be readily determined. But it is possible that their poor Verbal IQ is basically a reflection of not using successive processing properly.

7.6   CONCLUDING REMARKS

The purpose of cross-cultural studies in simultaneous–successive processing was not to assess various cultural samples in terms of how efficiently they use one or both processes. Comparison of levels of efficiency was never an objective of the cross-cultural studies. We were not interested in the question of relative superiority in cognitive processing. The major question that animated our various research projects was: Do cultural differences show up as differences in processing when the same set of tasks is used? It was fully expected that for some samples and for some tasks, processing differences would be displayed; it could not always be predicted which tasks these might be.

Our approach to cognitive-processing differences has been characterized as nomothetic rather than idiographic or etic rather than emic. However, we did not assume that the same cognitive processes were available to children in all cultures, or universally used processes were identically used by all children. Cultural preferences were exhibited as early as ages 8 and 9. Elementary school children were shown to habitually use, for instance, successive rather than simultaneous processes in solving a problem in one culture. In another culture, that of the native children in Canada, children did not choose successive processing because, probably, it was not the preferred mode in the culture. By relating the preferred method of processing to cultural factors which influenced cognition, one could learn more about both the task and the cultural variables. The aim was to understand, nomothetically, what salient variables in the culture interacted with the demands of the task.

8

Comparison with
Alternate Models

The discussion of the theory of simultaneous and successive syntheses in previous chapters has outlined the support for the theory in terms of essentially two sources. First, the physiological evidence for the two forms of cognitive integration has been presented, drawing heavily from Luria's investigations of the effects of brain lesions. Second, the results of a series of factor-analytic studies have been reviewed, in which it has been suggested that the theory of simultaneous and successive syntheses accounts parsimoniously for the factors that have been found in these studies.

The results from the factor-analytic studies raise a host of questions, however, regarding the strength and validity of the theory of simultaneous and successive syntheses vis-à-vis other theories of cognitive abilities. Indeed, the consistency between the Soviet physiological investigations and the factor-analytic studies reviewed encourages us to reassess the strength of some of the theories of intelligence mentioned briefly in Chapter 1, with a particular focus on those that are seen to be most closely associated with the present line of research. As a first step in these reassessments, we turn now to the general problem of validity in psychological testing and theory.

8.1 CONSTRUCT VALIDITY

Most contemporary psychometricians divide test validity into three broad, well-known categories (e.g., Anastasi, 1976; Cronbach, 1970). The first of these is content validity, which is the extent to which a domain of behavior or learning is represented proportionally in the composition of a test. Content validity is often of particular importance in the construction of achievement and teacher-made tests, where the intention is to measure sets of educational objectives by representing the objectives systematically in the test. The second type of validity is criterion validity, which is an individual-differences concept based on the extent to which a test correlates with another test. Criterion validity may be either concurrent, based on correlations with a second test given at the same point in time, or predictive, as in correlations with tests given at later points in time.

Content and criterion validity have tended to be the principal concern of educators, by virtue of their implications for achievement measurement and prediction. The third type of validity, however, construct validity, has been mainly a psychologist's concept (Messick, 1975), and is the most complex of the three varieties. In brief, construct validity refers to the collection of evidence to support a particular theoretical interpretation for some empirical results, usually results derived from psychometric instruments. Stated more simply, this form of validity is based on the interpretation of observable data in terms of nonobservable entities, or psychological constructs. Because the nature of these psychological constructs generally takes the form of a theoretical network, dependent on which theory is considered, strict operationalism is discouraged in the process of construct validation. A single test is not said to measure a single construct, therefore, but rather, empirical relationships of different varieties between tests and measurement conditions reflect the underlying theoretical framework. Thus, in construct validation we do not claim that test x measures construct y, either exclusively, or by itself, even though in less formal parlance this suggestion is often made. Rather, in construct validation it is recognized that any given psychometric instrument may measure elements of several psychological processes, by virtue of its content and task demands, and therefore evidence for the validity of both the instrument and the theory itself must be collated from a series of sources (see Cronbach, 1971; Cronbach & Meehl, 1955; Loevinger, 1957, 1965).

The means by which the evidence for construct validity is compiled involve two fundamental requirements, as first suggested by Campbell and Fiske (1959). One requirement is the collection of convergent evidence, which is data indicating substantial empirical relationships between different psychological measures and variables as expected on the basis of the theory. Thus, for example, if two measures are both said to sample the same construct, these measures should be highly related empirically. Similarly, if the construct is said to be theoretically related to some subject classification variables, such as sex or height for example, convergent evidence would be the demonstration of this relationship.

It follows from this need for convergent evidence that construct validation also requires the second and converse type of evidence, known as discriminant evidence. Data which form the basis for discriminant evidence demonstrate a lack of empirical relationship between measures and variables when this lack of relationship is predicted on the basis of the theory. Thus, if constructs x and y are functionally independent in theory, and measures of these constructs are found to be empirically unrelated, this constitutes discriminant evidence. As an example, if a theory predicts that males and females will not differ in construct z, and it is found that sex is not related to a measure of construct z, this becomes discriminant evidence.

In the assessment of a theory, then, it is necessary to evaluate the supporting body of both convergent and discriminant evidence. Both of these types of evidence are used in establishing the status of the theory in terms of its different sources of support, as well as evaluating the merit of the theory in comparison to others of its class. In earlier chapters, a series of factor analyses were presented that were suggested to be consistent with a theory of cognitive processes based on entirely different evidence, namely Luria's physiological investigations. The basis for this attempt to wed a physiological theory with factor-analytic evidence is both forms of construct evidence. Convergent evidence was used heavily in noting that some of the tasks used by Luria to detect deficits in simultaneous synthesis correlated highly in normal populations. Thus, Luria's research on deficits was generalized to a continuous and full range of individual differences. Similarly, it was noted that successive forms of syntheses, which were identified by Luria primarily in terms of correct sequential order in behavior, could be found in high intercorrelations among tests scored for correct sequence of recall. Drawing from other sources of theories outside of Luria's formulations, we have also compiled convergent evidence based on Paivio's (e.g., 1975) dual coding hypothesis, and more generally, on the long history of dichotomies in cognitive processes summarized by Ornstein (1972). In brief then, the relationships found among the measures of both simultaneous and successive syntheses form convergent evidence consistent with many different theoretical sources, including Luria's theory.

In addition, discriminant evidence is also supplied, primarily in terms of the relationship of simultaneous synthesis to successive synthesis. The closely related theoretical positions noted previously vary somewhat in their definition of the dual constructs, but all share the common premise that these cognitive processes are essentially independent of one another.

The many philosophical and theoretical positions reviewed by Ornstein (1972) imply this independence, Paivio's dual coding theory suggests this also, as do Luria's formulations of simultaneous and successive processes. Discriminant evidence then would be the demonstration that tests which purport to measure these constructs are uncorrelated with one another across many populations. We have presented data in previous chapters which demonstrate this lack of correlation, and, as noted here, consider it one form of support for the theory.

Beyond the consistency of the theory with data, broader questions must be asked. Stated simply, if the theory of simultaneous and successive syntheses is an accurate description of cognitive processes, what is the status of the other theories of intelligence and human abilities? More particularly, how might the results of other research based on these theories be explained in terms of the simultaneous–successive model? It is to these questions that we now turn, with the assistance of the concepts of convergent and discriminant validity as tools. In so doing, however, we do not intend to analyze all of the major theories of cognitive ability, many of which have been noted in our introductory chapter. Rather, we will confine ourselves to those theories which have direct implications for the simultaneous–successive model, and particularly those for which some comparative empirical results are available.

8.2   RELATED MODELS OF COGNITION

We will consider related models of cognition within five topical areas: intelligence and abilities, cognitive styles, cognitive learning theory, cognitive developmental theory, and theories of brain function. In examining the other theoretical systems, we will stress their relationships with our own theory. We accept these other theories as legitimate theoretical perspectives. We are not seeking in any way to "disprove" them by examining the many systems; however, we would stress the advantages of a comprehensive integrated model over those that are less general.

Intelligence and Abilities

There are two models within this area that will be examined: the multifactorial, hierarchical model typified by Horn (1976), and Jensen's theory of Level I and II abilities.

MODELS OF ABILITIES

Horn's Model. In his comprehensive review of theories of human abilities Horn (1976) describes the following general model, which we have described previously in Chapter 1. At the lowest of three levels are the *primary abilities,* including such factors as verbal comprehension, numerical, inductive reasoning, spatial orientation, perceptual speed, flexibility of closure, speed of closure, associative memory, mechanical knowledge, divergent production, and so on. These primary factors are subsumed by a smaller number of *broad abilities* at a secondary level: verbal productive thinking (including creativity, divergence, etc.), general crystallized intelligence, general fluid intelligence, general visualization (including field independence), and general memory (or, in Horn's terms, short-term acquisition functions). General speediness may be a sixth broad ability (Horn & Cattell, 1966; Royce, 1973). Finally, even these broad second-order factors are subsumed at the highest level by *g,* or *general intelligence.*

Broadly speaking, we conceive of simultaneous and successive as modes of processing that would in effect cut across these ability factor lines. Functionally speaking, both forms of processing, at some level of complexity, would be required in virtually all cognitive tasks. This does not mean, of course, that individual differences in both forms of processing generally account for individual differences in all task performances. In most normal individuals, performance on different cognitive tasks will primarily result from individual differences in only certain cognitive processes and components (of which simultaneous and successive processing are two), much in the way that the flow of water from a pipe is related primarily to the narrowest part of the pipe. The water is functionally dependent upon the whole length of pipe, but its amount (i.e., individual differences) is most related to the most constricted part of the pipe. Similarly, for instance, the successive aspects of a particular task may be easily within the competence of all subjects while the simultaneous aspects are those which produce individual differences in performance. Thus simultaneous and successive processing can be expected to be more related to some variables than to others, without restricting their generality as constructs.

Because of the generality that we have ascribed to these methods of processing, they would seem to be best related to factors at the broad ability level. The construct of simultaneous processing would share with general visualization the characteristic of maintaining a complex stimulus array in a form that permits immediate access to all parts of it. Simultaneous processing would not, however, be limited to figural stimuli or to the visual mode. It should manifest itself in the variety of spatial primaries that are subsumed by general visualization. Furthermore, by virtue of the tests that are used to measure simultaneous processing, it should also be related to a number of other primary factors. Raven's Matrices, for instance, has commonly been used as a measure of inductive reasoning. Memory-for-Designs would appear to tap a nonverbal memory function, perhaps the visual memory factor that Ekstrom (1973) has tentatively suggested. Figure Copying might be considered a measure of spatial orientation (in the nonmanipulative, nontransformational sense), or of the recently identified factor representational drawing (Hakstian & Cattell, 1974).

Successive processing is more difficult to relate among the broad abilities. The essence of successive processing is temporal order or sequence, while the general memory factor subsumes a variety of primaries that do not require retention of order information. No other second-order ability seems to measure this successiveness adequately. At the primary level, successive processing would be related to span memory (in that the Digit Span test is said to measure both), associative memory (which involves the sequential linking of elements in pairs), and perhaps best of all to the less well identified memory-for-order factor (Ekstrom, 1973). It is also possible that successive processing is involved in a number of verbal primaries (e.g., verbal closure), due to the sequential nature of language tasks, and perhaps in others (e.g., verbal comprehension) due to the sequential–associative structure of semantic memory (Anderson & Bower, 1973).

The speed factor that we have discussed briefly in previous chapters is relatively easy to relate to the broad ability of general speediness, or to the perceptual speed primary, although the Color Naming and Word Reading tests have not been specifically used.

Our planning, or executive function, on the other hand, is much less well represented in the traditional models of abilities. While planning is involved in the selection of strategies within many of the tests of the cognitive factors (cf. Carroll, 1976), there has been little effort to isolate that aspect of the tasks. In fact, the search for culture-fair measures of intellectual ability has resulted in the avoidance of measures that are dependent upon learned strategies (cf. Hunt, 1975). Though perhaps well motivated, this lack of a strategic component is the least appealing aspect of the traditional abilities model, particularly from an information-processing point of view.

Traditional abilities models have similarly avoided concepts that would represent what we have referred to as Block 1 functions. Again, many tasks, if not all, can be seen to be dependent upon an appropriate arousal level. Arousal variables would seem to have been studied more within traditional models of personality (e.g., Eysenck, 1967a) or under the general topic of cognitive styles (see the following).

In the one study to date designed to assess the relationships among simultaneous and successive processing and traditional abilities (Kirby, 1976; Kirby & Das, 1978a), tests of inductive reasoning, memory (associative), and spatial abilities were selected from the Primary Mental Abilities battery (French, Ekstrom, & Price, 1963; Thurstone & Thurstone, 1962). While those factors were then related to the simultaneous and successive factors in a variety of ways (see Kirby, 1976), the most concise analysis simply correlated the factor scores of the two batteries (see Table 8.1). The results confirm the important relationship between simultaneous processing and spatial ability, other relationships being far less strong. These results are also relevant to our discussion of Jensen's two-level theory of abilities.

Jensen's Theory of Level I and II Abilities. Jensen's two categories of mental abilities are defined and distinguished in terms of the amount of transformation of stimulus input that is required in any task. Level I ability involves relatively little transformation and is measured by tests of rote learning and short-term memory. Level II ability requires transformation of and abstraction from stimulus inputs; Jensen has used tests of general intelligence (e.g., 1974a) as measures of Level II ability.

As the constructs are defined, there is little overlap between simultaneous–successive processing and Level I and II abilities, because both simultaneous and successive processing are conceived of as means of coding, of transforming stimulus input. Both simultaneous and successive processing occur in simple and complex cognitive tasks.

Confusion can arise, however, because Jensen has used tests very similar to those in the simultaneous–successive battery as measures of Level I and II ability. In a 1973 study, for instance, Raven's Coloured Progressive Matrices and Figure Copying were used as Level II measures, while a variety of Digit Span tasks were the Level I measures. It would seem that more consistent tests of Level II ability in particular should be employed to validate the construct of stimulus transformation (see Lawson & Jarman, 1977; Jarman, 1978a for a more extensive critique of Jensen's theory).

Jensen himself has suggested (e.g., 1973b, p. 264) that Levels I and II can be well measured, respectively, by tests of associative memory (specifically paired-associate learning) and of reasoning (particularly of the culture-fair variety). Thus it would seem that the study (Kirby, 1976; Kirby & Das, 1978a) referred to briefly in the previous section would be of relevance to the relationship between simultaneous–successive processing and Level I and II abilities (see Table 8.1). The results of that study indicate that simultaneous processing (as measured by Raven's Coloured Progressive Matrices, Figure Copying, and Memory-for-Designs) is far more related to spatial ability than to inductive reasoning. Furthermore, simultaneous is no

Table 8.1
Correlations among Simultaneous–Successive (Varimax Rotation) and Primary Mental
Abilities (Promax Rotation) Factor Scores[a][b]

	Inductive reasoning	Memory	Spatial
Simultaneous	.376	.345	.541
Successive	.215	.350	.165
Speed	−.244	−.143	−.197

[a] From Kirby and Das, 1978a.
[b] $N = 104$; r ($p = .01$, two-tailed) $= .254$.

more related to the reasoning factor than it is to memory (as measured by paired-associate tests). Paired-associate memory (supposedly a good measure of the rote associative function Jensen refers to as Level I ability) is no more related to successive processing than to simultaneous. At the very least, these results suggest that more care must be taken in selecting tests to define Level I and II abilities. More specifically, they do not support any contention that simultaneous processing can be identified with reasoning ability, or that successive processing can be identified with memory (see Jarman, 1978a).

Cognitive Styles

Cognitive styles can be conceived of as individual differences in preferred (or habitual) ways of processing information. As such, they will be intimately related to what we have termed Block 3 functions, the control and sequencing of cognitive operations in the solution of a task. We have seen in previous chapters how subgroups can differ in their approaches to cognitive tasks, particularly with regard to the use of simultaneous and successive processing. From this perspective, simultaneous and successive processing can be seen as cognitive styles, or as ways of processing information.

At the most general level, then, cognitive styles can be related to the planning function, or to the sequence of cognitive operations that is selected by the individual in response to a problem situation. In this section, however, we will attempt to relate a number of particular cognitive style variables more specifically to aspects of our model.

FIELD DEPENDENCE–INDEPENDENCE

Without a doubt the most frequently studied cognitive style has been that of field dependence–independence (Witkin, Lewis, Hertzman, Machover, Meissner, & Wagner, 1954). It is essentially a measure of the individual's ability to overcome embedding contexts in perception, but Witkin and his colleagues (e.g., Witkin & Berry, 1975; Witkin, Moore, Goodenough, & Cox, 1977) have extended the concepts to encompass the general construct of psychological differentiation. Horn (1976) discusses evidence from a number of studies (e.g., Vernon, 1972) that leads him to suggest that field independence can be broken down parsimoniously into the broad ability of general visualization and a visuokinesthetic function.

If Horn is correct in this suggestion, it would seem likely that field independence is related to simultaneous processing, just as general visualization is. However, it is possible to relate the general construct of field independence (as perceptual disembedding) to simultaneous processing in such a way as to include the visuokinesthetic functions.

It will be remembered (cf. Chapters 2 and 3) that simultaneous processing was described as operating in three cortical zones, the primary—projection, secondary—association, and tertiary—overlapping. In the tertiary zones, information from all sensory modalities is integrated; while we have concentrated upon the visual and auditory modes, particularly in relation to language, these areas are also responsible for the integration of tactile and vestibular information. Luria (1975b, p. 38) provides a good description of the integrating functions of this area (the "gnostic" area) in his extended case study, *The Man with a Shattered World*.

The essence of field independence, as traditionally measured by Witkin with the Rod-and-Frame and the Body Adjustment tests, would seem to be the coordination of visual and vestibular (balance) information. This dependence of both field independence and simultaneous processing upon the same cortical areas suggests a strong relationship between these constructs. Furthermore, the importance of these tertiary zones in cognition helps to explain the relationships between field independence and general intelligence (e.g., Vernon, 1972), as well as those between field independence and cognitive development (e.g., Case, 1975; see the section entitled Neo-Piagetian Cognitive Development Theories).

As of yet there has been no attempt empirically to relate field independence with simultaneous processing. We would anticipate that simultaneous processing would be manifested in tests of field independence to a degree similar to that to which it is manifested in tests of spatial ability or general visualization.

SERIALISM-HOLISM

In the context of developing computer-assisted-instruction materials, Pask and Scott (1972; Pask, 1975) observed how adult learners chose to explore a domain of knowledge. They state that learners can be divided unambiguously into two groups: *serialists,* who form and test relatively simple hypotheses and learn the information in an orderly, step-by-step fashion; and *holists,* who form and test more complex hypotheses about the material to be learned, and seem to jump from one area of the material to another. Pask and Scott found that when subjected to linear instructional programs that were deliberately either serial or holistic in nature, groups whose learning style was congruent with the learning program far outperformed those who were mismatched. Daniel (1975) has summarized the work of Pask and Scott, and has characterized the errors made by the mismatched serialists as resulting from being unable "to see the wood for the trees," while the holists tended to overgeneralize (Daniel, 1975, p. 85).

Little information is available about the relationship of this cognitive (learning) style to other psychological variables. However, if Pask and Scott are correct that serialists and holists attain similar levels of achievement when learning in their preferred manner, they may have discovered a useful aptitude variable for ATI research. Furthermore, this style is important because it describes *how* individuals learn, rather than relying upon a total score in a performance test.

Pask's research leads us to suspect that his holists are high in simultaneous-processing ability, and his serialists in successive-processing ability. His results would support our finding (Kirby & Das, 1977, described in Chapter 5) that individuals high in only one of the two modes of processing can achieve moderate levels of success in academic tasks. His work also suggests that such individuals differ not only in the way that they process information that they have received, but also in the way in which they seek information to process. Such speculations must await further research.

REFLECTION–IMPULSIVITY

Another well-studied cognitive style is Kagan's reflection–impulsivity (Kagan, Rosman, Day, Albert, & Phillips, 1964), which is normally assessed by the Matching Familiar Figures (MFF) test. In that test, subjects must select from a number of options the figure that is identical to a given figure. Both errors and response times are recorded. Impulsive children are those below the median in response time and above the median for errors, whereas reflective children are those above in response time and below in errors. Messer (1976) has comprehensively reviewed both the evidence for these constructs and a variety of methodological problems in the area. For our present purposes, we need only consider the suggestion that there is a dimension of impulsiveness in children, with low impulsiveness (reflection) being associated with greater success in school (see Kagan, 1965).

Impulsiveness as measured by the MFF seems to be related to a syndrome of behaviors: hyperactivity, poor selective attention, poor impulse control, and perhaps, learning disability (see Ross, 1976, for a review of this point of view). All of these behaviors can be caused by low cortical arousal, in turn a function of the reticular formation, and, in our terms, a Block 1 structure. As we saw in Chapter 6 when discussing the work of Williams (1976), behaviorally hyperactive children are cortically under-aroused. It would seem that Kagan's reflection–impulsivity is largely a measure of the first block of the brain.

We can do little more than suggest that this relationship exists, as the necessary data do not. Several points can, however, be made. Most importantly, impulsiveness seems subject to behavioral remediation (e.g., Meichenbaum & Goodman, 1971). It appears that reinforcement and modelling can help children to slow down, though there is little evidence to suggest that this results quickly in improved school performance.

A second point is that the MFF can also be seen as a test of planning, in that it requires the orderly scanning of a set of alternatives and an appropriate strategy. Impulsive children do not scan in as orderly a fashion as reflective children, but do seem to benefit from being given an appropriate strategy (Egeland, 1974). Other common tests of impulsiveness, such as the Porteus Mazes (Palkes, Stewart, & Freedman, 1971), share this relationship to planning ability. This functional relationship between Blocks 1 and 3 of the brain is an important aspect of Luria's model of the brain, and suggests that a Block 1 problem may be first manifested in tasks requiring Block 3 functions.

CONCEPTUAL LEVEL

The fourth cognitive style which we shall consider is based upon the theory of personality development described by Harvey, Hunt, and Schroder (1961). An individual's conceptual level, or degree of cognitive complexity, is indexed by the complexity of his information processing and by his preference for an unstructured learning environment (D. E. Hunt, 1971). Those of high conceptual level profit more from a learning environment that is of low structure, because that allows them to impose their own cognitive structure upon the material. Those of low conceptual level profit more from a structured learning environment, seemingly because they are unable or unwilling to generate their own structure (Hunt & Sullivan, 1974).

The individual's degree of cognitive complexity would appear to depend upon his ability to plan, a Block 3 function. The relationship is more complex, however, because individuals of low conceptual level rely upon recall of facts, as they were presented, in difficult situations, whereas those of higher conceptual level are able to analyze and synthesize (Hunt & Sullivan, 1974). Thus an inability to plan (Block 3 problem) is manifested by overreliance upon successive processing (Block 2), whereas competent planning relies upon simultaneous processing. This pattern supports the complex interdependence of the units in our functional model, but further speculation must depend upon future research.

Cognitive Learning Theories

In this section we will briefly explore the relationships between our model and some other recent attempts to characterize individual differences of cognitive variables in terms common to experimental psychology. We will examine the work of Carroll (1976), Estes (1974), and E. Hunt (Hunt & Lansman, 1975), all of whom have related traditional ability variables to performance in experimental tasks. (This research was reviewed in Chapter 1.)

Hunt, Frost, and Lunneborg (1973), and Hunt, Lunneborg, and Lewis (1975) applied E. Hunt's (1971, 1973) *distributed memory model* to the study of a number of college students for whom Verbal Ability and Quantitative Ability composite scores were available. They found that Quantitative Ability was related to resistance to interference in a paired-associate learning paradigm, though this was possibly due to the use of backward-counting (involving numbers, with which the high-quantitive-ability subjects might have been more adept) as the interference task. Their more interesting results concerned verbal comprehension ability, which they found to be related to a variety of short-term memory (STM) processes. Briefly, they found that subjects of high verbal ability were faster in converting a visual stimulus to its semantic meaning, more able to retain order information in STM, more rapid in searching STM, and more rapid in manipulating information held in STM.

Hunt et al. (1975) conclude that the verbal comprehension tests indirectly tap a number of more basic information-processing skills, in addition to the linguistic knowledge that they directly measure. From this they infer that the individual differences in verbal ability have arisen because of individual differences in information-processing characteristics.

E. Hunt's approach to intellectual abilities has been extended by Carroll (1976) to encompass 24 of the *primary mental abilities* listed by French, Ekstrom, and Price (1963). Carroll has subjectively analyzed the ability tests to determine the cognitive processes which would produce individual differences in those abilities. For instance, he describes the Spatial Orientation factor as requiring the ability (capacity of STM) and rate (temporal parameters) of a process occurring in STM whereby a spatial representation is "mentally" rotated (Carroll, 1976). Visualization involves the same processes, with the addition of the performance, in executive and STM, of serial operations upon the results of mental operations (Carroll, 1976).

Verbal Comprehension is said to depend upon retrieval from lexicoseman-tic information in long-term memory (LTM); Carroll does not include Hunt's empirically derived STM characteristics of Verbal Comprehension. Induction entails the searching of LTM for relevant hypotheses, though some subjects operate upon STM contents to construct new hypotheses. All cognitive factors are said to depend upon particular memory stores, differ-ent sorts of cognitive operations, and various strategies or control pro-cesses.

Estes (1974) has performed a similar analysis, though less systematically than Carroll, of four Stanford-Binet and WAIS subtests. He suggested that the Digit Span, Digit–Symbol Substitution, Vocabulary, and Word Naming subtests are far more complex, in terms of cognitive processes, than they appear to be. Among the factors that he stresses in these tests are the retrieval of information from LTD semantic networks, and the nature of the processing strategies that the subject employs.

While it would be a very extensive task to detail the relationship be-tween our model and the analyses that Hunt, Carroll, and Estes have performed, it is possible to note some general similarities. These similarities will form the basis for the integrated perspective that we will suggest later in this chapter.

The cognitive learning or memory models that Hunt, Carroll, and Estes employ consist of a processor (similar to our Block 2) and of an executive (our Block 3). Within the processing unit, they detail a structure of short- and long- (and sometimes intermediate-) term memories, as well as the processes (coding) by which information is transferred and transformed. Such a structure is very compatible with our concept of the second block of the brain, particularly in that simultaneous and successive processing are conceived of as means of coding. As broad categories of coding processes, simultaneous and successive processing would operate within and be-tween the various memory stores. They could be similarly conceived as coding processes operating within and between levels in a levels-of-processing framework (Craik & Lockhart, 1972).

More specifically, Hunt et al.'s (1975) description of the information-processing correlates of high verbal ability would appear to agree with our findings (Kirby & Das, 1977) with regard to simultaneous–successive pro-cessing and reading comprehension. Just as we found successive process-ing correlated with comprehension, they found retention of order informa-tion in STM important. Their finding that speed of STM information manipulation is important might well correspond to our correlation of simultaneous processing with reading achievement.

The work of Hunt, Carroll, and Estes is very important for understanding the nature of intellectual abilities. Hunt's experimental approach to subjects of different demonstrated levels of ability suggests a direction for future research. Estes' and Carroll's extensive elaborations of the contents, structures, and processes underlying psychometric test performance supply much greater detail to our Block 3, and, in particular, our Block 2 functional systems.

Neo-Piagetian Cognitive Development Theories

A fourth area which we will mention briefly concerns recent efforts to develop a functional theory of cognitive development, to complement Piaget's structural theory (Case, 1972, 1974, 1975, 1977; Pascual-Leone, 1970). The purpose of a functional theory is to describe "the devices or mechanisms by which human knowledge is actually acquired and utilized [Case, 1974, p. 544]," and so an information-processing framework has been used. In Case's (1974) terms, executive schemes are used to coordinate the activation of series of figurative and operative schemes in the solution of a problem. Executive schemes are said to correspond to plans and figurative schemes to chunks of information, while operative schemes are means of transforming information. The individual's functional system is limited in a particular problem situation by three factors:

1. The existence in his repertoire of schemes of appropriate schemes
2. The number of schemes which can be deployed at any one time; this is termed *mental* (or M) space and is measured by tests requiring sequential memory (memory span)
3. The field independence of the subject, which determines how likely he is to use his full M space and how likely he will be to avoid perceptual traps in selecting an executive scheme

Our interest in this neo-Piagetian model stems from two of its characteristics. First, its general outline stresses the executive or planning processes, and the information-transforming (coding) processes. To this extent, then, it recalls our discussion of Block 3 and Block 2 functions.

More importantly, however, Case's functional model refers to two limiting factors, M space and field independence, which may be seen to correspond to our successive and simultaneous processing. The construct of M space is different from that of successive processing, in that it is a capacity, not a means of coding information, but the two constructs are measured by similar tests and are not that conceptually remote. Case claims that M space is taken up by figurative and operative schemes, the former corresponding to information and the latter to transformational processes. His typical measures of M space (e.g., Backward Digit Span), however, like our measure of successive processing, relate to the retention of what he would term *figurative schemes*. This underscores the difficulty of accurately measuring the more complex manifestations of these sorts of processes in normal individuals. His suggestion that tasks of different developmental difficulty require numerically different M space capacities recalls similar suggestions by others (McLaughlin, 1963; Halford, 1972), and may provide a direction for further research with successive processing.

We have previously suggested that field independence is related to simultaneous processing. This would correspond to Case's description of field-independent subjects avoiding the perceptual traps contained in conservation tasks. Such perceptual information would be integrated, perhaps in figurative and operative schemes, through simultaneous processing. Direct evidence linking simultaneous processing to conservation tasks is provided by Carlson and Wiedel (1975). By factor analyzing conservation tests with simultaneous and successive tests, they showed that the conservation tests loaded on a simultaneous factor. The further characterization of field-independent subjects as being more likely to employ their full M space derives from their more analytic approach to tasks: They are less likely to accept given information, more likely to operate on it to create new information. In our model this would correspond to an active executive system, which would in turn rely upon successive (i.e., M space) and simultaneous processing in the analysis of information.

We have examined only a few interesting relationships between this functional developmental model and our own, but they do suggest an application of the simultaneous–successive model to developmental phenomena. An individual's ability to perform successive processing may well develop, as M space does, allowing the person to succeed in increasingly complex tasks. Similarly, simultaneous processing should develop, perhaps starting later than successive (Luria suggests that the temporal–parietal–occipital tertiary zones only become operative around age 7).

Theories of Brain Function

The last decade has seen a resurgence of interest and research concerning the functional organization of the brain, particularly with regard to the differences between cerebral hemispheres (e.g., Sperry, 1968). The basic verbal–nonverbal distinction in functioning between, respectively, the left and right hemispheres (in most right-handed people) has been extended by some (e.g., Ornstein, 1972) to suggest the existence of two different modes of consciousness, two different kinds of symbolic thought processes. This hemispheric asymmetry has been said to be the cause of a number of cognitive models, including Paivio's (1971, 1975) theory of imagery and verbal processes. We will first examine recent theories of hemispheric functional asymmetry and then concentrate on Paivio's work.

THEORIES OF HEMISPHERIC ASYMMETRY

Our major reason for considering the laterality differences theories is that, superficially, they appear to resemble ours strongly. This is particularly true of more recent formulations (Cohen, 1973; Nebes, 1974; Semmes, 1968) which have emphasized *processing* differences between hemispheres, the left (verbal) specializing in serial processing, and the right (nonverbal) in parallel processing. Luria's model of brain function describes simultaneous (parallel?) processing zones in the temporal–parietal–occipital regions, and successive (serial?) processing zones in the fronto–temporal regions, of both hemispheres; this essentially back-to-front distinction is clearly not the same as the familiar left-to-right one in the laterality differences literature. We will discuss how these two models can be resolved, and propose that our simultaneous and successive processing factors do not represent, respectively, nonverbal and verbal processes.

As with Luria's model, the basic information concerning laterality differences has come from clinical patients with clear brain damage, and the research elaborated in normals. Early investigators (e.g., Broca, 1888) observed that damage to the left hemisphere disrupted language functions, receptive, expressive, or both. Much more recently (e.g., Kimura, 1963, 1969; Milner, 1971) it has been noticed that right hemisphere damage results in similar disturbances of nonverbal, visuospatial functions. A similar pattern of results emerges from studies of split-brain patients (e.g., Nebes, 1974; Sperry, 1968) and of normals (e.g., White, 1969).

While early investigators interpreted these results as meaning that the left hemisphere processes verbal input and the right hemisphere nonverbal, more recent researchers (Cohen, 1973; Nebes, 1974; Semmes, 1968) have instead begun to propose what can best be termed a processing distinction. The earlier formulations have disappeared for a number of reasons: The right hemisphere has been shown to have at least some verbal abilities (Sperry, 1968, p. 731), the left hemisphere can deal with nonverbal stimuli more efficiently than the right if the task can involve verbal coding (Wyke & Ettlinger, 1961), and the right hemisphere can deal more efficiently with language stimuli if the task does not require verbal coding (Gibson, Dimond, & Gazzaniga, 1972). Perhaps most important has been the difficulty of ascribing a neurophysiological difference to stimulus characteristics.

The result has been an increased interest in the nature of the coding which each hemisphere is more capable of applying to incoming stimuli. Nebes' (1974) conclusions of his review of split-brain research are that "the type of information processing required to solve the problem" determines which hemisphere is dominant for a particular task, that the left hemisphere "sequentially analyzes input, abstracting out the relevant details to which it associates verbal symbols," and that the right hemisphere "is seen to organize and treat data in terms of complex wholes, being in effect a synthesizer with a predisposition for viewing the total rather than the parts [Nebes, 1974, pp. 12–13]."

This reference to sequential and wholistic processing, and Cohen's (1973) use of the terms *serial* and *parallel* processing, are reminiscent of Luria's two modes of processing, or at least our description of them as means of coding. It seems that most language is in some sense "stored" or controlled in the left hemisphere. This may be because, as Semmes (1968) suggests, the left hemisphere is neuroanatomically arranged in a "focal" manner, specializing in codes which are different only in minor ways (e.g., speech codes). With this focal arrangement, the left hemisphere must proceed from point to point in processing, that is, serially. The right hemisphere, according to Semmes (1968), is organized more diffusely, specializing in codes that represent overall patterns. Because information is used in the right hemisphere in this way, information appears to be processed in parallel.

There is a crucial difference between the laterality model and Luria's, however: The former is at least to a large extent *code content* specific, while the latter is not. By code content we mean not the stimulus content (verbal, spatial, etc.), but the characteristics of the code (verbal, etc.). The simultaneous–successive model states that both forms of processing (simultaneous–parallel, successive–serial) can be applied to codes of all sorts.

Luria has demonstrated this cross-content generality in clinical cases. He has found, for instance, the comprehension of a variety of logico-grammatical constructions to depend upon simultaneous processing (cf. Chapter 2). In our work with the simultaneous–successive battery, we have avoided the use of verbal–linguistic tests, so as not to disadvantage subjects of younger age or different cultural groups. However, we have shown simultaneous processing to be related to the recall of paradigmatic clusters of words (Kirby, Jarman, & Das, 1975), and to a variety of measures of reading vocabulary and comprehension (cf. Chapter 5). While it is difficult to prove a distinction between concepts such as these, we would propose that simultaneous and successive processing do represent means of coding that are at least theoretically independent of the code content. In practice, however, particular forms of coding may be more regularly applied to certain types of information (e.g., successive to verbal–acoustic).

A possible resolution to the problem would be to suggest that the serial and parallel processing postulated by both models exists. In that case, the temporal–parietal–occipital area of the right hemisphere would be "more" parallel than the corresponding area of the left hemisphere, and the fronto–temporal area of the left hemisphere "more" serial than that of the right. Such relationships may be difficult to demonstrate empirically, however.

PAIVIO'S THEORY OF IMAGERY AND VERBAL PROCESSES

Paivio (e.g., 1969, 1971) has proposed a dual coding model, wherein verbal input can be coded as the abstract proposition which it represents, or as an image which it evokes. Input which is coded both ways is more likely to be recalled than that which is coded in only one. This model can be seen as an example of the verbal–nonverbal distinction discussed previously, and in fact Paivio (e.g., 1974) suggests that the two forms of coding are based in the two halves of the brain.

In 1975 we suggested that most of what Paivio refers to as imagery processing probably involved simultaneous processing. In support of our argument we quoted an exploratory study with high school students by Cummins (1973), who factor analyzed a battery of tests that included concrete and abstract paired-associate tests, among others. Cummins identified his factors as divergence, simultaneous, and successive processing (see Table 8.2). The most interesting aspect of his results was that the concrete and abstract paired associates loaded on separate factors, suggesting that the high school students employed different cognitive processes in solving these tasks. We suggested, after Cummins, that simultaneous processing was used to remember concrete pairs, and successive processing to remember abstract pairs.

At the same time, however, we suggested that the imagery mode was by

Table 8.2
Cummins' Factor Analysis (Varimax Rotation)

	Factors		
Test	Divergence	Simultaneous	Successive
Digit Span	−.055	−.184	.577
Syllogisms	.243	.702	−.008
Similarities	.354	.548	.175
Paper Folding	−.067	.711	−.313
Concrete Paired Associates	−.011	.739	.348
Abstract Paired Associates	.113	.224	.640
Memory Span (concrete words)	.038	.154	.727
Memory Span (abstract words)	.135	−.037	.691
Utility (flexibility)	.890	.220	−.003
Utility (fluency)	.731	−.093	.191
Utility (originality)	.757	.191	−.010
Percentage of total variance	19.3	18.6	18.5

no means the same thing as simultaneous processing, nor was the verbal mode identical to successive processing. We thought it feasible for both imagery and verbal mediation to involve simultaneous or successive processing. While examples of successive processing in imaginal tasks have been difficult to find (the successive transformation of a complex figure may be such an example), there have been several examples of simultaneous processing in verbal tasks—paradigmatic clustering (Kirby, Jarman, & Das, 1975) and the Similarities test (Cummins, 1973) being two examples. In principle, mode of processing (simultaneous or successive) is orthogonal to code content (spatial or verbal). In practice, however, it is likely that simultaneous processing is more frequent with imaginal material, and successive with verbal (see also Kirby & Das, 1976).

There has since been a study which included both the simultaneous–successive battery and tests of concrete and abstract paired associates (Kirby, 1976). While concrete paired associates were strongly related to simultaneous processing (as both we and Paivio would suggest), abstract paired associates were not strongly related to successive processing (see Table 8.3). If anything, these results would suggest that success in both tasks was most dependent upon simultaneous processing, upon forming the two associates into some sort of unitary representation. While our theory could not claim to have predicted these results, it is far more comfortable with them than is Paivio's.

A similar result was found by Ernest and Paivio (1971). Their subjects were required to produce an image or, in the alternate condition, a verbal associate, in response to a series of concrete and abstract nouns. Response latencies in the four conditions (concrete-image, concrete-associate, abstract-image, and abstract-associate) were then correlated with tests of spatial ability and an imagery questionnaire. Interestingly, latencies in all four conditions were highly related to spatial ability (correlations were in the range .393 to .629). If anything, spatial ability was more related to performance under instructions to produce a verbal associate! Given the relation of spatial ability to simultaneous processing, it is difficult to see in these data any verbal-successive and imagery-simultaneous identification.

Table 8.3
Correlations of Simultaneous, Successive, and Speed Factor Scores with Concrete and Abstract Paired Associate Tests[a]

	Simultaneous	Successive	Speed
Concrete	.452	.166	−.214
Abstract	.264	.196	−.213

[a] $N = 104$.

Paivio (1975, 1976) disagrees with our proposed separation of codes and modes of processing. He states (1975) that the essence of imaginal processing is "synchronous" processing and that of verbal processing "sequential" processing, synchronous and sequential being equivalent to our simultaneous and successive. While we might conceive of verbal and imaginal systems existing at one level of analysis and of simultaneous and successive processing at a more basic level, Paivio equates these two levels.

There are a number of difficulties that result from this equation of the two processing models. The foremost is that it is very difficult for verbal information to be synchronously organized, or for imaginal information to be sequentially organized. Such processing can only take place if the information is translated into the other system, and presumably into the other cerebral hemisphere. This suggestion would seem to contradict Luria's observations of simultaneous processing disturbances of language from left hemisphere (temporal–parietal–occipital) damage. We are also unaware of any evidence in the split-brain literature to support this contention (presumably one would be far less able to use synchronous processing on verbal information, etc.).

If one seeks to identify the simultaneous and successive processing dimensions with spatial (imaginal) and verbal processing, this can only be done by stretching the meaning of the terms *spatial* and *verbal* beyond their normal meanings. Both most obviously refer to types of information, and can be of great use in this respect. To extend these concepts *isomorphically* to methods of information integration does violence both to the types of codes and the types of coding. The statement that "spatial processes" are involved in language comprehension (in the sense that simultaneous processing is so involved) suggests that "spatial" is not the correct word. "Quasi-spatial" (which we have used as a partial description of simultaneous processing) would be an improvement, but the crucial point is to avoid the identification of a type of content with a means of processing information. This of course does not deny that a particular type of processing may be more common with a particular type of content or code; this could certainly be true in the tasks commonly used by psychologists, and also true of the problem-solving strategies of Western subjects.

The greatest difficulty with Paivio's argument is that it attempts to equate a left-brain–right-brain formulation with a back-brain–front-brain one. Luria has demonstrated simultaneous and successive processing in both hemispheres, in both verbal and nonverbal tasks. This cannot be reconciled with Paivio's attribution of synchronous processing to the right hemisphere and sequential processing to the left, unless one accepts our suggestion, made in the previous section, that the fronto–temporal regions of the left hemisphere are more specialized for successive processing than those of the right, and that the temporal–parietal–occipital regions of the right hemisphere are more specialized for simultaneous processing than those of the left. At the very least, however, one cannot deny the importance of simultaneous processing in language, as will be evident in Chapter 10.

8.3 TOWARD AN INTEGRATED PERSPECTIVE

We have reviewed a number of theories of cognition in this chapter in order to show both their similarities and dissimilarities to our theory. It should be noted, however, that each, our own included, was intended to relate to a particular realm of phenomena, to answer particular questions. If a general cognitive model is to be envisaged, it must be an integrated perspective derived from these diverse theoretical positions. We can only sketch the broad outlines of such a model in this section.

The Three-Block Model

Luria's conception of three functional systems within the brain would provide a good basis for any integration. At the moment, while much is known about the first (arousal) system, particularly physiological information, this system has not often been explicitly included in models of cognition. A modern integrated model must include such a system, and in the future provide more detailed information about the interaction of this system with the other two.

The second functional unit is the one that has been best explored in cognitive models. At the moment there are two perspectives on the substructure of this system, one emphasizing time of processing (STM–LTM) and the other depth of processing (physical–phonemic–semantic). Any legitimate model of cognition must include such substructure and make explicit reference to how information is transferred from structure to structure (or state to state).

A major function of this second system is to encode input information. Our review of other theories has shown a great deal of interest in characterizing these codes. Some theorists (e.g., Jensen) have concentrated on how much coding is involved; others (not examined here) have discussed qualitative aspects of coding such as breadth of coding; still others (e.g., Paivio) have looked at what we have referred to as different types of code content (verbal, imaginal). Whichever of these descriptions is accepted, the inescapable conclusion is that coding (and thus storage) is multidimensional. Input is analyzed on a number of dimensions, and this analysis cannot be adequately summarized dichotomously. Codes themselves are manipulated and transformed (recoded, processed). We have studied two major categories of processing, simultaneous and successive, which subsume a number of component operations.

The third functional system is a crucial component of any general model. The explicit inclusion of an executive system, with a physiological locus (the prefrontal lobes), can be a framework for understanding many cognitive phenomena. The frequent references to an analytic tendency in people (e.g., Witkin), for example, may better be understood in terms of planning rather than of processing ability. The tendency of individuals or groups to process task information in characteristic ways may reflect ability as much as strategy, though of course there are likely to be strategy or planning abilities. Many cognitive styles may be characterized as reflecting strategy differences.

A final aspect of Luria's three-block model must be emphasized: These functional systems are highly interdependent. Each unit, to some extent, controls and is controlled by the other. This characteristic will make the experimental study of these systems in isolation very difficult in normal individuals. Furthermore, although all systems may be involved in a particular task, individual differences in performance in that task may only be due to individual differences in one system, or in one part of one system.

The Place of Abilities

The three-block model can be applied quite successfully to describing the cognitive processes which underlie psychometrically derived mental abilities. In this regard, it would rely heavily upon the work already done by Estes (1974) and Carroll (1976), but would include a Block 1 arousal system.

General ability or intelligence is more difficult to describe functionally, as it would depend upon the smooth operation of all systems. The role of planning and decision making is stressed, however, taking some of the emphasis away from simple processing power.

The cognitive processes and structures in the model would undergo development, that development being the basis for the normally observed qualitative changes in behavior with age. The consistent deployment of a set of processes (thus a strategy) in a series of problems would produce correlations among performances in those problems and thus potentially an ability factor. Such factors need not be immutable, and may in fact lose all importance if appropriate training is given.

The Educational Emphasis

By far the most important aspects of this functional model of cognitive processing are the optimistic suggestions it makes regarding the training of these cognitive processes. Three qualitatively different hypotheses were advanced in previous chapters. The first discussed the possibility that some individuals may be inadequate in a certain form of processing, or more generally, in a certain aspect of cognition. Identification of that weakness and appropriate training to improve the processes involved may be one remedial route. Regular educational programs should of course seek to minimize such processing weaknesses.

The second remedial hypothesis concerned aptitude–treatment interactions. In this case, an individual might be weak in a form of processing that was resistant to improvement. Depending upon the locus of the weakness, alternative educational environments may be designed to exploit the individual's cognitive strengths. Such programs must make every attempt to bring all individuals to similar goals, not to let "alternative educational environments" become "second-rate educational environments."

The third remedial route relies heavily upon the planning and strategy-forming unit. It suggests that all processes exist or potentially exist in all individuals, and that many observed weaknesses can be eliminated by proper instruction in how to orchestrate these processes in the solution of a task.

8.4 SOME CAUTIONS

In describing an integrated cognitive model, a number of cautions must be exercised. Because we wish the model to encompass the psychometric models of ability and intelligence, cautions that should be employed in those areas should also apply to the general cognitive model. In particular, assumptions of genetic determination and immutability should be avoided where possible. Such assumptions are often unstated, and lead to data collection which tends to confirm those same assumptions.

A second caution must be advised concerning the premature equation of dichotomies. Judging by sheer popularity, it seems that the most frequent manner of conceptualizing human behavior is to say: "It is of two types . . ." Different psychologists (and philosophers) over the years have described different dichotomies (see Ornstein, 1972, p. 67, for an extensive list), most of which have the tempting characteristic of seeming to be strongly related: verbal/spatial, active/receptive, analytic/gestalt, left hemisphere/right hemisphere, focal/diffuse, lineal/nonlineal, etc. (even intellectual/sensuous!). While many of these dichotomies may be isomorphic, the majority may at best be only correlated. Furthermore some of them (such as the left hemisphere/right hemisphere and successive processing/simultaneous processing dichotomies) relate to structures which are simply not the same. To suggest that they are similar (and they may be, in function) is to avoid the conclusion that they are different in actuality.

9

Can Strategies Be Taught?

9.1 APPLICATION OF SIMULTANEOUS–SUCCESSIVE MODEL

An efficient manner in which to discuss remediation strategy is to look upon cognitive incompetence in children as due to either a *mediational* or a *production* deficiency (Flavell, 1970). A mediational deficiency is closer to the notion of a deficiency in capacity—the capacity to use verbal processes in order to solve a problem at hand. Verbal processes, which mean largely linguistic processes, are essential for integrating information. Perhaps it is a new way of saying that one has to think and understand before performing an intellectual task. At higher levels of understanding, language becomes the only important tool. Production deficiency relates to a block in performance rather than in ability. Competence has to be inferred from performance, but incompetence may be removed by "prosthetic" devices such as rehearsal for better recall. A limited capacity for recall is assumed to exist if the deficiency is mediational. But production deficiency will be indicated by the fact that the individual does not lag behind in associative skills. Such an individual may need help to keep the stimulus items active in the STM store; hence rehearsal is effective in improving upon production.

Much has been made of production deficiency; sometimes the success of prosthetic devices in improving performance calls into question the very existence of a limited capacity. Curiously enough, the advocacy of production and not mediational deficiency has the same implication as the advocacy of behavior modification techniques to improve the performance of groups known for cognitive deficit (such as the mentally retarded). Bijou's

157

(1966) often quoted statement that there is no mental retardation, only retarded behavior directly implies the absence of an ability deficit. One may expect that a zealous utilization of devices to remove production deficiency may achieve the same objective, that is, the rejection of cognitive deficits of any kind.

Failure to teach appropriate skills for academic tasks leads to poor performance on the part of a child. If one accepts this (and as such, it seems to be a simple statement of the cause of academic failure), then remediation consists of better teaching. The skills to be taught are those that are required, and those on which the child is tested. Hence, if one seeks to improve reading, teach reading skills rather than cognitive processes such as memory and sequential analysis, which underlie reading. This view is the guiding principle in Bereiter and Engelmann's (1966) procedure. Often this takes the form of teaching the test or a closely related version of the test. Improvement is guaranteed if the teaching has been properly done. Thus, there is nothing wrong in teaching to do the test if one can show some amount of transfer to a similar test—this statement is in line with the Bereiter and Engelmann program. We do not necessarily agree with such a view. Neither do we think that the retarded or the severely learning disabled child can be characterized by production deficiency alone, and not by mediational deficiency. It would be difficult to conceive of a retarded child whose only problem is that he does not use rehearsal or some other production strategy until he is taught to do so. Ellis, McCartney, Ferretti, and Cavalier (1977) express doubt that the retarded person has a production deficiency in recognizing pictures because normal–retardate difference in recognition was found even immediately after the picture was exposed. Mediational deficiency seems to be present.

Mediational deficiency must refer to deficiency in processing information, to central processes, independent of the demands of output. In the simultaneous–successive model, mediational deficiency is largely a matter of defects in coding. Coding can be made more efficient by teaching simultaneous and successive strategies when information is to be analyzed. Barring structural limitations which impose a lower boundary on competence in coding, it is possible to improve performance through teaching both how and when to use simultaneous and successive processes. When to use which process, however, lies beyond coding; it must refer to the third unit of the brain, the decision and planning component. In terms of the model, then, remediation consists of teaching the use of simultaneous–successive coding as and when these are appropriate. Such an approach to remediation obviates the necessity of teaching production skills alone. In fact, it would view the teaching of prosthetic devices to be of limited value. The objective of remediation is to remove learning difficulty, in essence to teach an individual how to learn. A first step in remediation would be to analyze the processes underlying an academic skill such as reading; the next step would be to assess an individual with reading problems in terms of those processes. As a final step, training in the appropriate use of those processes is recommended.

Two studies in which this approach has been used successfully will be reported here. We note that this approach is similar to several other studies, such as Spiker (1971) who found that teaching cognitive processes rather than perceptual–motor skills or language skills (of Bereiter & Engelmann type) improved IQ in a comparison of all three methods.

A Word about Strategies

Strategies have been defined as ways of selecting, storing, manipulating, managing, and outputting information which occur at all levels of behavior. The definition of strategies is in line with the model that has been used in this book. It is possible to determine if training in some of the crucial strategies such as grouping, categorization, or memory will improve the efficiency of performance. For example, Reese (1962) suggested that instruction in the use of verbal mediation may facilitate learning in children who have not yet learned how to use mediational processes. In those days mediational deficiency was thought to be one of the primary causes for poor learning among the mentally retarded. Reese's position is in direct contrast to a production deficiency hypothesis (Flavell, Besch, & Chinsky, 1966). What has been noted by several investigators in the field, including Bortner and Birch (1970), is that instructions to use proper strategies lead to great improvement in task performance. Performance, as Bortner and Birch correctly point out, does not necessarily reflect cognitive competence accurately. Performance can be altered by changes in training procedure, in organization of the task, and in motivation. As we have described in the chapter on achievement, the low-achieving child seems to have two major difficulties—(1) he not only does not organize his material, but he may not realize the necessity to do so; (2) he does not use whatever verbal–successive skills he has in solving a problem. Thus, if a child is to be trained in strategies for improving his academic performance, the two important aspects of remediation are verbalization of what the child is trying to do and of feedback, and skills for successive processing.

9.2   ESSENTIAL FEATURES OF INTERVENTION

In both Krywaniuk (1974) as well as in Kaufman (1978) the use of successive strategies was emphasized in the intervention program. However, in Kaufman's study, in addition to teaching successive strategies particular attention was paid to training the child to verbalize his actions while attempting to solve a task. The training tasks in both studies were primarily successive tasks. But, while training on these tasks, some amount of simultaneous training also occurs. By asking the child to verbalize as he is solving a task, one can at least partially monitor the strategy that is being used. It is extremely difficult for a child verbally to order his actions and visually or manually to act in opposition (Jensen, 1966). Thus, verbalization served two functions: (1) It indicated to the experimenter the strategy that was being used; (2) it regulated subsequent actions.

In both of the intervention studies, verbalization was introduced into the training program, generally in the following manner. During each session the child was encouraged to verbalize the strategies and give a verbal summary. At the beginning of each training session the child was asked through direct questioning to recall the strategies used in previous sessions. Since items in any task were equally spaced in time, if a child finished an item quickly more time was spent between tasks with the experimenter in verbal training. As mentioned previously, verbal training was emphasized to a certain extent by Krywaniuk, and much more so in Kaufman's study.

Krywaniuk's Study

Subjects.   The children for the intervention study were Canadian native Cree children in Grades 3 and 4 in a school on a Reserve. According to teachers' rating they constituted the lowest third of the class in terms of school achievement. The children were randomly divided into two groups. One, to receive maximum training (14 to 15 hours) and the other to receive minimal training (3 hours). Training was administered individually. The groups were comparable on their IQs: mean Verbal = 78.39 for Group 1; 77.54 for Group 2; mean Performance = 94.33 for Group 1; 92.55 for Group 2. On full scale IQ there were also comparable means, 84.55 and 83.95. Both groups received three test measures which consisted of the simultaneous–successive battery and Schonell's Word Recognition Test. The tests are shown in Table 9.1.

The Tasks.   The tasks used in the intervention program were selected on the basis of their similarity with successive tasks. Also, they were selected in such a way that they did not reflect competence in any subject area such as mathematics or reading. Finally, the tasks were uncomplicated to produce or use and were easily available for classroom use.

Sequence Story Boards.   There were three separate stories, each consisting of 12 pictures which could be arranged to tell a complete story. The completed form took the form of three rows of four pictures each, similar in arrangement to a page of printed material. On three separate occasions the child was given one story (12 pictures) in random order and asked to arrange the pictures into the prescribed format. He was encouraged to examine each picture and to verbalize during their arrangement. A minimum of help was given; usually an indication of the first picture was sufficient where any help was needed. The child was also required to tell the completed story. Anomalies in the arrangement were pointed out, and the child was required to correct them and proceed toward the end until the complete story was told.

Parquetry Designs. The materials for this task consisted of a number of squares, triangles, and rhombuses of various colors, which could be fitted together to form visual patterns, as well as templates providing the patterns to be made. At first, the child built patterns by placing colored tiles directly upon the colored template, then proceeded to construct patterns by using the colored templates only as a reference. For subsequent sessions, color was removed as a cue, along with the internal lines. Several series of outline forms were developed, one of which is presented in Figure 9.1. Each outline form was presented on a separate sheet of paper. The series progressed by the addition of more and more pieces to an already completed pattern. In each case, the total pattern was to be reconstructed. The most efficient strategy was to remember the relationships involved in the previous pattern and then add new pieces. Each subsequent series presented was more difficult than the previous one and thus reinforced the importance of memory as a strategy.

Serial Recall. In this task 12 common objects were shown to a child for a short time and then taken away. The child was required to recall as many objects as possible. As each one was recalled, it was placed in front of him. He was shown the remaining articles and again they were removed. This procedure was repeated until he could name all objects. In the second presentation, 12 different objects were used. The child was encouraged to group them according to some criterion before they were removed. They were then recalled in the procedure just described.

Coding. Hand and knee "claps" were coded as dots and squares, respectively, and presented in rhythmic patterns similar to those on the

Figure 9.1. Parquetry designs.

Figure 9.2. Hand "claps" (dots) and knee "claps" (squares) sequences.

Cross-modal Coding test. Each pattern was presented separately and the child was expected to "decode" the pattern into the appropriate rhythm of claps. The series of patterns was graded in difficulty. Some examples are provided in Figure 9.2.

Matrix Serialization. During the administration of the Visual Short-Term Memory test, it was noticed that the children did not have a consistent recall pattern in terms of spatial organization. For this reason, it was decided to establish a search and recall pattern consistent with the reading pattern: top to bottom, left to right. To achieve this, several series of matrices were developed, as shown in Figure 9.3, that were identical in format to those used in the Visual Short-Term Memory test. The first five matrices in any one series were presented singly, and the child was required to read each number as it appeared. He was asked to repeat the whole series from memory, in the order presented. He was then shown the complete matrix for confirmation. If he made an error, he read the correct series aloud from the complete matrix and then recalled it again. The number sequences were graded in difficulty. In later sessions, he was shown only a complete matrix and was asked to read it in the prescribed order, and then recall it.

Filmstrips. A total of five filmstrips were prepared: Visual Discrimination and Spatial Orientation, Visual–Motor Coordination, Visual Memory, Figure and Ground, and Visualization. These filmstrips formed the basis of the Group 2 intervention and were also done by Group 1. As in all the intervention tasks, verbalization was encouraged. One of the filmstrips (Figure and Ground) will be described.

Each filmstrip consists of approximately 36 frames, graded in difficulty, and building on concepts learned in previous ones. This is fourth in the series and is designed around the conjunctional forms "only in," "and in," and "but not in." One frame and the accompanying questions, from near the end of the filmstrip, are shown in Figure 9.4. The filmstrips were shown to groups of three or four, and the questions were asked verbally. The

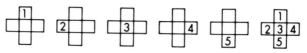

Figure 9.3. Successive matrices for teaching serialization strategy.

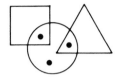

Figure 9.4. Teaching conjunctional skills through filmstrips. Which dot or dots are in the square and the circle but not in the triangle? Which dot is in the triangle but not in the circle or square? Which dot is in the square and triangle but not in the circle?

children were required to respond verbally or, in certain circumstances, by raising colored blocks.

As mentioned before, these tasks were all done individually. In general, the children were encouraged to use verbal mediation and were encouraged to verbalize their thinking. At all times the experimenter attempted to encourage the use of an appropriate strategy and to lead the learning tasks in such a way as to point out how these strategies were used in the solution of the problem.

RESULTS OF THE INTERVENTION PROGRAM

Although the training started with 20 children in each group, at the time of posttest following intervention, complete records were available for 15 children in the experimental group and 20 in the control group. The groups were compared on posttest means but their pretest means were adjusted for initial differences by a covariance technique. The resulting F ratios and probabilities are shown in Table 9.1. The analysis of variance with covariance adjustment showed that Group 1, which was the maximum intervention group, showed significant gains on the Schonell, Serial Learning and Visual Short-Term Memory tests over Group 2. Both Serial Learning and Visual Short-Term Memory are successive tasks in the battery. Thus, improvement in these tasks would be taken as an index of success for the training in successive strategies which Group 1 received. Improvement in Schonell's Word Recognition may be attributed to better use of successive strategies.

The main conclusion drawn from Krywaniuk's study is that both visual and auditory memory showed significant improvement, attributable to the intervention program.

Kaufman's Study

Since this study has not been published previously, it will be described in some detail here.

Subjects. Sixty-eight Grade 4 children were selected as subjects. All children had been tested on Metropolitan Achievement tests, Elementary

164

Table 9.1
Analysis of Variance with Covariance Adjustment between Groups 1 and 2 at Posttest (Hobbema)[a]

	F ratio	p
WISC Verbal	.002	NS
Performance	.390	NS
Full score	.001	NS
Stroop Word		
Schonell	11.470*	.002
Serial Learning	15.83*	.001
Raven's Coloured Progressive Matrices	.09	NS
Cross-modal Coding	2.69	NS
Figure Copying	3.14	.085
Visual Short-Term Memory	6.00*	.020

[a] Significant change is indicated by asterisk.

Battery Form G, and an achievement score was available for the children. On the basis of testing a larger sample of the Grade 4 children, Kaufman divided them into three groups in terms of their performance on the Metropolitan Achievement Test. The groups were: average, having grade equivalent composite score means between 3.7 and 5.5; below average with means between 2.5 and 3.2; and above average having means above 5.6. For purposes of remediation or intervention Kaufman decided to exclude the above average group. Thus, the remaining 68 children were rank ordered and categorized into 34 average and 34 below average children. For purposes of intervention, 17 children from each group were randomly assigned to either an intervention or a no-intervention group. They were balanced for age and sex within each group. The intervention and no-intervention groups, that is, the experimental and control groups, had comparable IQs as judged from their scores on the Otis–Lennon test. Their IQs ranged from 95 to 127 with a mean of 109.38. One might consider the below average group to be similar to a group of learning disabled children. All groups were administered five tests from the simultaneous–successive battery. These were Raven's, Memory-for-Designs, Digit Span Forward, Serial Recall, and Color Naming. In addition to these, the Bender Visual Motor Gestalt Test and the Schonell Reading tests were also administered. These could be referred to as marker tests. Improvement in these tests as a result of intervention was examined following the posttest.

Following intervention all the marker tests as well as the Metropolitan Achievement Test were readministered in order to determine the effectiveness of intervention.

The intervention group received 10 hours of individual training on the tasks to be described below. The no-intervention or control group did not receive training, but continued in the regular class program for those 10 hours. A point that should be noted in regard to the intervention tasks in Kaufman's study is that the tasks were not copies of the marker tests nor did they include materials which were similar in content to the academic tasks in the Metropolitan Achievement tests.

DESCRIPTION OF INTERVENTION TASKS

People Puzzles. These consisted of four 8½- × 11-inch colored picture puzzles of people: a facial view of a toddler boy; a young teen-aged boy in full view; a facial view of a man; and a facial view of a woman. Rather than being true jigsaw puzzles, these puzzles were composed of horizontal strips which extended the full width, one-half of the width, or one-third of the width of the puzzle. This made the puzzle more amenable to sequential attack, for example, top to bottom. Each puzzle picture was on a solid background of a different color, and the back of each puzzle was composed of a different green design on a white background, that is, green vertical lines, green checkered lines, green dots, and green horizontal lines, respectively. In addition, the upper side of each puzzle had a solid line, of a different color from the background color, along the extreme right-hand side.

The task was timed, after familiarizing and desensitizing the child to the stop watch. Initially, all pieces from all four puzzles were mixed together in a large envelope. The child's task was to put together the puzzles, one at a time.

Picture Story Arrangement. The task was similar to Krywaniuk's Sequence Story Boards. Picture Story Arrangement consisted of seven series of pictures, the first three series being on 2¾- × 2¼-inch hardbacked cards, the last four series being on 4- × 4-inch squares of paper. The first series consisted of three cards, while the other six series consisted of six cards each. Each series depicted a complete story. In each series, the author had numbered each card in the sequence they were to be presented to the child, and had letter-coded each card according to the correct response, in the same manner as that used in the WISC-R Picture Arrangement subtest (Wechsler, 1974). The series were ordered according to probable degree of difficulty, beginning with the easiest and ending with the most difficult. The child's task was to order each of the series into sensible stories.

Matrix Numbers. Quite similar to Matrix Serialization (Krywaniuk, 1974), the task consisted of four items. Each item was a five-cell matrix which had one number per cell. Numbers were chosen randomly, but so that no one number appeared more than once in any one cell. Each matrix was presented in the shape of a cross, with one central cell, and one cell on each of its sides.

Each matrix in the present task was presented on sheets of white 8½- × 11-inch paper. The matrix was placed on the center of the paper, with each cell being 1-inch square. In each case, the child was shown a complete matrix, containing one digit in each cell. Thereafter, the child was shown the matrix broken down into its five component parts, with each part being presented separately on a single page, but in its correct position on an otherwise empty matrix. In this way, the child was taken sequentially through the matrix. After he/she had viewed the entire matrix, then the five component parts separately, he/she was asked to recall and write down the complete matrix on a sixth, blank matrix. The sixth page was covered with an acetate sheet upon which the child wrote with a washable marker. After each completed response, the sheet was wiped off with a damp sponge.

Matrix Letters.   This task was similar, and was presented in the same manner as Matrix Numbers. The task consisted of four items. Each item was a five-cell matrix which had one letter per cell. However, letters were not chosen randomly, although no one letter appeared more than once throughout the four matrices. Letters were chosen so that the top and far left letter could be grouped, and the middle and the far right letter could be grouped. Generally, the groupings were standard abbreviations (e.g., PS). The bottom (and final) letter of each matrix was the only vowel in the matrix, and as such, could be a word, or phonetically associated to a word (e.g., U-you).

Once again, the child's response and cell order of each response were recorded by the experimenter.

Matrix Pictures.   This task was similar to Matrix Numbers and Matrix Letters. The task consisted of four items. Each item was a five-cell matrix which had one stimulus per cell. Three of the stimuli were pictures, one stimulus was a design, from the same set of cards as the pictures, and the fifth stimulus was a letter, printed by the author on the background card in block, filled-in letters. The pictures and designs were taken from Memory Game (Instructo). Each 2- × 2-inch card was of heavy cardboard, and was mounted on a background 2½- × 2½-inch card of light brown cardboard. The matrices were presented on reinforced white 8½- × 11-inch paper. The pictures, design, and letter were different for each matrix, and were arranged so that neither the design nor the letter appeared more than once in any one cell.

Picture (Number) Arrangement. This task consisted of 12 series of pictures, presented 3 series to a card on four cards. The 8½- × 5½-inch cards are from Memory Tasks for Reading (Wise Owl), and were covered with clear acetate sheets so that after completion by each child, responses made with a washable marker could be erased with a damp sponge.

Each series was lettered and consisted of four 1½- × ⅞-inch black-and-white pictures, spaced ⅜ inch apart, which, when properly arranged, would depict a story or sequence. Under each picture was a blank ½·inch line on which the child could write a number, depicting the order of that particular picture in the story. To facilitate scoring, the author had placed a duplicate card on the back side, putting in the correct sequencing in the blank spaces. The child's task was to number the pictures in each series so that the order depicted a sensible story.

Serial Recall of Pictures. This task consisted of five items. The first item was composed of 6 cards, while the last four items were composed of 10 cards each. Each 2½- × 2½-inch card was of light brown cardboard and each had a different black-and-white picture of an object or person affixed in the center. These pictures (approximately ½ inch × 1 inch) were from cards found in Memory Tasks for Reading (Wise Owl), which were cut apart and used in an order devised by the author. Each series of cards was composed of pictures of objects that could be paired (e.g., a key and a lock), so that the first series contained three pairs and the other four series contained five pairs. Objects were arranged so that one item from each pair was in the first half of each series while the other item from each pair was in the identical order in the second half of the series. Each card in a series was numbered, and the object was named on the back in the order in which they were to be placed in front of the child. The child's task was to recall, in serial order, all of the pictures in each series.

Free Recall of Pictures. This task consisted of six items. The first two items were composed of 6 cards, the following two items were composed of 8 cards, the fifth item was composed of 10 cards, and the sixth item was composed of 12 cards. Each 2½- × 2½-inch card was of light brown cardboard, and each had a different black-and-white picture of an object or person affixed in the center. These pictures (approximately ½ inch × 1 inch) were from cards found in Memory Tasks for Reading (Wise Owl), which were cut apart and used in an order devised by the author. In the first series, all pictures belonged to the same category, for example, sweets or desserts. In each of the other series, pictures could be equally distributed into two categories. In these series, the items were arranged so that an item from one category was always followed by an item from the other category. Items were arranged in this way to facilitate ease of reorganization by the child into groups, that is, items from one category could be moved up and pushed together while items of the second category could be left in the line presented and pushed together. The categories were different for each series. Each card in a series was numbered, and the object named, on the back in the order in which they were to be placed in front of the child. The child's task was to recall, in any order, all of the pictures in each series.

Follow-the-Arrows.   This task consisted of five items presented on 8½- × 5½-inch cards from Memory Tasks for Reading (Wise Owl). The cards were covered with clear acetate sheets so that after completion by each child, responses made with a washable marker could be erased with a damp sponge.

Four of the cards had five black-and-white pictures which were ordered sequentially to make a story. The pictures were ordered, in a clockwise manner, by means of heavy black arrows. The fifth card consisted of six black-and-white pictures ordered in a counterclockwise manner. The first two cards, on which all of the pictures were joined by arrows, had the word *start* at the beginning point to direct the child. The remaining three cards did not have all the pictures connected by arrows, and had obvious beginning points.

On the back of each card the pictures presented on the front had been rearranged into a different order, and the arrows had been removed. The child's task, after viewing and verbalizing the sequence on the front of the card, was to mark in the arrows on the back so that the sequence was the same as on the front.

Film Strips.   These were the same ones used in Krywaniuk's study. The seven filmstrips, distributed by Classroom Materials Company (310 North Second Street, Minneapolis, Minnesota 55401) were designed to be used in the development of visual perception skills. The seven filmstrips were designed to include seven factors of visual perception.

The filmstrips were all shown on the white wall of the nurse's office at the school at a distance of 7 feet. The child was seated in a comfortable chair next to the projector, and was responsible for turning the strip to the next frame once a frame had been correctly responded to. Each child saw the films individually, and responded verbally. In cases where the child encountered difficulty, he/she was asked either to step closer to the screen or to trace with his/her fingertip on the wall screen for that response.

Only the child's errors were recorded by the experimenter. In instances where there was an error, the child was asked to verbalize the repeated question, then verbally to work through the question and response step-by-step. Each frame received a correct response before the child went on to the next frame. The experimenter ensured, on the first few frames of each filmstrip, that the child knew what he/she was to do. In each filmstrip, the frames proceeded from easy to fairly difficult for these particular children. Questions, on those filmstrips using them, and all responses were included with the distributor's instructions.

Details of procedure including step-by-step methods of training for each task is given in Kaufman (1978).

RESULTS

Did intervention improve the performance of the children on the successive tasks and, to a lesser extent, on the simultaneous tasks?

For purposes of analysis, the group which received training, the experimental group, was compared with the control group in a three-way analysis of variance. The factors in ANOVA were Experimental and Control, within each group, Above and Below Average as determined by the Metropolitan Achievement tests, and Pre versus Posttest scores on the marker tests. The last factor is repeated.

In Table 9.2 a summary of ANOVAs for marker tests is given. Obviously if the interaction between Experimental/Control and Pre/Post measures is significant, then it can be inferred that intervention was effective in improving the performance of the experimental group. As the table shows, except for Raven's Coloured Progressive Matrices, the interaction term was highly significant. The table includes the results of analyses on Bender–Gestalt and on Schonell's Word Reading, which are not parts of the simultaneous–successive battery.

The intervention procedure appeared to have a facilitatory effect on performance on all the successive and all but one of the simultaneous tasks. It also improved Color Naming speed and performance on the Bender–Gestalt, which loads on the simultaneous factor. One may conclude from these results that the intervention training encouraged the use of appropriate strategies. None of the training tasks were purely successive; in fact, it is nearly impossible to devise training tasks which would be exclusively successive. Throughout the training period, verbalization was encouraged. Suppose the child in the experimental group learned where and when to use successive strategies. It is reasonable to expect, then, that by not using a successive strategy where a simultaneous strategy is appropriate, improvement in both kinds of tasks would occur.

The two intervention studies are enough to convince one that strategies can be taught. There is no need to assume that the only way to improve performance in a test is to teach the test. Clearly, the children who improved were learning to use generalized strategies. Two things may be

Table 9.2
Summary of Analyses for Marker Tests: Three-Way Analyses of Variance with One Factor Repeated

Marker tests	Source (expressed as calculated F Ratio)						
	A(Exp/Cont)	B(AV/Below AV)	AB	C(Pre/Post)	AC	BC	ABC
Raven's Coloured Progressive Matrices	—	—	—	23.04***	—	—	—
Memory-for-Designs	—	—	—	48.42***	25.78***	—	—
Serial Recall	—	—	—	59.56***	50.54***	—	—
Free Recall	4.92*	—	—	89.02***	44.86***	4.87*	—
Digit Span Forward	—	—	—	7.55**	11.99***	—	6.29*
Color Naming	—	5.20*	—	17.17***	17.48***	—	—
Bender Gestalt	4.13	—	—	13.28***	13.92***	—	—
Schonell	6.70*	28.40***	—	112.22***	14.76***	—	—

* $p < .05$.
** $p < .01$.
*** $p < .001$.

noted, however. First, in as much as every task is only relatively more or less successive than another task, perhaps it would be unnatural to teach only successive strategies even if it were possible to devise simple training procedures to do so. Second, it may be worthwhile to consider the role of verbalizing one's immediately past activity and future course of action. When verbalization is associated with any teaching, of successive or of simultaneous strategies, it can only enhance the efficacy of teaching. The foregoing studies have demonstrated this.

9.3   CONCLUSION

Our foregoing discussion of the two studies on the teaching of strategies may be viewed in retrospect in terms of three related issues. These issues are first, some empirical considerations regarding the nature of the teaching process as related to assessments of performance; second, theoretical assumptions on which this research has been founded; and finally, some comments regarding the ontogeny of strategic behavior.

The most specific issue in our two studies is concerned with the relationship between the characteristics of the tests used to assess the cognitive level of the subjects of the studies, and the nature of the intervention activities. This issue, of course, concerns the extent of transfer demanded between the instructional activities and the assessment procedures. Transfer is a key issue in studies of educational intervention, and indeed, some psychologists would claim that transfer is the primary phenomenon which any theory of learning must explain (Buss, 1973b).

Our procedures in these two studies have been to avoid teaching the content of the pre and posttest assessment procedures, and yet to incorporate similar task demands in the instructional activities. In this regard, we find ourselves most closely aligned with what Scott (1978) has termed the assessment–intervention model. The instructional demands have not been manipulated systematically, however, so we have not provided data on the form and degree of generalization that it is possible to develop by our instructional techniques. Nonetheless, we must also note that the areas of assessment to which this learning has generalized are fairly broad and represent some important elements of school learning.

The second, and slightly more general issue, concerns our theoretical assumptions in the two studies. These assumptions were relatively few and therefore largely unrestrictive. Flavell's (1970) distinction between production and mediational deficiencies was seen to relate, respectively, to our distinction between the propensity to use a simultaneous or successive cognitive strategy in a particular situation, and individual differences in ability in coding in these processes. The question begged by this distinction and our results in these two studies, then, is which of these two characteristics of the children was changed as a result of the intervention procedures? Granting that this question is impossible to answer categorically, we would be hard pressed to suggest that generalized changes in coding ability were the consequences of our procedures. This may be true to a limited extent, but related research would suggest, instead, that our procedures were primarily responsible for inducing the use of cognitive strategies which were effective for given classes of tasks. That is, we have proceeded in both studies to help children develop effective techniques of structuring task information in order that performance in completion of the task can be improved. It is this strategic aspect of children's behavior that we have focused on, for it is this aspect which is most responsive to educational intervention. This focus on the mutability of strategic behavior, we recognize, is parallel to many areas of research using alternate theoretical perspectives, as for example, memory in the retarded (Brown, 1974), and rule learning (Siegler, 1976).

We may note, further, that our procedures of intervention combine elements of cognitive–educational theory (Klahr, 1976) with a behavioral approach. This reflects our primarily pragmatic view of the instructional process itself, as distinct from our slightly more theoretical view of cognitive processes. We adopt this position because there appears little chance of the development of a general instructional theory which will take account of all of the situational variables in a given instructional sequence (Snow, 1977). Looking ahead, however, it is quite possible that a formative and situation-specific view of instruction will yield more effective procedures than those that have been used in the two studies discussed here. It is in this respect that we must say that research of the variety reported in this chapter has hardly begun, but would add also that it appears to have a highly optimistic future.

Turning to the third and final issue in our studies, that of the origins of strategic behavior, we find a general problem for contemporary cognitive psychology. It has been noted earlier that research on techniques for the development of optimal learning strategies has emerged in recent years as an area of vigorous activity. A wealth of training and intervention studies have been completed, with frequent findings of increased effectiveness of cognitive strategies, particularly in memory tasks (e.g., Brown, 1975). Furthermore, various new assessment techniques for strategic behavior have been developed, even including the use of introspection (Yalow & Webb, 1977), contrary to Hebb's (1960) predictions.

Despite these developments, and rather paradoxically, remarkably little is known concerning the antecedent variables responsible for the pattern of cognitive strategies characteristic of any particular individual. It may be seen that this problem is dealt with slightly by that portion of the research literature dealing with cognitive complexity and cognitive style, and may also be related to questions of the interrelationship between personality and cognitive ability (see Messick, 1972). These sources notwithstanding, an integrated view of the origins of particular patterns of strategic behavior remains to be developed.

10

Language Functions and Cognitive Processing

JAMES P. CUMMINS

A theory of cognitive functions should indicate how it regards language processes since systems of mediation based on linguistic symbols undoubtedly play a major role in processing information. One must consider, therefore, how linguistic functioning relates both to simultaneous and successive forms of coding and also to Luria's third block of the brain, which is concerned with planning or executive functions. We have only recently begun to investigate this complex area but our preliminary results are encouraging in that they are remarkably consistent with the findings of Luria's clinical research into different patterns of aphasic disorders.

10.1 RESEARCH ON APHASIA

Luria (1975a) has argued on the basis of these studies that all grammatical constructions can be divided into two completely different groups, comprehension of which depend on different brain mechanisms. The first type of construction Luria terms *contextual grammatical structures,* while the second type is classified under the heading *communication of relationships.* Individuals suffering from lesions of the anterior sections of the speech zone (fronto–temporal areas) experience disruption of "successively automatized organized speech [1975, p. 68]" in both receptive and expressive language functioning. Although these patients are capable of understanding the logical grammatical constructions involved in communication of relationships, they experience difficulty in evaluating the correctness of contextual grammatical structures, that is, "those forms that link together the elements of a statement into a single concrete whole [1975, p. 68]." For example, they would find it difficult to say which of the following two statements is in accordance with the rules of connected discourse: "I am writing along the papers" or "I am writing on the paper." Disturbances of the contextual or syntactic structure of expressive speech are also characteristic of individuals with left hemisphere fronto–temporal lesions. Luria suggests that underlying these disruptions of receptive and expressive speech "is impairment of inner speech, which is abbreviated in structure, predicative in function and affords the most important means of converting thought into the linear pattern of the sentence [1975, p. 66]." Patients with fronto–temporal lesions experience no disruption of the nominative function of speech, that is, the naming of separate objects, but are often unable to find the predicate forms (verbs) to link the designation of separate objects or events into a unified statement.

While successive synthesis clearly underlies the processing of contextual grammatical structures, simultaneous synthesis is involved in processing the second class of logical–grammatical structures that Luria terms *communication of relationships*. Patients with lesions in the parietal–occipital sections of the speech areas experience no impairment in the predicative function of inner speech nor in the linear pattern of the sentence but are unable to comprehend certain types of quasi-spatial logical grammatical constructions. For example, these patients have difficulty in understanding comparative constructions (e.g., "taller than") and spatial prepositional constructions (e.g., "above," "below," "inside," etc.), and are also unable to distinguish between relationships of the type "the father's brother" and "the brother's father." The essential characteristic of the linguistic processing deficits of these patients is "impairment of their ability to turn information received sequentially into synchronic quasi-spatial arrangements [1975, p. 71]." The quasi-spatial character of the processing involved in these logical–grammatical constructions is confirmed, according to Luria, by the fact that patients with lesions in the parietal–occipital area also have difficulty in grasping spatial relationships (e.g., right–left, east–west) and in carrying out arithmetical calculations "that presuppose the preservation of the interior quasi-spatial distribution of numerical elements [1975, p. 70]."

Luria's contention that simultaneous processing is involved in comprehension of logical grammatical constructions is supported in a study carried out by Caramazza, Gordon, Zurif, and DeLuca (1976). Caramazza et al. reported that patients with right-hemisphere damage and no obvious linguistic impairment were relatively incapable of solving two-term syllogistic problems in which comparative adjectives in the premise and question were antonymic ("John is taller than Bill, who is shorter?"). The authors suggest that this type of verbal reasoning depends, in part, upon nonlinguistic imaginal processes subserved by the right hemisphere. This interpretation is clearly consistent with Luria's contention that understanding of comparative constructions involves simultaneous processing.

On the basis of Luria's clinical research, then, we would predict significant relationships between successive processing and performance on linguistic tasks which require either analysis of the sequential linear structure of the input or syntactically mature expressive speech. We would predict that simultaneous processing, on the other hand, would be involved in linguistic tasks which require the grasping of quasi-spatial conceptual relationships. Further predictions regarding the roles of simultaneous and successive synthesis in linguistic processing can be generated from the theoretical extensions of Luria's work by Jakobson (1971) and Reid (1974).

Jakobson (1971) proposed that aphasic disorders could be classified as either similarity disorders or contiguity disorders and states (p. 119) that this distinction corresponds to the distinction between paradigmatic (e.g., horse–pony) and syntagmatic (e.g., horse–gallop) relations between words. It is also similar to Luria's (1975) distinction between disorders of the nominative and predicative functions of speech which, Luria argues, are subsumed by different brain mechanisms. Consistent with this general distinction is Reid's (1974) theory that the paradigmatic–syntagmatic dichotomy constitutes a fundamental distinction in the structure of internal representations. The rationale for exploring the relationships between simultaneous and succesive processing and paradigmatic and syntagmatic relations between words derives from Jakobson's (1975, p. 90) proposal that, although the dimensions are not identical, most similarity aphasic disorders involve disruption of simultaneous processes whereas most contiguity disorders involve disruption of successive processes.

Thus, in investigating the relationships between simultaneous and successive processing and linguistic functioning, our procedure was first, to generate hypotheses based largely on Luria's neuropsychological findings, and second, to devise a battery of tests to test these hypotheses in a sample of normal Grade 3 children.

10.2 EXPERIMENTS ON SOME LINGUISTIC FUNCTIONS

Subjects. The sample consisted of 32 boys and 28 girls of mean age 108 months. The mean verbal, quantitative, and nonverbal IQs on the Canadian Cognitive Abilities Test (available only for 50 subjects) were 108, 103, and 105, respectively.

Story Recall. Two short stories, adapted from two of Aesop's Fables, were read to the subjects who were required to retell each story in their own words. The first story, "The Lion and the Mouse," consisted of 196 words and the second, "The Ant and the Grasshopper," consisted of 132 words. Subjects' recall of the stories was recorded on cassette tape.

Hunt's (1970) method of assessing syntactic maturity in written and oral speech was used to score the protocols. Hunt proposed the "minimal terminable unit" (T-unit) as a reliable device for segmenting expressive language. The T-unit was defined as "one main clause plus any subordinate clause or nonclausal structure that is attached to or embedded in it [1970, p. 4]." The T-unit is "minimal" and "terminable" in that it represents the shortest units which it is grammatically allowable to punctuate as sentences. In addition to T-units the number of clauses was measured. Hunt defines a clause as "any expression containing a subject or coordinated subject and a finite predicate or coordinated predicates [1970, p. 4]." Thus, the expression "Jim and I went home and rode our bikes" would be counted as just one clause.

The measures assessed in the present study were

1. mean number of words (for the two stories)
2. mean number of clauses
3. mean number of T-units
4. words per T-unit
5. clauses per T-unit
6. words per second

Several studies (Braun & Klassen, 1971; Hunt, 1970; O'Donnell, Griffith, & Norris, 1967) have reported developmental increases in T-unit length and in indices of subordination (such as clauses per T-unit), suggesting that these measures can be regarded as measures of syntactic maturity or complexity. Based on Luria's description of "the grammatical structure of speech as one of the most obvious examples of serially organized cerebral activity [1966b, p. 78]," we predicted that these indices of syntactic organization would relate significantly to successive processing.

Ambiguities. This 12-item test was taken directly from Kessel (1970) and assessed children's sensitivity to lexical (L), surface structure (SS), and underlying structure (US) ambiguities. The subject was shown four line drawings, two of which depicted different meanings of a sentence which was read aloud by the experimenter. (See Figure 10.1.) Examples of each of the types of ambiguous sentences are: L—"The boy picked up the bat" (baseball bat, flying bat); SS—"He told her baby stories" (he told *her* baby-stories, he told her *baby* stories); US—"The eating of the chicken was

Figure 10.1. Drawing for the ambiguous sentence, "He told her baby stories." (From F. S. Kessel, The role of syntax in children's comprehension from ages six to twelve, *Monographs of The Society for Research in Child Development, 1970, 139.* Copyright 1970 by The Society for Research in Child Development, Inc.)

sloppy" (chicken eating sloppily, girl and boy eating chicken sloppily). Children were scored 2 if they gave the two meanings and correct justifications spontaneously, 1 if they gave the two meanings and justifications after probing, and 0 if they chose the wrong pictures or only one correct picture or if their justifications showed they had not grasped both meanings. The probing procedure for each item is described in Kessel (1970, pp. 30–32) and was used to ensure that the child had, in fact, understood the two meanings of the sentence. Also, if the child either completed or altered his answer during the probing procedure (so that he now chose the correct drawings) he received 1 point for the sentence.

It has been shown in several studies (Brodzinsky, Feuer, & Owens, 1977; Goldstein, 1976; Kessel, 1970; Shultz & Pilon, 1973) that lexical ambiguities are grasped much earlier than either surface structure or underlying structure ambiguities. In addition, the processing requirements for the latter two types of ambiguities appear to be similar to each other and different from those of lexical ambiguities (Goldstein, 1976). This is most likely due to the fact that for lexical ambiguities the ambiguity resides in just one word rather than in the entire sentence.

The Ambiguities task was included in the linguistic battery because different relationships between the three types of ambiguous sentences and simultaneous and successive processing could be predicted on the basis of Luria's hypothesis that different brain mechanisms underlie the nominative and predicative aspects of linguistic processing. Because analysis of the sequential pattern of the entire sentence was required in processing surface structure and underlying structure ambiguities, it was hypothesized that these types of ambiguity would involve the predicative aspect of language and consequently relate significantly to successive processing. Processing of the one-word lexical ambiguities, on the other hand, appears to involve the nominative rather than the predicative aspect of language and thus may relate to simultaneous processing.

Word Association. This task was included in order to test the hypothesis that simultaneous processing is involved in generating paradigmatic relations between words. The shift between ages 6 and 9 from syntagmatic or sequential responses to paradigmatic responses in word association has been well established (e.g., Ervin, 1961; Nelson, 1977). Thus, we predicted that children with high levels of simultaneous processing would be more advanced in this respect than children low on simultaneous processing.

The 20 stimulus words were all high-frequency words and consisted of eight nouns, six verbs, and six adjectives. Responses were scored as paradigmatic only if they could occur in the same form class as the stimulus work and if they did not occur in immediate sequence or separated only by a determiner in ordinary continuous speech (e.g., front-door).

Class Inclusion. This Piagetian test consisted of two parts with four items in each. In the first part the child was shown line drawings of two groups of objects each of which formed a subclass of a larger superordinate class. There were four objects in one subclass and two in the other, and subclasses were spatially separated. Children were asked questions of the type "In this picture are there more spoons or more things to eat with?" (see Figure 10.2). The second part consisted of four questions on the type "In the whole world are there more animals or more cows?" On the second part children were required to justify their responses and justifications were given a score of 0, 1, 2, or 3 according to the following criteria: 0 = wrong response, for example, saying there are more cows than animals; 1 = correct response but inappropriate justification, for example, "There are more animals than cows because cows live on farms"; 2 = correct response but personalized or incomplete justification, for example,

Figure 10.2. Drawing for class inclusion question, "In this picture are there more spoons or more things to eat with?" (From F. S. Kessel, The role of syntax in children's comprehension from ages six to twelve, *Monographs of the Society for Research in Child Development*, 1970, *139*. Copyright 1970 by The Society for Research in Child Development, Inc.)

"There are more animals because you see all kinds of animals around"; 3 = correct superordinate response, for example, "More animals because cows are animals."

Since the major requirement in the class inclusion task is grasping the relationship between superordinate and subordinate classes, we predicted that it would relate primarily to simultaneous processing.

In addition to the linguistic tasks, Raven's Coloured Progressive Matrices and Figure Copying were administered as marker tests for simultaneous processing while Serial Recall and Digit Span were markers for successive processing.

The correlation matrix is presented in Table 10.1, and the principal-components analysis is presented in Table 10.2. The first factor could be described as a general language factor with loadings from the Ambiguities and Story "quantity" variables. The second factor is defined by the two indices of organizational complexity in story recall. Number of Words and Number of Clauses also load on this factor as do Digit Span and Figure Copying. The third factor confirms the predicted relationship between simultaneous processing and class inclusion performance while the fourth factor has high loadings from Words per Second, Word Association, and the two simultaneous processing tasks. Factor V is defined by the successive processing tasks and by surface structure and underlying structure ambiguities.

These results are consistent with the predictions which were derived from Luria's neuropsychological research. Simultaneous processing was clearly involved in grasping the relationship between subordinate and superordinate classes in the Class Inclusion task. There was also evidence

Table 10.1
Correlation Matrix of Cognitive Processing and Language Tasks

Test	1	2	3	4	5	6	7	8	9	10	11	12	13	14	15	16
1. Raven's Coloured Progressive Matrices	1.00	.51	.27	.14	.30	.15	.13	.03	.33	.42	.22	.20	.18	.10	.09	.30
2. Figure Copying		1.00	.26	.24	.12	.21	.24	.06	.28	.21	.39	.31	.24	.36	.25	.32
3. Serial Recall			1.00	.64	.00	-.10	.16	.20	.20	.11	.06	.04	-.04	.22	.20	.10
4. Digit Span Forward				1.00	.04	-.03	.25	.32	.27	.20	.24	.21	.07	.46	.38	.10
5. Word Association					1.00	-.02	.09	.07	-.04	.10	.21	.27	.27	-.04	.11	.39
6. Ambiguities (L)						1.00	.22	.33	.22	.26	.35	.39	.34	.11	.27	.13
7. Ambiguities (SS)							1.00	.30	.07	.18	.27	.33	.28	.14	.23	.18
8. Ambiguities (US)								1.00	.20	.22	.38	.41	.31	.29	.38	-.09
9. Class Inclusion (Part I)									1.00	.64	.34	.28	.20	.35	.20	.16
10. Class Inclusion (Part II)										1.00	.30	.30	.27	.17	.14	.16
11. Number of Words											1.00	.94	.88	.53	.41	.34
12. Number of Clauses												1.00	.91	.37	.50	.38
13. Number of T-units													1.00	.11	.12	.36
14. Words per T-unit														1.00	.61	.08
15. Clauses per T-unit															1.00	.17
16. Words per Second																1.00

r .95 (two-tailed) = .25.
r .99 (two-tailed) = .33.

182

Table 10.2
Principal-Components Analysis of Processing and Language Tasks (Varimax Rotation)

Test	I	II	III	IV	V
Raven's Coloured Progressive Matrices	−.03	−.04	.61	.53	.17
Figure Copying	.04	.35	.40	.47	.13
Serial Recall	−.23	.22	.17	.15	.75
Digit Span Forward	−.04	.47	.13	.05	.72
Word Association	.15	−.12	−.11	.70	.11
Ambiguities (L)	.61	−.01	.32	−.12	−.03
Ambiguities (SS)	.44	−.11	.01	.13	.56
Ambiguities (US)	.58	.13	.06	−.27	.51
Class Inclusion (Part I)	.13	.27	.81	−.05	.04
Class Inclusion (Part II)	.26	−.03	.81	.03	.11
Number of Words	.74	.48	.15	.32	−.03
Number of Clauses	.82	.38	.08	.34	.02
Number of T-units	.82	.09	.07	.39	−.07
Words per T-unit	.12	.88	.15	−.03	.14
Clauses per T-unit	.28	.70	.00	.02	.24
Words per Second	.15	.11	.10	.75	−.02
Percentage of total variance	19.3	13.5	12.9	12.8	11.3

that paradigmatic responding on the word association task was related to aspects of simultaneous processing. Possibly due to the relatively high proportion of noun stimuli, there was a high rate of paradigmatic responding on the Word Association task (mean = 14 out of 20). A stronger relationship between simultaneous processing and paradigmatic responding might be obtained with a more challenging set of stimulus words.

The relationship between Words per Second and simultaneous processing was not predicted, and consequently attempts at explanation are post hoc. Hesitation phenomena in speech are frequently regarded as indicative of verbal planning functions (see, e.g., Goldman-Eisler, 1961; Hawkins, 1973). Hawkins (1973), for example, suggests that relatively long pauses occurring at clause boundaries in story-telling are indicative of deficient verbal planning. If this is the case then one would expect that rate of speech output would primarily involve Luria's third block of the brain, which is responsible for executing plans and programs. However, the executive function interacts with the coding processes in constructing and implementing programs and the relationship between rate of speech output and simultaneous processing can be interpreted as the result of this interaction. Thus, in the Story Recall task, effective planning of speech output and consequent fast rate of speech may be dependent upon the formation of a unifying Gestalt embodying the relationships between different parts of the story.

On the basis of previous findings involving the Ambiguities task, it was predicted that different processing requirements were involved in comprehension of lexical ambiguities as compared to surface structure and underlying structure ambiguities. From the point of view of Luria's theory, it was suggested that the one-word lexical ambiguities might involve the nominative aspect of speech whereas the latter types seemed more likely to involve the predicative aspect. These predictions were clearly supported in the factor analysis. Surface structure and underlying structure ambiguities loaded on the successive factor while there was a small loading from lexical ambiguities on one of the simultaneous factors. The variance in lexical ambiguities was small due to a ceiling effect (mean = 7.3 out of 8, SD = 1.1), a factor which may have limited the strength of its relationship with the simultaneous-processing variables.

Finally, it was predicted that successive processing would be related to syntactic organization in the Story Recall task. This prediction is partially supported by the loading of Digit Span on Factor II which is defined by the two indices of syntactic organization. One might have expected Serial Recall which involves words, rather than Digit Span, to relate to indices of syntactic organization. Also, the loading of Figure Copying on Factor II, although small, was not predicted. Nevertheless, the results provide some preliminary support for Luria's claim that successive processing is involved in the organization of narrative speech.

10.3   THE NATURE OF SUCCESSIVE PROCESSING

One of the wider implications of these findings is that they support a "processing" rather than an "abilities" interpretation of cognitive functioning. For example, our analysis strongly suggests that different forms of cognitive processing underlie the comprehension of lexical as opposed to surface structure and underlying structure ambiguities. These findings reinforce our contention that successive processing cannot be equated with simple rote memory. There are no differences between the memory demands of the three types of items, but our analysis shows the *processing* requirements to be clearly different. An abilities model such as Jensen's (1969) model of Level I and Level II abilities would predict that the simultaneous or Level II dimension would relate more to surface structure and underlying structure ambiguities than to lexical ambiguities since considerably more transformation of the input is required in comprehension of the former. Also, the involvement of successive processing in complex aspects of both receptive and expressive language functioning belies Vernon, Ryba, and Lang's (1978) assertion that successive processing is of relatively little theoretical significance in accounting for individual differences in cognitive behavior.

In conclusion, the results of this study are generally highly consistent with predictions derived from Luria's clinical research. Theoretically, the study appears to be important in that it considerably expands the scope of the successive processing dimension and makes an identification of successive processing with rote or associative memory much less plausible. We are currently following up this research by investigating the role of executive functions and coding processes in the organization of both written and oral speech and also in the comprehension of a variety of linguistic structures. We are also comparing the developmental relationships between simultaneous and successive processing and linguistic functioning in groups of normal, EMR, and reading disabled children. We believe that the relationships between modes of cognitive processing and linguistic and academic performance are not invariant but will vary as a function of task and population characteristics. Our hope is that by examining the interaction between basic modes of cognitive processing and linguistic and academic performance at different grade levels this research will provide a more adequate basis for remediating learning difficulties in different diagnostic groups.

11

Retrospect and Prospect

Throughout this book we have attempted to propose the beginnings of an information-processing theory of intelligence. Our theory has relied upon recent work in the areas of clinical neuropsychology, human abilities, learning, and cognition. We have suggested, after Luria, that the human brain can be described as consisting of three functional, interdependent systems responsible for arousal, processing, and planning. We have concentrated upon the action of the second system, which engages in two types of information processing, simultaneous and successive. The third functional system controls the planning of processing, thus emphasizing a strategic component in cognition.

In this concluding chapter we will not review the conclusions of the many studies that have been presented in the preceding chapters. Instead we will emphasize a few major themes of a general nature.

1.1 INTELLIGENCE REVISITED

The concept of a global general ability has not been discredited, but has been proved to be of little use in the work we report in this book. For example, consider Weschler's (1958) view of general ability; g is involved in so many different types of ability that it is, in essence, not an ability at all. According to Weschler, it is a property of the mind. We think this is the logical end of the notion of a general ability; it ceases to be an ability and becomes a property of any and all mental processes. It is difficult to use this concept to generate research hypotheses or formulate explanations for specific processes such as coding.

Mental processes, in general, are used in acquiring knowledge. They are also utilized in creating knowledge. Not only do we react to stimuli from the enviornment, trying to structure our experience, but often we engage in what has been called original or creative thinking. We do not only solve problems, but we also create problems to challenge our thinking. All of these mental activities can be subsumed under intelligent behavior, and labeled "intelligence." The concept of g, or IQ, however, is defined by IQ tests, and some people see IQ as the only index of intelligence.

We cannot measure intelligence by the conventional tests for IQ, partly because the notion of a general ability is questionable. The notion is similar to the discarded notion of the strength of the soil. Neurologically it is untenable. Damage to a part of the occipital lobe does not damage something called symbolic activity. It produces an identifiable dysfunction, for instance, in spatial perception. Damage to the temporal lobe, on the other hand, may result in disturbances in speech and movement. "Strength" of mental processes means little, then, unless one specifies the processes and the tasks, and, above all, the components of behavior which are being measured, as Sternberg (1977) has done. The components are processes which can be measured. In this book, these are broadly called simultaneous, successive, and planning. Sternberg rightly points out that so long as components can be indexed by speed and accuracy measures, they will not be considered arbitrary. In contrast, abilities are arbitrary; they could be called by any other name, as we have listed them in Chapter 1: fluid, crystallized, verbal, mechanical, and induction.

Our basic premise has been that a cognitive, process-oriented theory of intelligence is needed. This position explicitly rejects the doctrine of "mindless prediction" which has become common within the study of intelligence, and instead seeks to understand *why* or *how* intelligence tests predict.

The information-processing approach argues further that any description of how intelligent acts are produced will be complex, consisting of many interacting processes and components. In this way terms like *reasoning, verbal and spatial abilities,* and *memory* are not used as explanatory constructs, but rather become the constructs to be explained. Monolithic general intelligence similarly becomes something to be explained, and as such loses much of its appeal as an explanatory construct.

11.2   HALSTEAD, LURIA, AND
THE NEUROPSYCHOLOGICAL APPROACH

The Luria model of three blocks of brain functions and three levels of functions (projection, associative cum projection, and associative) within the coding block is one of several neuropsychological models. There are some other models, notably that of Halstead (1947), and more recently that of Pribram (1971).

We shall discuss Halstead's model briefly in order to demonstrate, subsequently, the advantages of Luria's model. Our final goal is to summarize how the simultaneous–successive processing approach can advance the understanding of cognitive competence and incompetence. We will not discuss the value of Halstead's clinical tests. The Halstead–Reitan battery has been widely used for diagnosis of brain damage. It has recently been compared with Luria's tests (Luria & Majovski, 1977).

Halstead (1947) wrote an entire book on tests of frontal lobe functions, a remarkable book at that time. On the basis of specific psychological tests, he identified four major mental processes. One of these, the most general one, was the Central integrative function, or factor C, as typically indicated by category tests. Since the category tests usually do not differentiate between frontal and other cases of brain damage satisfactorily, they cannot be regarded as tests of decision making or planning. Factor C does not seem to have a roughly corresponding brain structure. One of the tests in the literature, however, the Porteus Maze, is often found to distinguish between frontal and nonfrontal damage. It is not clear, though, how far impulsivity or overarousal, which are the functions of Block 1 rather then Block 3 in Luria's model, are responsible for poor performance on the Porteus Maze. The best test of decision and goal directed behavior is Halstead's speed component in the performance test. This is a score derived from the speed of solving formboards. Halstead names it the D or directionality factor. Probably it is directionality, and not the central integrative factor that has an identifiable location. Halstead's factor of abstraction, A factor, has for its measures, oddity learning, consistency in space, and location. All of these can be measures of simultaneous processing, although this has to be determined empirically. Halstead also proposes a power factor, measured by critical flicker fusion, visual field, and contour. He suggests that P is a component of biological intelligence. In Luria's model, P may be understood as a Block 1 activity, which affects coding functions in Block 2 and motivational aspects in Block 3 functions.

The concept of P as a biological endowment has been reinterpreted as the power to postpone or inhibit a response (Stenehouse, 1973). It is similar to the internal inhibition concept of Pavlov. Stenehouse conceives of it as an affective–conative function. Perhaps this is a reasonable interpretation in as much as the regulation of inhibition is crucial for all sorts of intellectual behavior. At least, its failure, inhibition deficit, leads to impulsivity. Poor discrimination learning has been attributed to an inhibitory deficit in the retarded. According to Stenehouse, the inhibition factor distinguishes between the criminal and the creative person. In many other respects they are similar—they are aggressive, risk taking, etc.

Compared to Halstead's model of brain functions, Luria's model is more in line with recent developments in neuropsychology, which is only to be expected. The functional organization of the brain into three blocks, and the vertical organization of functions within each block, provide an adequate framework for considering all facets of intelligence described by Halstead. For instance, Halstead's integrative function, C, can be identified as a function of Block 3, perhaps of the prefrontal area. Dysfunction in this area is characterized by many of the characteristics of frontal cases described by Luria. One of these is that the patient persists in doing what he has been doing in the face of errors; normals usually change after discovering an error. Halstead's D, or directionality factor, could be identified as a Block 3 function. Abstraction, or the A factor, is clearly a Block 2 function, which is concerned with synthesizing information as well as coding and retrieving. Halstead's factor of power or P, however, cannot easily be located in one of the blocks. It is a biological factor as indexed by the critical–flicker–fusion test. Most probably it would have a strong arousal component, and if so could be mostly a Block 1 function. As critical–flicker–fusion is related to personality (see Eysenck, 1967a), one may describe P as an interaction between Blocks 1 and 3.

A neuropsychological approach to cognitive processes has its strengths and weaknesses. One may question the necessity of relying on evidence which has been gathered from studies on brain lesions. Do these add anything substantial to the conceptualization of cognitive processes? Obviously, our inclination is to treat cognitive processes in terms of the functional organization of the brain, even though neuropsychological research into these functions is still at a rudimentary stage. The model draws upon Luria's findings at different points, such as regarding linguistic and planning behavior. Neuropsychological work provides a direction for our search for processes which may be involved in apparently diverse behaviors such as narrative speech and comprehension of ambiguous sentences. The model is also useful for understanding theoretical concepts such as temporal integration, or, to go a step further, futuristic thinking in terms of temporal integration (Hearnshaw, 1956). Hearnshaw (1956) predicted that "the concept of temporal integration is likely to illuminate many aspects of human psychology—language, . . . conceptual cognition, planning and foresight [p. 18]." An understanding of these psychological processes is the major goal of the simultaneous–successive model.

11.3   COMMENTS ON SUCCESSIVE PROCESSING

Lashley (1951), in his influential paper on serial order, was discussing the nature of temporal integration. That serial ordering was much more than associative chaining was clearly indicated by Lashley. He might have anticipated the important role ascribed to successive processing by Luria; serial ordering was to explain the comprehension of spoken language, according to Lashley. Clearly, serial ordering was not a simple task like rote memory.

Recently, Blumenthal (1977) has treated temporal order in an insightful manner, suggesting that the basis of cognition is temporal. Mental processes can be understood in terms of temporal characteristics, and "consciousness" and "continuity" arise out of our ability to integrate the constantly changing experiences. Speaking philosophically, the experiences of the world are fleeting. As the Greeks said, you cannot step into the same river twice—the river was analogous to reality. To this, the Buddhists added that the same *you* cannot step into the same river twice, because of changes occurring within oneself moment by moment. What gives us and our experiences of reality some amount of continuity is memory.

Returning to modes of information processing, *all* information arrives in succession, but it is ordered either simultaneously or successively. This is how Luria begins the discussion on simultaneous and successive processing (see Chapters 2 and 3). The results of both modes of processing can be called *cognition*. Viewed from this perspective, successive processing need not be inferior to simultaneous; it need not provide merely a prop for higher order thinking. By demonstrating that successive processing is related to reading and linguistic functions (see, especially, Chapter 10), we have essentially reiterated the importance of serial order (Lashley's). By the same token, we have dispelled the notion that associative memory for meaningful material does not call for organization and transformation.

The memory processes become progressively amodal as these proceed from sensory input to integration. Estes (1976a) mentions this in summarizing some contemporary research in memory: "Whether or not a conception of separate short- and long-term stores is accepted, there is substantial agreement among current investigators . . . concerning the idea of a succession of encodings or other transformations whereby the representation of the original stimulus input is progressively removed further from the original modality-bound form [p. 8]."

This description of encoding and processing agrees with Luria's neuro-psychological account of vertical levels of processing in the occipital or temporal lobes—that the primary area is responsible for projection, leading up to a projection cum associative area, which still retains some traces of modality, and above this the associative area for the zones of overlapping functions.

To conclude this discussion on successive processing, then:

1.   It is an integral part of cognition, or as described in our model, a central processing unit. It is neither higher nor lower than simul-taneous processing as ability models (see Vernon *et al.*, 1978) would attempt to place it. The important consideration is where the pro-cessing is employed and how its use can be encouraged (see Chap-ter 9).

2   The neuropsychological approach to successive processing is consis-tent with research on thinking and memory.

11.4   LEARNING DISABILITY, HYPERACTIVITY, AND THE FUNCTIONAL ORGANIZATION OF THE BRAIN

In retrospect, how do we understand learning disability and hyperactiv-ity? To be more precise, is reading disability a coding disorder and hyperactivity mainly a defective relationship between arousal and planning functions? Reading disability does not occur alone. It is associated with other symptoms of cognitive incompetence which were discussed in Chap-ter 6. Cited in that chapter was Leong's work, which showed that reading disabled children were inferior to the nondisabled in several coding tasks, despite the fact that they were matched on nonverbal IQ. Not all of those tasks were verbal. Leong's research made it clear that since the reading disabled children were matched on IQ, part of the reason for their poor performance may be found outside coding, perhaps in the strategies and plans of attack employed when the child is faced with a new problem to solve. Reading disability is manifest in poor word recognition skill and in comprehension; the first is related to successive and the second to simul-taneous processing (see Chapters 6 and 10). In addition to this, a reading disabled child often is not proficient in planning composition. For good comprehension and planned composition the child needs to construct a *gestalt* of what he is reading or composing, an overall plan.

Research to establish this empirically is still lacking. We have begun to construct tasks to test decision-making and planning behavior. We have also started to look at narrative speech (Chapter 10). But intuitively, it would appear that both coding and planning functions are involved in reading disability. If one may conjecture further, the weakness in these functions stems from the general weakness of the verbal system of the reading disabled child. Most of these children are known to have a substantially lower verbal IQ in comparison with their performance IQ. Leong (1974) really wanted to show that the left hemispheric functions of the reading disabled children were weaker than those of the nondisabled children. He used dichotic listening tasks for this purpose, and was partially successful. Similarly Witelson (1976) studied the hemispheric functions of dyslexic children by using the visual and the tactile modes (left versus right visual fields and hands) and found that the dyslexics were not clearly better in their right hemispheric function than they were in left hemispheric function. A weakness in left hemispheric function was suggested, however. If planning and goal setting are mediated verbally, as it seems they are, it would be worthwhile to specify how the "weakness" in left hemispheric function of the reading disabled may adversely affect those functions.

Turning to hyperactivity, it would appear that the hyperactive child may have difficulties in choice behavior in addition to such obvious behavioral signs as impulse control. The child at each choice-point does not wait long enough until he has considered all aspects of the situation thoroughly. He is impatient, ready to act before he is sure of the solution. Perhaps, when stimulants such as amphetamines have a beneficial effect on the hyperactive child, the drug may be acting to raise the threshold of tolerance for ambiguity, to delay the child's choice response. Amphetamines quiet down some (not *all*) hyperactives; they also calm down normal children (Kolata, 1978). It is probable that amphetamines increase the regulatory function of Block 3 in relation to Block 1, although this is speculation at the present time. It does seem that the dynamic relation between these two blocks in the case of hyperactive children is worth studying.

Our discussion up to this point has been concerned with neuropsychological theory, successive processing, and learning disability. What binds these diverse considerations, admittedly in a loose integrative bond, is an underlying theoretical orientation. The necessity of having any theoretical orientation cannot be overemphasized. Without it, clinical diagnosis and remediation become haphazard and uneconomical, if not totally ineffective. The Halstead–Reitan approach to diagnosis, for example, is based on an extensive battery of tests, but the tests are not developed as measures of homogeneous mental functions. In fact, the mental function which a test may measure is not typically defined when the test is being constructed. In contrast, Luria's tests are constructed to measure a specific dysfunction that is widely noticed in a clinical condition, for example, the loss of nominative or predicative functions, or of sequencing one's behavior, and so on.

In the next two sections, we shall discuss further the theoretical development of coding and planning processes, and their relevance in understanding the development of cognitive competence. In the course of doing so, we shall consider again some of the theories of intellectual behavior mentioned in Chapter 1.

11.5   DEVELOPMENTAL ISSUES

Our discussion in the previous chapters has touched only tangentially on problems related to the study and conceptualization of cognitive–developmental issues. It is of interest, therefore, to ask a general question at this point concerning the developmental implications of the views that we have presented. More specifically, one may ask which contemporary cognitive–developmental perspective is most closely aligned to the previously described studies. Further, one may also ask if there are areas of research related to the present investigations which in the future may shed some further light on the developmental implications of simultaneous and successive cognitive processes.

It has been noted frequently in recent years that developmental research on cognitive ability tends to fall into two broad varieties. One type is the age–stage research, as best exemplified by Piaget's studies and the flood of investigations based on his theory. These studies, of course, stress the qualitative changes that the individual passes through in the course of cognitive development. Recently, this research has been directed to investigating the invariance of these stages, that is, the extent to which there is a sequence of progression from stage to stage with each stage as a necessary but not sufficient condition for the next. The role of individual differences in these studies is primarily in terms of rate of development through the stages, and more broadly, group differences are viewed similarly, particularly in the case of cross-cultural comparisons (e.g., Dasen, 1972). Prediction is not emphasized in age–stage theory then, except in very general terms for stages attained by children from different cultural backgrounds.

In contrast to the age–stage investigations of cognitive development, psychometric studies stress the predictability of cognitive processes at one point in time from assessments made at earlier points. The foundation of this procedure is the use of individual differences within a given age grouping. Researchers in this mode have tended to ignore, or even explicitly disagree with, the premise of stages of cognitive development, and so in its strongest form, this research adopts the position that increases in cognitive ability with age represent changes in degree rather than in kind. An extension of this view then is that most fundamental cognitive abilities are present throughout life, but with age they become increasingly complex and efficient.

These two traditions in developmental research have coexisted for several decades. The psychometric view predates Piagetian research in familiarity in North America, but at present, both perspectives are in clear evidence (Elkind, 1974). Recent attempts to synthesize these views, though, have been made from primarily the psychometric side. Indeed, one may say that the psychometricians appear more amorous toward their Piagetian colleagues than the opposite!

A pervasive issue for the psychometrician attempting this synthesis is the problem of how to conceptualize and measure developmental differentiation and integration. Developmental differentiation is the progressive emergence of distinct cognitive processes with age, such that new and more specific processes exist at a later point in time than existed previously. Developmental integration, on the other hand, refers to the combining of discrete cognitive processes with age in order that generalized abilities may emerge. The question of the relationship between these two functions can be traced back to Werner's (1948) early work, but has been dealt with most recently by Buss and Royce (1975a). Three distinctions in the emergence of cognitive abilities are possible, according to Buss and Royce; these may be labeled *parallelism, convergence,* and *divergence.* Parallelism refers to two or more cognitive abilities that develop independent of one another, with no common origin nor any common point of integration. These abilities, then, remain distinct from one another throughout the cognitive–developmental period under investigation. Convergence refers to an integration of two or more abilities over time, such that a set of abilities that began as distinct from one another combine with increasing development to form a higher order or more complex ability. Finally, divergence refers to the progressive emergence of specific abilities from a generalized ability, with the result that an increase in the number of abilities is found with increasing cognitive development. These distinctions between parallelism, convergence, and divergence are readily evident in the developmental literature in terms of the assumptions made in different varieties of research. The psychometric literature appears implicitly to adopt a parallelism view, although factor-analytic studies are mixed in this regard (Horn, 1973). Piagetian studies appear to combine elements of convergence and divergence, although this is somewhat idiosyncratic to any particular interpretation of Piaget. If we turn to Luria's clinical studies of simultaneous and successive processes specifically, we find a view which is not easily classified in this three-fold scheme, but could be said to represent parallelism. Perhaps by virtue of his clinical concerns with atypical cognitive processes, Luria does not emphasize a developmental function approach in his neuropsychological investigations. Rather, similar cognitive processes are examined in patients of many ages, although most frequently adults have been the subject of his studies. One is left, then, with a sense of parallelism in Luria's studies; simultaneous and successive processes neither emerge from a common cognitive ability, nor converge with one another with developmental increases in cognitive competence.

Similarly, the broad areas of literature related to simultaneous and successive processes, as summarized by Ornstein (1972), are clearly in the parallelism tradition. These areas represent, for example, the different roles of the two hemispheres in the brain (e.g., Levy, 1974), Levy and Sperry's distinction between analytic and Gestalt processes, Bogen's dichotomy of propositional and appropositional logic, and Kant's suggestion that space and time are the two primary dimensions of thought. The history of dichotomies similar to these can be traced as far back as ancient Chinese and Indian philosophy, and may be found currently outside of our own work in the research on serial and parallel processes (Neisser, 1967), and in research on the role of sensory modalities (Freides, 1974). The dominant picture that emerges through this literature is one of parallelism, therefore, with the basic dichotomy between two cognitive processes maintained as an assumption for all developmental periods.

Despite the weight of the parallelism evidence that has accumulated from these sources related to our studies of simultaneous and successive processes, however, it is clear that further and more detailed descriptions of the developmental characteristics of these processes are required. The need for this detail is highlighted by our previous discussion on language, and particularly those portions that deal with syntagmatic and paradigmatic processes. An interesting split is evident in this body of literature, namely, its origins are from two markedly different lines of research and these two lines represent different assumptions regarding parallelism, convergence, and divergence. One source of knowledge on syntagmatic and paradigmatic processes is the literature on aphasia. From their investigations of disrupted language functioning, Jakobson (1964), Luria (1973c), and Pribram (1971) have suggested that dysfunctions tend to fall into the two varieties syntagmatic and paradigmatic, and that the cognitive processes that are disturbed, as manifested by these language dysfunctions, are successive and simultaneous processes, respectively. Thus, this body of literature suggests a direct subsidiary relationship such that successive processes are the basis for syntagmatic language functions, and simultaneous cognitive processes are responsible for paradigmatic language functions.

The second area of literature on syntagmatic and paradigmatic language processes is made up of studies on memory and verbal learning. Where the first area has dealt with language dysfunction, this second area has been largely both normative and experimental with subjects from a full range of abilities. The types of tasks used in this second area have included the traditional paradigms for this purpose such as paired-associates, free and serial recall, and most heavily, word association. The tradition of this research may be traced particularly to studies by Brown and Berko (1960) and Ervin (1961), who fostered investigations of a phenomena which became known as the *syntagmatic–paradigmatic shift*. This label refers to the finding that, in studies of free association, young children tend to respond with words from different word classes, and therefore exhibit primarily syntagmatic associations, but at approximately the ages of 5–7, a change takes place in typical response patterns, such that the words generated may also be from the same word class as the stimulus word, and therefore are paradigmatic responses. The syntagmatic–paradigmatic distinction was placed in a broader perspective by White (1965), who reviewed many areas of research in an attempt to derive a developmental view of learning processes. White concluded that learning processes were primarily of simple associative varieties up to the point of ages 5–7, following which a higher-order cognitive layer developed as a second type. Syntagmatic responses as a case in point were seen as mainly associative, and the later emergence of paradigmatic responses manifested this cognitive function. In turn, White's (1965) analyses formed the basis for Jensen's (1970) model of Level I and Level II abilities, where Level I corresponds to associative learning and Level II corresponds to cognitive learning. Jensen (1970) also suggested a set of hypothetical growth curves that corresponds to White's analyses and accounts for both the later emergence of Level II and the more powerful group discrimination function of this ability. Finally, as Jarman (1978a) has argued, the model of simultaneous and successive processes is proposed in part as an alternative to Jensen's (1970) theory of Level I and Level II.

A clear contrast is formed by these two bodies of literature on syntagmatic and paradigmatic processes, and this contrast suggests both some broader theoretical implications and some future research directions related to developmental issues. The aphasia literature has adopted a largely parallelism view of both simultaneous and successive processes and syntagmatic and paradigmatic language functions. This literature proposes specific ties with the model of simultaneous and successive processes, and is consistent with the simultaneous–successive literature to date on its assumption of parallelism. Studies of memory and word association, in contrast, appear to be in the divergence mode, with two distinct processes emerging from one following a cognitive–developmental shift period. Thus, despite the sequence of theoretical developments from White's (1965) work to Jensen (1970), and then to the simultaneous–successive model, a general inconsistency regarding this assumption remains.

One possible way to explain the inconsistency between the divergence model of syntagmatic and paradigmatic language functions and the parallelism model of simultaneous–successive processes is to consider the different roles of the three zones of the brain, as discussed by Luria (1973d). These zones, as noted earlier, are the primary, secondary, and tertiary types, and are responsible respectively for modal-specific associations, coding of information, and higher-order amodal associations. Viewed developmentally, one may hypothesize that the primary projection zones process information both simultaneously and successively from the very early years onward, but the role of the tertiary nonmodal zones would not emerge until the shift period of ages 5–7. At this point also, language assumes more of a controlling influence in cognitive activity (Luria, 1961). Thus, the emergence of the "cognitive layer" in White's (1965) analyses may correspond to the combined role of language and the tertiary functions, rather than the emergence of a qualitatively different ability. Simultaneous synthesis may not be later in its time of emergence then, but rather, be present early in life. The role of simultaneous synthesis in the infant years would primarily be in perceptual analysis of visual forms, and would proceed to more complex types with the integration of language as the cognitive–developmental shift takes place. In this view, the syntagmatic–paradigmatic shift becomes one of conceptual growth in two already existing processes, such that the latter becomes of equal primacy to the former. This proposal of conceptual reorganization is a plausible alternative, we note, in explanations of the syntagmatic–paradigmatic phenomenon (Nelson, 1977).

This view of the developmental changes in simultaneous and successive processes suggests several possible areas of future developmental research. At present, relatively little is known regarding the predictability of simultaneous and successive processes from measures taken in the preschool years. If both processes can be measured in elementary forms in the early years, as suggested, then the problems of prediction and early assessment becomes one of the measurement of primary-associative functions which are to form the basis later for higher-order conceptual functions. Research designed to illuminate the differentiation between these processes would be valuable for general application to the field of early screening for learning difficulties.

A second related area of future developmental research concerns the progressive development of simultaneous and successive processes in terms of functional dependence on external input. One may posit, for example, that the development of simultaneous synthesis proceeds from elementary visual analysis of spatial forms (Pick, Pick, & Klein, 1967), through early memory including object permanence (Flavell, 1963), on to the visual synthesis of discrete spatial information (Birch & Lefford, 1967), and further, to the simultaneous integration of discrete information presented successively (Hearnshaw, 1956). The progression represents, in part, a growing ability in cognitive representation, although the details of its etiology are only slightly understood.

For both of these suggested areas of research longitudinal and combinations of longitudinal and cross-sectional studies (Baltes, Reese, & Nesselroade, 1977) are required. The use of multiple measures appears essential in view of the changing functions of simultaneous and successive syntheses with increasing age. Finally, it appears to be particularly important to include tasks of both language and nonlanguage varieties, in order that a clearer perspective can be gained of the developmental characteristics of simultaneous and successive processes.

In the following sections we have suggested a framework for research on early detection of cognitive deficits, which is based on some of these developmental considerations. The simultaneous–successive model has been used to construct tasks which will not only test central processing but will be varied in terms of their input and output characteristics. In this concluding section, then, we wish to demonstrate another practical use for the model.

11.6 EARLY DETECTION AND REMEDIATION: A FRAMEWORK FOR RESEARCH

The research on simultaneous and successive processes that has been discussed in the previous chapters has been largely concerned with both describing and, to a lesser extent, modifying the patterns of cognitive processes characteristic of normal and atypical children. An important question raised by our previous discussion, particularly that on developmental trends, is the degree to which early assessments and predictions can be made regarding these patterns. That is, we may ask the extent to which the patterns of processes that we have typically found can be predicted from assessments taken at earlier points in development. Research on this question is of obvious importance because of its direct implications for both the validation of tests for screening and assessment of learning difficulties and the design of remedial programs. In this final section, we describe the rationale of a 4-year longitudinal project by Jarman (1978c), which is currently in progress and is designed to focus on the foregoing topic.

The research in progress is an extension of some historical trends in the prediction of cognitive ability, and a departure from others. Prior to the 1960s, a substantial body of research on the question of the temporal stability of general intelligence accumulated. Broad age ranges were represented longitudinally in these studies, and theoretical interest was based in large part on the hoary issue of nature versus nurture. Bloom (1964) supplied a cogent summary of this line of research and his analysis became a point of reference for several shifts in focus that took place in subsequent years.

One area of change in prediction research is the subject populations, which have become narrower than in the early studies of intelligence. As an extension of the efforts of Project Headstart, research attention has focused more heavily on young children (Akers, 1972), particularly those between the ages of 3 and 8. Concentration on this age range, of course, is due to the increased recognition of the importance to developmental processes of environmental conditions in the early years (see Shipman, 1972; Shipman, Barone, Beaton, Emmerich, & Ward, 1971; Shipman, Boroson, Bridgeman, Gant, & Mitovsky, 1976).

A second area of change is the operational models and definitions used in predictive research. Early studies employed the general variable of IQ as defined by many different tests for both the prediction and criterion measures. Partly as a consequence of the recent upsurge of information-processing theory (Estes, 1976a), and recommendations to utilize these theories in predictive studies (Gallagher & Bradley, 1972) some current research studies attempt to refine general cognitive ability by using a series of specific instruments and operational definitions.

A third area of change is the primary purpose and application of predictive research. In the early years, data were used to answer questions on the long-term stability of degrees of mental competence. Thus, these types of studies tended not to emphasize environmental change in terms of social and educational programs and their possible effects on human development. At present, there is more of an emphasis on the predictive validation of tests and instruments for the purpose of early assessment and screening of various learning and behavioral problems. The applied implication of this movement is to design beneficial environments for children who require them, in the form of remedial and special purpose programs. For learning disabilities particularly there are a plethora of studies recently completed and in progress which attempt to discover predictors and early warning assessment techniques so that selection for remedial programs is effective (see Meier, 1975; Zeitlin, 1976).

Despite these changes of focus, however, it appears that predictive studies are reaching an asymptote in their contribution to both applied and theoretical knowledge. This is particularly true in the prediction of the cognitive abilities responsible for individual differences in learning in the early years, and it is this area of research that comprises the vast majority of current predictive studies. Progress is hindered in part by problems that plague all prediction research, from statistical and design viewpoints. These include well-known factors such as subject attrition and differential subject learning histories between the time of prediction and criterion measures.

There are other difficulties present in the current prediction research, however, which are due to problems in the underlying conceptual rationales of the studies. These problems are even more critical than the former varieties, but little progress has been made toward their amelioration. In brief, they can nearly all be traced to the central need for a theoretical model to guide the selection, validation, and interpretation of measurement instruments. Predictive research of the last decade has not produced such a model, nor have models been adopted from other independent areas of research. Most notably, the advances in knowledge of human abilities (Horn, 1976) have largely been ignored as a possible rationale for predictive studies, particularly in the case of attempts to develop early assessment techniques for learning disabilities. This is unfortunate, because most early assessment research projects implicitly conceive of abilities as mediators for short- and long-term learning, and this conception has a long history in the study of individual differences (Buss, 1973b) and experimental research (Estes, 1970).

Without information from contemporary human abilities research as a conceptual framework, predictive analyses of the last 10 years have proceeded almost exclusively by pure empiricism. Predictor tests have typically been selected for varying or often unstated reasons, assembled into large batteries, and their statistical effectiveness has been determined in a longitudinal design. Subsequent investigators have then adopted the tests which have been shown to be most effective, added a new set of tests of their own, and repeated the process of predictive validation. The overall result of this trend is a growing array of tests available for the early assessment of learning problems, with no theories on which to interpret results, and no sense of the relationships among the tests. Further, the lack of a theoretical rationale has pre-empted the logical design of subsequent remedial and special programs.

An alternative approach is clearly required then, one that does not rely solely on individual differences data as a source of guidelines for the selection and validation of tests. Indeed, this need has been recognized generally in the derivation of theories of human abilities (Carroll, 1976). A potentially more powerful procedure is to use human abilities theory to derive a task-analysis framework for the selection of tests, and then to validate and interpret the tests according to the theory. In adopting this approach, it is necessary to employ a theory of human abilities that satisfies at least three criteria.

The first criterion is that the theory be based on multiple forms of independent evidence, not just a single research paradigm, in order to maximize its generalizability. This criterion is important in order that the theory hold potential for integration of information in diverse areas of research. In terms of this criterion, as we have described earlier, the concepts of simultaneous and successive processes have a long history in many diverse fields. In cognitive psychology, constructs comparable to these, but labelled as serial and parallel processes, are quite prevalent (Neisser, 1967). Many theoreticians in the philosophy of science and epistimology have proposed similar dichotomies (Ornstein, 1972) and current physiological research on the roles of the hemispheres in the brain also suggests these processes (Gazzaniga, 1970; Levy, 1974).

The second criterion is that the theory come to grips with the relationships between its basic premises and those of competing theories. This process is never complete of course, but the essential differences between theories and the potential for generation of testable hypotheses on their relative validities should be articulated. The relationship of the theory of simultaneous and successive syntheses to other research on human abilities was described earlier, consistent with this recommendation. We have expanded on Luria's concepts by relating them to current research on language, memory, and imagery. Recent studies, for example, have compared the theory to Jensen's (1969, 1970) model of Level I and Level II abilities (Jarman, 1978a; cf. Lawson & Jarman, 1977), Cattell's theory of fluid and crystallized intelligence, and begun to relate these processes to Piaget's (1961) work on perception (Jarman, in press a). The future metatheoretical implications of the theory as well as its potential for research on mental retardation and learning disabilities have been suggested also.

Finally, the theory should be sufficiently detailed that it may be translated to guidelines for the selection, validation, and interpretation of psychometric tasks. It is this criterion that makes possible the application of knowledge in human abilities to problems in individual assessment. This translation could take the form of a schematic model, utilizing the basic parameters of a theory. An initial form of such a model using simultaneous and successive processes is proposed here as shown in Figure 11.1. This model constitutes a rudimentary translation of the features of Figure 1 of Das, Kirby, and Jarman (1975) into a chart for classifying the task demands of a given psychometric instrument.

For exploratory application to the general area of prediction of cognitive abilities, the possible sensory systems are restricted to the auditory and visual modalities. This is consistent with established views of the dominance of these two modalities in children's learning processes in the school years and their current importance in research on sensory modalities (Jarman, 1977a, 1977b, 1978c, in press b). As shown at the top of the classification chart, within each of these modalities information may be presented simultaneously or successively. The central processes involved in a given task are enumerated vertically in the figure. Tasks may involve simultaneous or successive forms of processing, and within each of these may be classified as mnestic (memory), perceptual, or conceptual. To the extreme left of the chart, a further dimension is added concerning the form of output, which is simultaneous or successive. As shown in Figure 11.1, then, 48 possible combinations are generated for the classification of a given test by the factors of (a) modality of presentation and (b) form of presentation, crossed with (c) the type of task in terms of mnestic, perceptual, and conceptual, (d) the form of synthesis, and (e) the form of information output.

It should be noted that classification of test by the 48 cells in Figure 11.1 may not be completely representative or mutually exclusive. A complete representation of all cells may not be possible because in some cases tests have not been constructed according to the parameters of the chart. Most notably, few tests are available which would fit in cells 13–24. Dichotic listening tasks, in which different auditory information is presented simultaneously to each ear, are the main example of these tests at present (e.g., Kimura, 1973; Schulhoff & Goodglass, 1969). Further, the classification of tests is not mutually exclusive because some tasks contain elements of more than one mnestic, perceptual, and conceptual processes. These tests are not restricted to one cell in categorization, therefore, although two cells are generally the maximum number required.

Jarman (1978d) has developed this chart to classify and select a group of tests for use with children in kindergarten and the early school years. The tests are drawn from a variety of sources; some are well-known

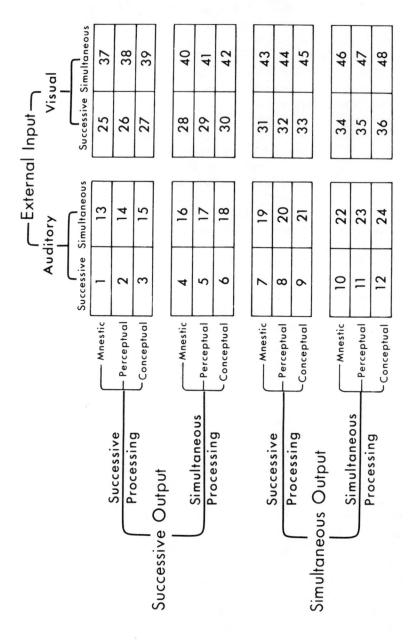

Figure 11.1. A chart illustrating task selection for measuring input, processing, and output components.

standardized tasks and others are still in experimental stages of development. The complete set of tasks used by Jarman will not be given here, but some examples of these tasks are described.

Cell 1 of the chart would be measured by a standardized digit span forward task. The input in this variety of task is auditory–successive, and the task measures successive processes in memory (mnestic), with successive output. In contrast, cell 4 of the chart may be measured by a digit span backward task. This task would be auditory–successive in input, but as suggested by Jarman (1978a), based on Jensen (1970), the task may measure simultaneous processes in memory. The output is of course successive. Similarly, as suggested in earlier discussions of Paivio (Kirby & Das, 1976; Paivio, 1976) abstract and concrete paired associates may fit in cells 1 and 4 respectively. Further corresponding additions to these cells may be the syntagmatic and paradigmatic tasks as described in our earlier discussion of developmental trends.

If we turn to the column headed by cell 25, several well-known tasks are seen to fit readily in some of these cells. The Knox Cubes subtest of the Arthur Point Scale of Performance would be placed in cell 25. In this task, a series of blocks that are arranged in a straight line are touched silently in a sequence by the experimenter. The child must recall the sequence by touching the blocks in the same order. Another interesting task that fits in this column in cell 34 is the Successive Shapes task by McDaniel (1972). This task involves the successive presentation of separate lines; the child must integrate the patterns formed by the lines in order to select the correct complete figure from a set of choices.

Finally, if we turn to the column headed by cell 37, several other examples may be noted. Well-known block pattern tasks, such as those in the Hiskey–Nebraska Test of Learning Aptitude, may fit in cells 41–42. In these tasks a model structure of blocks is built by the experimenter, and the child is required to build a pattern to match the model. The model remains in view at all times, and therefore the task does not emphasize memory. Due to the nature of the task, the output is, of course, successive. A second example is the very substantial number of tasks available for cells 46–48 that are psychomotor in origin. The Memory-for-Designs subtest of the Detroit Tests of Learning Aptitude, for example, would fit in cell 46; this task involves drawing geometric figures from memory. On the other hand, the Developmental Test of Visual–Motor Integration does not involve memory, and more likely fits in cells 47–48.

Several comments are necessary regarding the use of this model to classify tasks as exemplified here. First, experience has shown that the ease of classification of tasks by this chart varies considerably depending on the nature of the tasks. The classifications of concrete and abstract paired

associates, and syntagmatic and paradigmatic paired associates, for example, are based more on the related literature for these tasks than on any
obvious task demands in each test. In contrast, the Knox Cubes task, for
example, is easily classified in the model, based on its apparent cognitive
demands. There appears to be no easy solution to this problem of variation
of ease of classification, and perhaps test validation must always proceed
by an interaction of task analysis and empirical validation. Part of the
rationale of the project by Jarman (1978d) is that both are now necessary
in order to make a new contribution in the validation of early assessment
techniques.

Second, an interesting finding that was part of the process of task
classification by Jarman (1978d) was the relationship of the subtests of
many standardized intelligence tests to the classification scheme. In the
course of searching for appropriate tasks, most standardized tests were
surveyed and their subtests were classified. It was found that many of the
standardized tests had a structure which could be described in terms of the
model. This is intriguing, because these standardized tests are typically
developed by purely empirical means and are mainly atheoretical. This
finding will be explored in more detail in the future, for it lends both
meaning to the standardized tests, and further indirect empirical support for
the theory of simultaneous and successive cognitive processes.

Finally, the assumptions of the chart in Figure 11.1 should be noted. In
contrast to an orthogonal model of intelligence, as exemplified clearly by
Guilford (1967), the task-analysis chart presented does not assume independence of cells. In Guilford's scheme, cells in a schematic model represent separate abilities, and therefore Guilford has attempted to demonstrate
zero-order correlations between tasks in different cells. In contrast, the
model presented here is simply a schematic outline of the basic parameters
of the theory of simultaneous and successive processes. It is a scheme for
classifying tasks a priori, but it does not assume independence or nonin-
dependence of cells.

This question of the relationship between the cells is central, when
viewed in a developmental context. Cells that are independent at one age
level may not be independent at another age level. It is seen that the issue
underlying this problem is that of developmental integration and differentiation, as discussed earlier in developmental issues. For example, it may
be that learning is modality-specific in the early years, but changes to
modal-independent in the first years of school (Jarman, 1978c). The
schematic model used here would take this possibility into account, and
indeed, allow assessments of this changing relationship over time. Thus,
the relationships between the cells are not static assumptions, but rather,
are topics of research in their own right. This approach, then, allows a

systematic analysis of problems of developmental differentiation and integration when the model is applied in a developmental study, by using different age ranges and different tasks in the cells at varying developmental levels.

This developmental approach has been adopted by Jarman (1978d). Approximately 200 kindergarten children have been tested on 25 tasks, with these tasks chosen to fit a variety of cells in the model. The children will be followed longitudinally for 3 years, with assessments on all tasks made each year. In the final year, multiple measures of school learning will also be taken. Variations in factor structures will be measured year by year, and all data will be used to predict the school measures in the final year.

Thus, this project will supply information on the degrees of developmental differentiation and integration of simultaneous and successive processes in the early school years. This information is of interest for theoretical purposes, but it should also be useful in practical terms, by supplying a set of guidelines for the development of techniques for the early assessment of learning difficulties.

APPENDIX

A General Manual for Tests of Simultaneous and Successive Processing and Speed of Processing

A.1 DESCRIPTIONS AND INSTRUCTIONS

Tests of Simultaneous Processing

RAVEN'S COLOURED PROGRESSIVE MATRICES

Ease of administration and the requirement of few verbal instructions have resulted in Raven's Coloured Progressive Matrices (Raven, 1960) being a widely used culturally reduced test of intellectual reasoning for children aged 5 to 11 years. Consisting of 36 matrices or designs, each having a part which has been removed, the task is to choose the missing insert from six possible alternatives. The 36 matrices are grouped into three series, each series comprised of 12 matrices of increasing difficulty. The earlier series require accuracy of discrimination, while the latter series involve analogies, permutation and alternation of pattern, and other logical relations. Each child responds on the standard form. The total number of correct responses is recorded.

Instructions for Raven's Coloured Progressive Matrices
I am going to show you pictures of designs, each with a piece missing.
Look at this design [point to A1]. *You see, it is a pattern with a piece cut out of it. Each of these pieces* [point to each in turn] *is the right shape to fit the space, but only one of them is the right pattern. No. 1 is the right*

shape, but is not the right pattern. No. 2 is not a pattern at all. No. 3 is quite wrong. No. 6 is nearly right but it is wrong here [point to the white piece]. *Only one is right. Point to the piece which is quite right.* [If the child fails to do so, continue explanation until the nature of the problem to be solved is clearly grasped.] [Pointing to problem A2] *Now point to the piece which came out of this pattern.* [If the child fails to do so, re-demonstrate problem A1 and again ask him to do A2. Before allowing the child to continue with the rest of the test, ensure comprehension of the instructions.] *Begin and finish the booklet.*

MEMORY-FOR-DESIGNS

Developed by Graham and Kendall (1960), this test has become one of the most popular tests for the assessment of brain damage in both children and adults. However, in the present battery of tests, its purpose is merely to provide a memory task of designs. The test material consists of 15 simple straight line designs which the child is shown one at a time for 5 seconds each. The child's task is to reproduce from memory each of the 15 designs. Each child is given one sheet of 8½- × 11-inch white paper, placed lengthwise in the usual position for writing. The actual stimulus cards from the test (5 × 5 inches) are held at right angles to the child's line of vision, 18 inches from his eyes. An objective scoring system has been developed, which encompasses the designation and subsequent summing of numerical values to the qualitatively different errors.

Instructions for Memory-for-Designs
I am going to show you some cards with drawings on them. I will let you look at a card for 5 seconds. Then, I will take it away and let you draw from memory what you have seen. Be sure to look at the drawing carefully so that you can make yours just like it. Don't start to draw until I take the card away. Ready, here's the first one.

FIGURE COPYING

Adapted by Ilg and Ames (1964) as a means for determining developmental readiness for the traditional school learning tasks of the primary grades, the task requires the child to copy 10 geometrical forms which increase in difficulty and are visible to the child at all times. Each drawing is scored as 0, 1, or 2, according to the degree of correctness of reproduction. Scoring criteria emphasize the maintenance of geometric relations and proportions rather than exact reproduction.

Instructions for Figure Copying
I am going to show you 10 cards with drawings on them. I will place in front of you 1 card at a time. You are asked to make yours look just like the

one in front of you. After drawing each card, I will remove it and place another in front of you to draw. Ready? Here's the first card.

CROSS-MODAL CODING

The test was used by Birch extensively (Birch & Belmont, 1964) as a measure of auditory–visual integration. Birch used patterns of pencil taps by the experimenter with visual recognition of patterns of sound. The claim was made that his procedure yielded degrees of auditory–visual integration that were related to retardation in reading, as mentioned earlier. However, the problem with the study was that the testing situation was not very well controlled. There were two basic defects in the presentation of the stimuli. The first defect was that taps were made by the experimenter who presumably had practiced the timing of ½-second and 1-second intervals. The time and volume of the tap variation from one testing situation to another may have been rather large. The other defect was that, while the task was supposed to be an auditory–visual integration, the subjects *watched* the examiner tap out the sequence. The possibility exists then that a visual input mode was operative. Therefore, the task was at least partially a visual–visual integration. Possibly little or no cross-modal transfer was, in fact, functioning. These two difficulties were rectified in our adaptation of the task.

A standardized testing procedure was accomplished by tape recording the entire test. All the examiner had to do was turn on the tape recorder and present the visual stimuli at the proper times. Tones of 1000 Hz were of .15 seconds duration with .35 seconds between short pauses and 1.35 seconds between long pauses. The instructions for the test are presented later, along with the auditory and visual stimuli.

In some of our experiments, a total of 30 auditory patterns were presented to each subject. The position of the correct response on the 3- × 5-inch visual stimulus card was randomly assigned to each of the 30 test items. This required that each auditory pattern be presented three times, in the same order as shown in Figure A.1. In other experiments, 20 patterns, that is, two replications of the original 10 were presented. More recently, we have been using only 10 patterns as shown in the figure.

Cross-modal Coding cannot only be thought of as a task in auditory–visual integration, but also as a short-term memory task. Viewing the experiment as a short-term memory test, the input mode is auditory, which fits nicely into the acoustic nature of the short-term store, but the output mode is visual recognition. Therefore, encoding of stimuli is done to transform the information into a visual mode. Perhaps this is why Cross-modal Coding loads on both simultaneous and successive factors. But sometimes it loads only on the simultaneous, and rarely, only on the speed factor.

	AUDITORY STIMULI	VISUAL STIMULI		
	EXAMPLES			
	• •	••	• •	•••
	• ••	•••	• ••	•• •
	•• •	•••	• ••	•• •
	TEST ITEMS			
1	•• ••	• •••	• ••• •	•• ••
2	• •••	••••	• •••	••• •
3	••• ••	•••••	•• •••	••• ••
4	• •• •	• ••• •	•••••	•• ••
5	••• •• •	••• •• •	•• ••• •	• ••• ••
6	•• •••	••• • •	•• •••	•••• •
7	•• •• ••	•• •• ••	••••• ••	••• • ••
8	••• ••• •	•• ••• ••	••• •• ••	••• ••• •
9	•• • •••	•• •• ••	•• • •••	•• ••• •
10	• ••• ••	• •• •••	• ••• ••	•• • •••

Figure A.1. Stimuli and recognition test items for Cross-modal Coding.

Instructions for Cross-modal Coding

I am going to let you listen to some patterns of sounds. Listen carefully. [Examples 1, 2, and 3 without the visual stimulus cards were presented.] *Each of the patterns you heard are just like the dots you see on this card.* [Card shown.] *Let's take a look at each one. Here is what the first one sounded like.* [Example 1 presented.] *This is what the second one sounded like.* [Card 2 shown and Example 2 presented.] *You see. It is just like the dots that are on this card. Let's take a look at the other one that we listened to.* [Card 3 shown and Example 3 presented.] *Each pattern you hear is going to be like one of the dot patterns you see here. Let me show you. Listen!* [Card 4 shown, Example 1 presented. N.B.: Card 4 and all subsequent cards contain three possible sound patterns of which one is correct. Cards 1–3 contain only the correct pattern.] *Which one did you hear? It was this one.* [Examiner points to the correct pattern.] *Listen again then you show me which one you heard. Ready?* [Card 5 shown and Example 2 presented.] *Which one is it?* [Subject points.] *Let's listen to a different one.*

Ready? [Card 6 shown, Example 3 presented.] *Which one is it this time? Let's try another one. You show me which you heard. Ready?* [Example 1 presented, followed immediately by Card 7.] *Listen again and then show me which one you have heard.* [Example 2 presented, then Card 8 shown.] *Ready?* [Example 3, then Card 9.] *Ready?* [Example 1, then Card 10.] *Ready?* [Example 2, then Card 11.] *Ready?* [Example 3, then Card 12.] [If the subject did not correctly identify any of the last three stimuli, the instructions were repeated until he could.] *Listen carefully and pick out the dots that look like the tones you hear. Ready?* [Test item one presented followed by the rest of the test.]

Tests of Successive Processing

SERIAL RECALL

Presented individually by means of a tape recorder, the subject's task is to recall verbally, immediately following the presentation of a list of four words. Twenty-four groups of four words which are either acoustically similar (e.g., *man, mat,* and *mad*) or neutral (e.g., *day, hot,* and *cow*) are given. In some studies (cf., Orn, 1970), an additional set of 24 lists have been presented—12 neutral word lists and 12 semantically similar word lists. The semantically similar words were *wide, large, big, high, long, fat, great, huge,* and *tall*. Any four of these nine words were selected to make up a list, and no list was identical with the other.

Each series of four words is scored for words in the correct serial position. For instance, if the list is Number 1, and the subject recalled *key, cow, pen, hot,* then his/her score is 1. If the sequence of recall is *key, hot, pen, cow,* the score is 2. The maximum score is 96. As will be noticed from the lists of words given below, the acoustic lists were drawn from a pool of nine words; so were the neutral lists.

	Examples for practice session:	a.	*big*	*long*	*great*	*tall*
		b.	*cow*	*day*	*key*	*few*
		c.	*man*	*mad*	*map*	*pan*

1.	*key*	*hot*	*cow*	*pen*	9.	*tap*	*mat*	*pan*	*cat*
2.	*cab*	*cat*	*mad*	*can*	10.	*key*	*day*	*cow*	*bar*
3.	*day*	*cow*	*wall*	*bar*	11.	*cab*	*cap*	*cat*	*tap*
4.	*man*	*mad*	*pan*	*mat*	12.	*bar*	*pen*	*few*	*day*
5.	*pen*	*wall*	*book*	*key*	13.	*cab*	*man*	*mad*	*map*
6.	*book*	*bar*	*wall*	*hot*	14.	*mat*	*can*	*cap*	*man*
7.	*key*	*few*	*hot*	*book*	15.	*few*	*pen*	*hot*	*wall*
8.	*can*	*pan*	*tap*	*cab*	16.	*day*	*cow*	*bar*	*wall*

17.	*cap*	*pan*	*cat*	*can*	21.	*key*	*book*	*day*	*hot*
18.	*man*	*mad*	*mat*	*pan*	22.	*cab*	*tap*	*man*	*cat*
19.	*few*	*day*	*cow*	*book*	23.	*can*	*cap*	*pan*	*mad*
20.	*cap*	*man*	*mad*	*tap*	24.	*pen*	*few*	*wall*	*cow*

Rest for about 60 seconds between twelfth and thirteenth list

Instructions for Serial Recall (and Free Recall)

I am going to say some words. When I am finished I want you to say the words just the way I said them. There will be four words in each group. I'll repeat the instructions. I am going to say some groups of words. When I am finished I want you to say the words just the way I said them. Let's try a group of words. Ready? big long great tall. [Pause] You should have said, big long great tall. Each time I say a group of four words, I want you to say the words in exactly the same order that I do. Let's try another group of words. Ready? Cow day key few. [Pause] You should have said, cow day key few. Let's try one more group of words. Ready? Man mad map pan. [Pause] You should have said, man mad map pan. You see, when I say a group of words, I want you to say the same words just as I do. Now let's try some other groups of words. Ready? [Begin test.]

FREE RECALL

The list of words given in this test is identical to the list given in Serial Recall. However, each series of four words is scored for the total number of words correctly recalled. For instance, if List 1 is recalled as *key, cow, pen, hot,* the score is 4. The maximum score is 96. Thus, depending upon the scoring technique, one administration of the series of words will yield two scores, one of Serial Recall and the other of Free Recall.

DIGIT SPAN FORWARD

This task is similar to the WISC-R (Wechsler, 1974) Digit Span Forward subtest. The experimenter reads to the child series of digits of increasing length, beginning with three digits, to a maximum of nine digits. If the child is unable to recall correctly any series of digits, he is given a second series of identical length. When the child fails to recall correctly both series of any one length, the test is discontinued. The score is equivalent to the highest series of digits correctly recalled, with a maximum of nine points. The series of digits are as follows:

Series	Trial 1	Trial 2
(3)	4–9–7	7–2–3
(4)	4–5–2–8	7–2–6–9
(5)	9–5–3–4–8	6–3–2–9–7

(6)	4–9–7–2–8–5	8–6–9–5–4–7
(7)	6–2–8–5–3–4–9	8–7–5–3–2–9–4
(8)	2–7–5–6–3–1–9–4	3–8–6–5–4–2–9–1
(9)	6–4–9–8–2–3–5–7–1	5–3–7–8–1–9–4–6–2

Instructions for Digit Span Forward

I am going to say some numbers. Listen carefully, and when I am through say them right after me. Are you ready? [Pause; begin test.] [The digits are presented at the rate of one per second. All subjects are started with the three-digit series.]

VISUAL SHORT-TERM MEMORY

Presented individually by means of a slide projector are 12 items (2 practice and 10 test items), each of which is a five-cell cross-shaped matrix with one number per cell; this test requires the child to recall (write down) the cell items which are viewed for 5 seconds, after also being presented a 2-second filler task of color naming in order to prevent any rehearsal during this period of retention time (see Figure A.2). Scoring involves the sum of all the numbers correctly placed within each of the cells. The maximum score is 50. Some studies have used 20 rather than 10 items; the maximum, then, is 100.

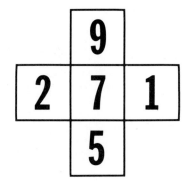

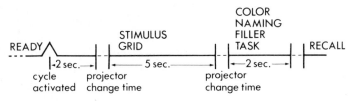

Figure A.2. Diagram showing sample Visual Short-Term Memory (VSTM) task grid and operation.

Instructions for Visual Short-Term Memory

I am going to show you some numbers and some colors. I want you to watch the screen and do as I tell you [project slide 1]. Look at these numbers. Try to remember each number [pause, then project slide 2]. Now name these colors starting at the top [pause, then project blank slide 3]. Now write the numbers you saw at first on this paper. Good. [If incorrect, repeat example 1.]

Now let's try another one [project slide 4]. Look at these numbers and try to remember them [pause briefly, then project slide 5]. Name these colors starting at the top [project slide 6]. Now write the numbers you have just seen. [Set Timers.]

Now we are going to try again, but we will go a bit faster. Ready? [Engage timers.] [As the first sequence progresses, say] Look at the numbers . . . Name the colors . . . Write . . .

Let's try another set. Ready? [Engage timers.] Good. Remember to look at the numbers, name as many colors as you can, then write the numbers.

[Start test with each trial preceded by a ready signal.]

Stimuli numbers for Visual Short-Term Memory

*1. 9 8 4 5 1	7. 5 4 8 1 6
*2. 9 2 7 1 5	8. 9 7 5 3 1
3. 2 4 9 7 1	9. 3 5 6 1 8
4. 7 2 3 9 6	10. 7 3 9 8 4
5. 7 5 2 9 4	11. 3 8 6 9 4
6. 4 8 9 3 1	12. 5 3 6 1 9

*Series 1 and 2 were for practice purposes and are not scored.

Tests of Speed of Processing

COLOR NAMING

This task is based on one of the three developed by Stroop (1935). The task is presented on a white background card (28 × 30 inches), having eight rows of colored bars with five positions in a row. The colored bars were 3 inches long and ¾ inch wide. Red, green, yellow, and blue bars were alternated, to a total of 10 presentations of each color, in replication of the Stroop task. The child is placed 7 feet from the card, and after being familiarized with the working of a stopwatch, is asked to name each color, successively by rows. The score is the time, in seconds, it takes the child to complete the task.

Instructions for Color Naming

I have here a board with strips of different colored bars. The colors are red, blue, green, and yellow. When I lift this cover, I want you to start here at the top left [point] and name the colors going across. When you finish the first row, go here [point to the second row left] and work across. Name all the colored bars in this way [demonstrate the pattern with your finger]. Remember, you are being timed, so name the colors as quickly as you can. Are you ready? [Lift cover.] Begin. [Start stopwatch.]

Color Chart

Red	Green	Yellow	Green	Blue
Green	Blue	Yellow	Red	Blue
Blue	Green	Red	Yellow	Red
Yellow	Red	Blue	Green	Yellow
Blue	Yellow	Red	Blue	Green
Yellow	Red	Green	Yellow	Blue
Blue	Green	Red	Yellow	Green
Red	Yellow	Blue	Green	Red

WORD NAMING

This task is based on one of the three developed by Stroop (1935). The task is presented on a white background card (28 × 30 inches), having eight rows of words, for example, red, blue, green, and yellow, with five positions in a row. The words are 3 inches long and ¾ inch wide. Words are alternated, to a total of 10 presentations of each word, in replication of the Stroop task. The child is placed 7 feet from the card and after being familiarized with the working of a stopwatch, is asked to read the words, successively by rows. The score is the time, in seconds, it takes the child to complete the task.

Instructions for Word Naming

I have here a board with names of different colors. [Make sure that the child can read the words red, blue, green, and yellow.] When I lift this cover, I want you to start here at the top left [point] and read the words going across. When you finish the first row, go here [point to the second row left] and work across. Read all the words in this way [demonstrate the pattern with your finger]. Remember, you are being timed, so read the colors as quickly as you can. Are you ready? [Lift cover.] Begin. [Start stopwatch.]

Word Chart

Red	Blue	Yellow	Blue	Green
Red	Green	Red	Yellow	Blue
Blue	Green	Yellow	Red	Yellow
Green	Yellow	Red	Green	Blue
Red	Green	Blue	Yellow	Green
Yellow	Blue	Red	Blue	Green
Blue	Green	Yellow	Red	Yellow
Blue	Red	Yellow	Green	Red

A.2 TEST MEANS, STANDARD DEVIATIONS, AND FACTOR LOADINGS

Since the tests have been given to different samples and have been included in many factor analyses, it will be helpful to report their means, standard deviations, and factor loadings. In Tables A.1 to A.10, the relevant data have been summarized. Where a test had loadings on more than one factor, the factor on which its major loading occurred has been given. Tables A.1–A.10 follow on pages 219–228.

Table A.1
Comparison of Means, Standard Deviations, and Factor Loadings of Raven's Coloured Progressive Matrices[a]

Authors	Groups	Means	Standard deviations	Factor loadings
Das, 1973	Gr. 4 (Edmonton; N = 60; high and low SES)	—	—	.740*
	Gr. 4 (Orissa; N = 90; high and low SES)	—	—	.624*
Molloy, 1973	Low SES—Gr. 1 (N = 30)	13.77	2.01	.784*#
	High SES—Gr. 1 (N = 30)	15.37	3.21	.784*#
	Low SES—Gr. 4 (N = 30)	25.57	4.24	.876*#
	High SES—Gr. 4 (N = 30)	26.93	4.87	.876*#
Krywaniuk, 1974	Low achievers— Gr. 3 (Canadian Native; N = 38)	23.08	4.11	.668**
	Low achievers— Gr. 3 (Edmonton; N = 56)	23.84	6.43	.792*
	High achievers— Gr. 3 (Edmonton; N = 56)	29.98	3.97	.745*
Leong, 1974	Severely disabled readers ($\overline{CA}$ = 9 − 3 yrs.; N = 58)	22.60	5.04	.802*
	Above average readers ($\overline{CA}$ = 9 − 3 yrs.; N = 58)	28.19	3.70	.817*
Jarman, 1975	Low IQ (males, Gr. 4; N = 60)	23.23	4.89	.600*
	Normal IQ (males, Gr. 4; N = 60)	26.08	5.04	.552**
	High IQ (males, Gr. 4; N = 60)	30.95	3.38	−.590**
Kirby, 1976	Gr. 4 (males, N = 104)	28.55	4.39	.753*
	Gr. 4 (females, N = 98)	29.04	4.47	.793*
Williams, 1976	Learning disabled (Gr. 2-6; N = 51)	27.00	4.14	.775*
Kaufman, 1977	Average and below average achievers— Gr. 4 (N = 68)	26.77	4.68	−.873*
Jarman, 1978	Educable mentally retarded (N = 67)	19.56	5.26	.943*

[a] * represents simultaneous factor loading; ** represents successive factor loading; # represents combined SES.

Table A.2

Comparison of Means, Standard Deviations, and Factor Loadings of Memory-for-Designs Test[a]

Authors	Groups	Means	Standard deviations	Factor loadings
Das, 1973	Gr. 4 (Edmonton; N = 60; high and low SES)	—	—	−.830*
	Gr. 4 (Orissa; N = 90; high and low SES)	—	—	−.809*
Molloy, 1973	Low SES—Gr. 1 (N = 30)	16.50	6.09	−.713*#
	High SES—Gr. 1 (N = 30)	12.67	5.82	−.713*#
	Low SES—Gr. 4 (N = 30)	3.00	3.39	−.750*#
	High SES—Gr. 4 (N = 30)	3.37	3.13	−.750*#
Krywaniuk, 1974	Low achievers— Gr. 3 (Canadian Native; N = 38)	3.82	2.84	−.831*
	Low achievers— Gr. 3 (Edmonton; N = 56)	5.52	4.29	−.764*
	High achievers— Gr. 3 (Edmonton; N = 56)	3.52	3.67	−.583*
Leong, 1974	Severely disabled readers ($\overline{CA}$ = 9–3 yrs.; N = 58)	8.57	6.48	−.808*
	Above average readers ($\overline{CA}$ = 9–3 yrs.; N = 58)	4.43	3.02	−.585*
Jarman, 1975	Low IQ (males, Gr. 4; N = 60)	3.43	3.35	−.798*
	Normal IQ (males, Gr. 4; N = 60)	3.10	3.11	−.632*
	High IQ (males, Gr. 4; N = 60)	1.70	2.11	−.909*
Kirby, 1976	Gr. 4 (males, N = 104)	7.77	2.63	.810*
	Gr. 4 (females, N = 98)	7.97	3.41	.793*
Kaufman, 1977	Average and below average achievers— Gr. 4 (N = 68)	4.61	3.35	.787*
Jarman, 1978	Educable mentally retarded (N = 67)	9.78	6.13	−.894*

[a] * represents simultaneous factor loading; # represents combined SES.

Table A.3
Comparison of Means, Standard Deviations, and Factor Loadings of Figure Copying Test [a]

Authors	Groups	Means	Standard deviations	Factor loadings
Das, 1973	Gr. 4 (Edmonton; N = 60; high and low SES)	—	—	.674*
	Gr. 4 (Orissa; N = 90; high and low SES)	—	—	*.800*
Molloy, 1973	Low SES—Gr. 1 (N = 30)	5.47	1.45	.762*#
	High SES—Gr. 1 (N = 30)	5.80	1.21	.762*#
	Low SES—Gr. 4 (N = 30)	9.13	1.50	.797*#
	High SES—Gr. 4 (N = 30)	8.93	1.28	.797*#
Krywaniuk, 1974	Low achievers— Gr. 3 (Canadian Native; N = 38)	12.08	4.94	.711*
	Low achievers— Gr. 3 (Edmonton; N = 56)	11.89	6.93	.685*
	High achievers— Gr. 3 (Edmonton; N = 56)	14.09	6.41	.654*
Jarman, 1975	Low IQ (males, Gr. 4; N = 60)	14.82	1.88	.767*
	Normal IQ (males, Gr. 4; N = 60)	14.55	2.46	.861*
	High IQ (males, Gr. 4; N = 60)	16.27	2.41	.483*
Kirby, 1976	Gr. 4 (males, N = 104)	13.60	2.92	.713*
	Gr. 4 (females, N = 98)	14.49	2.33	.629*
Williams, 1976	Learning disabled (Gr. 2-6; N = 51)	12.20	2.60	.866*
Jarman, 1978	Educable mentally retarded (N = 67)	9.17	3.39	.865*

[a] * represents simultaneous factor loading; # represents combined SES.

Table A.4
Comparison of Means, Standard Deviations, and Factor Loadings of Cross-Modal Coding Test[a]

Authors	Groups	Means	Standard deviations	Factor loadings
Das, 1973	Gr. 4 (Edmonton; $N = 60$; high and low SES)	—	—	.457**
	Gr. 4 (Orissa; $N = 90$; high and low SES)	—	—	.800*
Orn, 1970	Low SES—Gr. 3 ($N = 30$)	23.33[b]	4.85	—
	High SES—Gr. 3 ($N = 30$)	24.17[b]	4.99	—
	Low SES—educable mentally retarded (MA matched; $N = 30$)	16.97[b]	5.17	—
	High SES—educable mentally retarded (MA matched; $N = 30$)	15.63[b]	6.86	—
Molloy, 1973	Low SES—Gr. 1 ($N = 30$)	7.70[c]	2.61	.541**#
	High SES—Gr. 1 ($N = 30$)	6.63[c]	3.31	.541**#
	Low SES—Gr. 4 ($N = 30$)	16.47[c]	3.12	.677***#
	High SES—Gr. 4 ($N = 30$)	16.80[c]	3.42	.677***#
Krywaniuk, 1974	Low achievers— Gr. 3 (Canadian Native; $N = 38$)	10.40[c]	4.15	.585**
	Low achievers— Gr. 3 (Edmonton; $N = 56$)	15.32[c]	4.41	.521**
	High achievers— Gr. 3 (Edmonton; $N = 56$)	18.14[c]	2.60	.603*
Leong, 1974	Severely disabled readers ($\overline{CA} = 9\text{–}3$ yrs.; $N = 58$)	6.26[d]	2.07	.526**
	Above average readers ($\overline{CA} = 9\text{–}3$ yrs.; $N = 58$)	8.16[d]	1.62	.420*

[a] * represents simultaneous factor loading; ** represents successive factor loading; *** represents speed factor loading; # represents combined SES.
[b] Out of 30.
[c] Out of 20.
[d] Out of 10.

Table A.5
Comparison of Means, Standard Deviations, and Factor Loadings of Serial Recall Test [a]

Authors	Groups	Means	Standard deviations	Factor loadings
Molloy, 1973	Low SES—Gr. 1 (N = 30)	58.57[b]	25.51	.951**#
	High SES—Gr. 1 (N = 30)	60.47[b]	27.31	.951**#
	Low SES—Gr. 4 (N = 30)	84.73[b]	9.84	.950**#
	High SES—Gr. 4 (N = 30)	86.30[b]	10.87	.950**#
Krywaniuk, 1974	Low achievers— Gr. 3 (Canadian Native; N = 38)	92.39[c]	32.78	.863**
	Low achievers— Gr. 3 (Edmonton; N = 56)	130.43[c]	32.78	.917**
	High achievers— Gr. 3 (Edmonton; N = 56)	145.45[c]	26.40	.913**
Leong, 1974	Severely disabled readers ($\overline{CA}$ = 9–3 yrs.; N = 58)	57.12[b]	12.22	.888**
	Above average readers ($\overline{CA}$ = 9–3 yrs.; N = 58)	72.17[b]	8.48	.817**
Jarman, 1975	Low IQ (males, Gr. 4; N = 60)	68.00[b]	19.56	.656**
	Normal IQ (males, Gr. 4; N = 60)	78.30[b]	17.16	.731***
	High IQ (males, Gr. 4; N = 60)	86.15[b]	9.11	.582**
Kirby, 1976	Gr. 4 (males, N = 104)	54.42[b]	12.98	.642**
	Gr. 4 (females, N = 98)	60.85[b]	12.10	.560**
Williams, 1976	Learning disabled (Gr. 2–6; N = 51)	71.76[b]	18.92	.922**
Kaufman, 1977	Average and below average achievers— Gr. 4 (N = 68)	63.74[b]	9.89	.913**
Jarman, 1978	Educable mentally retarded (N = 67)	38.22[b]	21.87	.879**

[a] ** represents successive factor loading; *** represents successive cum speed factor loading; # represents combined SES.
[b] Out of 96.
[c] Out of 192.

Table A.6

Comparison of Means, Standard Deviations, and Factor Loadings of Free Recall Test [a]

Authors	Groups	Means	Standard deviations	Factor loadings
Molloy, 1973	Low SES—Gr. 1 (N = 30)	76.17[b]	13.86	.955**#
	High SES—Gr. 1 (N = 30)	76.93[b]	4.10	.955**#
	Low SES—Gr. 4 (N = 30)	90.40[b]	6.38	.941**#
	High SES—Gr. 4 (N = 30)	90.43[b]	6.87	.941**#
Krywaniuk, 1974	Low achievers— Gr. 3 (Canadian Native; N = 38)	125.39[c]	30.29	.852**
	Low achievers— Gr. 3 (Edmonton; N = 56)	147.61[c]	28.24	.905**
	High achievers— Gr. 3 (Edmonton; N = 56)	159.68[c]	18.23	.892**
Williams, 1976	Learning disabled (Gr. 2–6; N = 51)	83.17[b]	9.87	.916**
Kaufman, 1977	Average and below average achievers— Gr. 4 (N = 68)	72.30[b]	7.49	.895**

[a] ** represents successive factor loading; # represents combined SES.
[b] Out of 96.
[c] Out of 192.

224

Table A.7
Comparison of Means, Standard Deviations, and Factor Loadings of Digit Span Forward Test[a]

Authors	Groups	Means	Standard deviations	Factor loadings
Molloy, 1973	Low SES—Gr. 1 (N = 30)	4.10	.71	.811**#
	High SES—Gr. 1 (N = 30)	4.17	.75	.811**#
	Low SES—Gr. 4 (N = 30)	5.23	.86	.801**#
	High SES—Gr. 4 (N = 30)	5.57	.82	.801**#
Kirby, 1976	Gr. 4 (males, N = 104)	5.34	.94	.785**
Williams, 1976	Learning disabled (Gr. 2–6; N = 51)	5.15	1.07	.845**
Kaufman, 1977	Average and below average achievers— Gr. 4 (N = 68)	5.32	.81	.594**
Jarman, 1978	Educable mentally retarded (N = 67)	6.72	1.73	.809**

[a] ** represents successive factor loading; # represents combined SES.

Table A.8
Comparison of Means, Standard Deviations, and Factor Loadings of Visual Short-Term Memory Test[a]

Authors	Groups	Means	Standard deviations	Factor loadings
Das, 1973	Gr. 4 (Edmonton; N = 60; high and low SES)	—	—	.760**
	Gr. 4 (Orissa; N = 90; high and low SES)	—	—	.918**
Molloy, 1973	Low SES—Gr. 1 (N = 30)	18.43[b]	5.85	−.557***#
	High SES—Gr. 1 (N = 30)	21.57[b]	9.56	−.557***#
	Low SES—Gr. 4 (N = 30)	47.83[b]	11.98	.689**#
	High SES—Gr. 4 (N = 30)	51.87[b]	11.27	.689**#
Krywaniuk, 1974	Low achievers— Gr. 3 (Canadian Native; N = 38)	24.97[c]	10.24	−.624***
	Low achievers— Gr. 3 (Edmonton; N = 56)	28.09[c]	10.26	.601**
	High achievers— Gr. 3 (Edmonton; N = 56)	33.93[c]	9.30	−.623***
Leong, 1974	Severely disabled readers ($\overline{CA}$ = 9–3 yrs.; N = 58)	60.84[b]	15.4b	.934[p]
	Above average readers ($\overline{CA}$ = 9–3 yrs.; N = 58)	82.91[b]	11.58	.620**
Jarman, 1975	Low IQ (males, Gr. 4; N = 60)	57.28[b]	17.59	.652**
	Normal IQ (males, Gr. 4; N = 60)	63.38[b]	17.00	.672**
	High IQ (males, Gr. 4; N = 60)	64.90[b]	16.28	.714**
Kirby, 1976	Gr. 4 (males, N = 104)	77.09[b]	15.63	.838**
Jarman, 1978	Educable mentally retarded (N = 67)	35.61[b]	11.85	.977**

[a] ** represents successive factor loading; [p] represents perceptual organization factor loading; *** represents speed factor loading; # represents combined SES.
[b] Out of 100.
[c] Out of 50.

Table A.9
Comparison of Means, Standard Deviations, and Factor Loadings of Color Naming Test (in Seconds)[a]

Authors	Groups	Means	Standard deviations	Factor loadings
Molloy, 1973	Low SES—Gr. 1 (N = 30)	60.60	27.75	.801***#
	High SES—Gr. 1 (N = 30)	59.27	21.17	.801***#
	Low SES—Gr. 4 (N = 30)	36.40	7.03	.833***#
	High SES—Gr. 4 (N = 30)	36.37	6.39	.833***#
Krywaniuk, 1974	Low achievers— Gr. 3 (Canadian Native; N = 38)	97.29	26.17	.739***
	Low achievers— Gr. 3 (Edmonton; N = 56)	79.54	19.13	.855***
	High achievers— Gr. 3 (Edmonton; N = 56)	72.73	19.72	.765***
Kirby, 1976	Gr. 4 (males, N = 104)	33.36	6.77	.904***
	Gr. 4 (females, N = 98)	30.92	4.86	.573***

[a] *** represents speed factor loading; # represents combined SES.

Table A.10

Comparison of Means, Standard Deviations, and Factor Loadings of Word Naming Test (in Seconds)[a]

Authors	Groups	Means	Standard deviations	Factor loadings
Molloy, 1973	Low SES—Gr. 1 (N = 30)	94.23	50.41	.766***#
	High SES—Gr. 1 (N = 30)	70.90	25.10	.766***#
	Low SES—Gr. 4 (N = 30)	24.37	3.13	.842***#
	High SES—Gr. 4 (N = 30)	23.53	3.95	.842***#
Krywaniuk, 1974	Low achievers— Gr. 3 (Canadian Native; N = 38)	32.97	11.33	.856***
	Low achievers— Gr. 3 (Edmonton; N = 56)	25.52	5.30	.893***
	High achievers— Gr. 3 (Edmonton; N = 56)	22.14	4.29	−.571**
Kirby, 1976	Gr. 4 (males, N = 104)	21.87	4.09	.771***
	Gr. 4 (females, N = 98)	20.44	3.82	.916***

[a] *** represents speed factor loading; ** represents successive factor loading; # represents combined SES.

References

Akers, E. Prologue: The why of early childhood education. In I.J. Gordon (Ed.), *Early child-hood education. The seventy-first yearbook of the National Society for the Study of Education.* Chicago: National Society for the Study of Education, 1972.

Anastasi, A. Faculties *versus* factors: A reply to Professor Thurstone. *Psychological Bulletin,* 1938, *35,* 391–395.

Anastasi, A. *Psychological testing.* London: Macmillan, 1976.

Anderson, B.R. On the comparability of meaningful stimuli in cross-cultural research. *Sociometry.* 1967, *30,* 124–136.

Anderson, J.R., & Bower, G.H. *Human associative memory.* Washington, D.C.: Winston, 1973.

Ashman, A. The relationship between planning and simultaneous and successive synthesis. Unpublished Ph.D. dissertation. Department of Educational Psychology, University of Alberta, Edmonton, Canada, 1978.

Atkinson, R.C., & Shiffrin, R.M. Human memory: A proposed system and its control processes. In K.W. Spence & J.T. Spence (Eds.), *The psychology of learning and motivation* (Vol. 2). New York: Academic Press, 1968.

Baltes, P.B., Reese, H.W., & Nesselroade, J.R. *Life-span developmental psychology: Introduction to research methods.* Monterey, Cal.: Brooks/Cole, 1977.

Bartlett, F.C. The measurement of human skill. *British Medical Journal,* 1947, *1,* 835–838, 877–880.

Bayley, N. Behavioral correlates of mental growth: Birth to thirty-six years. *American Psychologist.* 1968, *23,* 1–17.

Bereiter, C., & Engelmann, S. *Teaching disadvantaged children in the preschool.* Englewood Cliffs, N.J.: Prentice-Hall, 1966.

Berry, J.W. On cross-cultural comparability. *International Journal of Psychology,* 1969, *4,* 119–128.

Berry, J.W., & Dasen, P.R. *Culture and cognition: Readings in cross-cultural psychology.* London: Methuen, 1974.

229

Bijou, S.W. A functional analysis of retarded development. In N.R. Ellis (Ed.), *International review of research in mental retardation* (Vol. 1). New York: Academic Press, 1966.

Bindra, D. *A theory of intelligent behavior.* New York: Wiley, 1976.

Birch, H.G., & Belmont, L. Auditory–visual integration in normal and retarded readers. *American Journal of Orthopsychiatry,* 1964, *36,* 852–861.

Birch, H.G., & Lefford, A. Visual differentiation, intersensory integration and voluntary motor control. *Monographs of the Society for Research in Child Development,* 1967, *32,* (2, Whole No. 110).

Blackman, L.S., Bilsky, L.H., Burger, A.L., & Mar, H. Cognitive processes and academic achievement in EMR adolescents. *American Journal of Mental Deficiency,* 1976, *81,* 125–134.

Blishen, B.R., Jones, F.E., Naegele, K.D., & Porter, J. *Canadian society.* Toronto: Macmillan, 1965.

Bloom, B.S. *Stability and change in human characteristics.* New York: Wiley, 1964.

Blumenthal, A.L. *The process of cognition.* Englewood Cliffs, New Jersey: Prentice Hall, 1977.

Bock, R.D. Word and image: Sources of the verbal and spatial factors in mental test scores. *Psychometrika,* 1973, *38,* 437–457.

Bortner, M., & Birch, H. Cognitive capacity and cognitive competence. *American Journal of Mental Deficiency,* 1970, *74,* 734–744.

Braun, C., & Klassen, B. A transformational analysis of oral syntactic structures of children representing varying ethno-linguistic communities. *Child Development,* 1971, *62,* 1859–1871.

Brislin, R.W. Comparative research methodology: Cross-cultural studies. *International Journal of Psychology.* 1976, *11,* 215–229.

Brislin, R., Lonner, W., & Thorndike, R. *Cross-cultural research methods.* New York: Wiley, 1973.

Broca, P. *Mémoires sur le cerveau de l'homme.* Paris: Reinwald, 1888.

Brodzinsky, D.M., Feuer, V., & Owens, J. Detection of linguistic ambiguity by reflective, impulsive, fast/accurate, and slow-inaccurate children. *Journal of Educational Psychology,* 1977, *69,* 237–243.

Brown, A.L. The role of strategic behavior in retardate memory. In N.R. Ellis (Ed.), *International review of research in mental retardation* (Vol. 7). New York: Academic Press, 1974.

Brown, A.L. Knowing, knowing about knowing and knowing how to know. In H.W. Reese (Ed.), *Advances in child development and behavior* (Vol. 10). New York: Academic Press, 1975.

Brown, R., & Berko, J. Word association and acquisition of grammar. *Child Development,* 1960, *31,* 1–14.

Bruner, J.S. *The relevance of education.* New York: Norton, 1971.

Burt, C. *Factors of the mind.* London: University of London Press, 1940.

Burt, C. Ability and income. *British Journal of Educational Psychology,* 1943, *13,* 83–98.

Burt, C. The structure of the mind: A review of the results of factor analyses. *British Journal of Educational Psychology,* 1949, *19,* 100–111: 176–199.

Burt, C. The evidence for the concept of intelligence. *British Journal of Educational Psychology,* 1955, *25,* 158–177.

Burt, C. Intelligence and social mobility. *British Journal of Statistical Psychology,* 1961, *14,* 3–24.

Burt, C. Is intelligence distributed normally? *British Journal of Statistical Psychology,* 1963, *16,* 175–190.

Burt, C. Inheritance of general intelligence. *American Psychologist,* 1972, *27,* 175–190.

Buss, A.R. A conceptual framework for learning effecting the development of ability factors. *Human Development,* 1973, *16,* 273–292. (a)

Buss, A.R. Learning, transfer, and changes in ability factors: A multivariate model. *Psychological Bulletin,* 1973, *80,* 106–112. (b)

Buss, A.R., & Royce, J.R. Ontogenetic changes in cognitive structure from a multivariate perspective. *Developmental Psychology,* 1975, *11,* 87–101. (a)

Buss, A.R., & Royce, J.R. Detecting cross-cultural commonalities and differences: Intergroup factor analysis. *Psychological Bulletin,* 1975, *82,* 128–136. (b)

Butcher, H.J. *Human intelligence: Its nature and assessment.* London: Methuen, 1968.

Butterfield, E.C., Wambold, C., & Belmont, J.M. On the theory and practice of improving short-term memory. *American Journal of Mental Deficiency,* 1973, *77,* 654–669.

Campbell, D.T., & Fiske, D.W. Convergent and discriminant validation by the multitrait-multimethod matrix. *Psychological Bulletin,* 1959, *56,* 81–105.

Caramazza, A., Gordon, J., Zurif, E.B., & DeLuca, D. Right hemispheric damage and verbal problem-solving behavior. *Brain and Language,* 1976, *3,* 41–46.

Carlson, J.S., & Wiedel, K.H. Modes of information integration and Piagetian measures of concrete operational thought. *Intelligence,* 1977, *1,* 335–343.

Carroll, J.B. Review of Guilford's *The Nature of Human Intelligence. American Educational Research Journal,* 1968, *5,* 249–256.

Carroll, J.B. Stalking the wayward factors. *Contemporary Psychology,* 1972, *17,* 321–324.

Carroll, J.B. Psychometric tests as cognitive tasks: A new structure of intellect. In L. Resnick (Ed.), *The nature of intelligence.* Hillsdale, N.J.: Erlbaum, 1976.

Case, R. Learning and development: A neo-Piagetian interpretation. *Human Development,* 1972, *15,* 339–358.

Case, R. Structures and strictures: Some functional limitations on the course of cognitive growth. *Cognitive Psychology,* 1974, *6,* 544–573.

Case, R. Gearing the demands of instruction to the developmental capacities of the learner. *Review of Educational Research,* 1975, *45,* 59–87.

Case, R. Responsiveness to conservation training as a function of induced subjective uncertainty, M-space, and cognitive style. *Canadian Journal of Behavioural Science,* 1977, *9,* 12–25.

Cattell, R.B. Theory of fluid and crystallized intelligence: A critical experiment. *Journal of Educational Psychology,* 1963, *54,* 1–23.

Cattell, R.B. *Abilities: Their structure, growth and action.* Boston: Houghton Mifflin, 1971.

Cattell, R.B. A culture-free intelligence test. In H.J. Eysenck (Ed.), *The measurement of intelligence.* Lancaster: Medical & Technical Publishing Co. Ltd., 1973.

Clarke, A.M., & Clarke, A.D.B. (Eds.) *Mental deficiency: The changing outlook.* London: Methuen, 1974.

Clarke, E., & Dewhurst, K. *An illustrated history of brain functions.* Oxford: Stanford Publications, 1972.

Coan, R.W. Facts, factors and artifacts: The quest for psychological meaning. *Psychological Review,* 1964, *71,* 123–140.

Cohen, G. Hemispheric differences in serial versus parallel processing. *Journal of Experimental Psychology,* 1973, *97,* 349–356.

Cohen, M.A., & Douglas, V.I. Characteristics of the orienting response in hyperactive and normal children. *Psychophysiology,* 1972, *9,* 238–245.

Cole, M., & Bruner, J.S. Cultural differences and inferences about psychological processes. *American Psychologist,* 1971, *26,* 867–876.

Cole, M., & Scribner, S. *Culture and thought: A psychological introduction.* New York: Wiley, 1974.

Cole, M., & Scribner, S. Theorizing about socialization of cognition. *Ethos,* 1975, *3,* 249–268.

Cole, M., & Scribner, S. Cross-cultural studies of memory and cognition. In R.V. Kail & J.H. Hagen (Eds.), *Perspectives on the development of memory and cognition.* Hillsdale, N.J.: Erlbaum, 1977.

Craik, F.I.M., & Lockhart, R.S. Levels of processing: A framework for memory research. *Journal of Verbal Learning and Verbal Behavior,* 1972, *11,* 671–684.

Crano, W.D., Kenny, D.A., & Campbell, D.T. Does intelligence cause achievement? A cross-lagged panel correlation. *Journal of Educational Psychology,* 1972, *63,* 258–275.

Cronbach, L.J. The two disciplines of scientific psychology. *American Psychologist,* 1957, *12,* 671–684.

Cronbach, L.J. *Essentials of psychological testing.* New York: Harper & Row, 1970.

Cronbach, L.J. Test validation. In R.L. Thorndike (Ed.), *Educational measurement.* Washington, D.C.: American Council on Education, 1971.

Cronbach, L.J. Five decades of controversy over mental testing. *American Psychologist,* 1975, *30,* 1–14. (a)

Cronbach, L.J. Beyond the two disciplines of scientific psychology. *American Psychologist,* 1975, *30,* 116–127. (b)

Cronbach, L.J., & Meehl, P.E. Construct validity in psychological tests. *Psychological Bulletin,* 1955, *52,* 281–302.

Cummins, J. Systems of mediation in memory and reasoning. Paper presented at the meeting of the Canadian Psychological Association, Victoria, Canada, June, 1973.

Cummins, J. & Das, J.P. Cognitive processing and reading difficulties: A framework for research. *Alberta Journal of Educational Research,* 1977, *23,* 245–256.

Cummins, J., & Das, J.P. Simultaneous and successive syntheses and linguistic processes. *International Journal of Psychology,* 1978, *13,* 129–138.

Daniel, J.S. Learning styles and strategies: The work of Gordon Pask. In N.J. Entwistle & D.J. Hounsell (Eds.), *How students learn.* Lancaster, U.K.: Institute for Research and Development in Post-Compulsory Education, 1975.

Das, G., & Broadhurst, P.L. The effect of inherited differences in emotional reactivity on a measure of intelligence in the rat. *Journal of Comparative & Physiological Psychology,* 1959, *52,* 300–303.

Das, J.P. Mental retardation in India. In N.R. Ellis (Ed.), *International review of research in mental retardation* (Vol. 3). New York: Pergamon Press, 1968.

Das, J.P. Patterns of cognitive ability in nonretarded and retarded children. *American Journal of Mental Deficiency,* 1972, *77,* 6–12.

Das, J.P. Cultural deprivation and cognitive competence. In N.R. Ellis (Ed.), *International Review of Research in Mental Retardation* (Vol. 6). New York: Academic Press, 1973. (a)

Das, J.P. Structure of cognitive abilities: Evidence for simultaneous and successive processing. *Journal of Educational Psychology,* 1973, *65,* 103–108. (b)

Das, J.P. The uses of attention. *Alberta Journal of Educational Research,* 1973, *19,* 99–108. (c)

Das, J.P., & Cummins, J.P. Academic performance and cognitive processes in EMR children. *American Journal of Mental Deficiency,* 1978, *83,* 2, 197–199.

Das, J.P., Kirby, J., & Jarman, R.F. Simultaneous and successive synthesis: An alternative model for cognitive abilities. *Psychological Bulletin,* 1975, *82,* 87–103.

Das, J.P., Manos, J., & Kanungo, R.N. Performance of Canadian Native, Black and White children on some cognitive and personality tasks. *Alberta Journal of Educational Research,* 1975, *21,* 183–195.

Das, J.P. & Molloy, G.N. Varieties of simultaneous and successive processing in children. *Journal of Educational Psychology,* 1975, *67,* 213–230.

Das, J.P., & Pivato, E. Malnutrition and cognitive functioning. In N.R. Ellis (Ed.), *International review of research in mental retardation* (Vol. 8). New York: Academic Press, 1976.

Das, J.P., & Singha, P.S. Caste, class and cognitive competence. *Indian* Educational Review, 1975, *10,* 1–18.

Dasen, P. Cross-cultural Piagetian research: A summary. *Journal of Cross-cultural Psychology,* 1972, *3,* 23–40.

Davids, A. An objective instrument for assessing hyperkinesis in children. *Journal of Learning Disabilities,* 1971, *4,* 499–501.

Dawson, J.L.M. Theory and research in cross-cultural psychology. *Bulletin of the British Psychological Society,* 1971, *24,* 291–306.

Doehring, D.G. *Patterns of impairment in specific reading disability.* Bloomington, Indiana: Indiana University Press, 1968.

Dyer, J.L., & Miller, L.B. Note on Crano, Kenny, and Campbell's "Does intelligence cause achievement?" *Journal of Educational Psychology,* 1974, *66,* 49–51.

Dykman, R.A., Ackerman, P.T., Clements, S.D., & Peters, J.E. Specific learning disabilities: An attentional deficit syndrome. In H.R. Myklebust (Ed.), *Progress in learning disabilities* (Vol. II). New York: Grune & Stratton, 1971.

Egeland, B. Training impulsive children in the use of more efficient scanning techniques. *Child Development,* 1974, *45,* 165–171.

Ekstrom, R.B. *Cognitive factors: Some recent literature.* Princeton, N.J.: Educational Testing Service, RB-73-30, 1973.

Elkind, D. Piagetian and psychometric conceptions of intelligence. *Harvard Educational Review,* 1969, *39,* 319–337.

Elkind, D. *Children and adolescents: Interpretive essays on Jean Piaget.* London: Oxford University Press, 1974.

Ellis, N.R., McCartney, J.R., Ferretti, R.P., & Cavalier, A.R. Recognition memory in mentally retarded persons. *Intelligence,* 1977, *1,* 310–317.

Ernest, C.H., & Paivio, A. Imagery and verbal associative latencies as a function of imagery ability. *Canadian Journal of Psychology,* 1971, *25,* 83–90.

Ervin, S.M. Changes with age in the verbal determinants of word-association. *American Journal of Psychology,* 1961, *74,* 361–372.

Estes, W.K. *Learning theory and mental development.* New York: Academic Press, 1970.

Estes, W.K. Learning theory and intelligence. *American Psychologist,* 1974, *29,* 740–749.

Estes, W.K. *Handbook of learning & cognitive processes* (Vol. 4). Hillsdale, N.J.: Erlbaum, 1976. (a)

Estes, W.K. Intelligence and cognitive psychology. In L.B. Resnick (Ed.), The nature of intelligence. Hillsdale, N.J.: Erlbaum, 1976. (b)

Eysenck, H.J. Review of primary mental abilities. *British Journal of Educational Psychology,* 1939, *9,* 270–275.

Eysenck, H.J. *The biological basis of personality.* Springfield, Ill.: Thomas, 1967. (a)

Eysenck, H.J. Intelligence assessment: A theoretical and experimental approach. *British Journal of Educational Psychology,* 1967, *37,* 81–98. (b)

Eysenck, H.J. Sir Cyril Burt. *British Journal of Mathematical and Statistical Psychology,* 1972, *25,* i–iv.

Eysenck, H.J. (Ed.) *The measurement of intelligence.* Lancaster, J.K.: Medical & Technical Publishing Co. Ltd., 1973.

Farnham-Diggory, S. Cognitive synthesis in negro and white children. *Monographs of the Society for Research in Child Development,* 1970, Whole No. 135, Vol. 35.

Ferguson, G.A. On learning and human ability. *Canadian Journal of Psychology,* 1954, *8,* 95–112.

Ferguson, G.A. On transfer and the abilities of man. *Canadian Journal of Psychology,* 1956, *10,* 121–131.

Flavell, J.H. *The developmental psychology of Jean Piaget.* New York: Van Nostrand, 1963.

Flavell, J.H. Developmental studies of mediated memory. In H.W. Reese & L.P. Lipsitt (Eds.), *Advances in child development and behavior* (Vol. 5). New York: Academic Press, 1970.

Flavell, J.H., Beach, D.H., & Chinsky, J.M. Spontaneous verbal rehearsal in a memory task as a function of age. *Child Development,* 1966, *37,* 283–299.

Freides, D. Human information processing and sensory modality: Cross-modal functions, information complexity, memory and deficit. *Psychological Bulletin,* 1974, *81,* 284–310.

French, J., Ekstrom, R., & Price, L. *Manual for kit of reference tests for cognitive factors.* Princeton, N.J.: Educational Testing Service, 1963.

Furneaux, W.D. *The Nufferno Manual of Speed and Level Tests.* Slough: National Foundation of Educational Research, 1956.

Furneaux, W.D. Intellectual abilities and problem solving behavior. In H.J. Eysenck (Ed.), *Handbook of abnormal psychology.* London: Pittman, 1960.

Gagné, R.M. Contributions of learning to human development. *Psychological Review,* 1968, *75,* 177–191.

Gagné, R.M. Learning and instructional sequence. In R.N. Kerlinger (Ed.), *Review of research in education* (Vol. 1). Itasca, Ill.: F.E. Peacock, 1973.

Gagné, R.M. Task analysis - Its relation to content analysis. *Educational Psychologist,* 1974, *11,* 11–18.

Gallagher, J.J., & Bradley, R.H. Early identification of developmental difficulties. In I.J. Gordon (Ed.), *Early childhood education: The seventy-first yearbook of the National Society for the Study of Education.* Chicago: University of Chicago Press, 1972.

Galton, F. *Inquiries into human faculty and its development.* London: Macmillan, 1883.

Gazzaniga, M.S. *The bisected brain.* New York: Appleton-Century-Crofts, 1970.

Gibson, A.R., Dimond, S.J., & Gazzaniga, M.S. Left field superiority for word matching. *Neuropsychologia,* 1972, *10,* 463–466.

Goldman-Eisler, F. The continuity of speech utterance: Its determinants and its significance. *Language and Speech,* 1961, *4,* 220–231.

Goldstein, D. Comprehension of linguistic ambiguity and development of classification. *Perceptual and Motor Skills,* 1976, *43,* 1051–1058.

Goodnow, J.J. The nature of intelligent behavior: Questions raised by cross-cultural studies. In L.B. Resnick (Ed.), *The nature of intelligence.* Hillsdale, N.J.: Erlbaum, 1976.

Gorsuch, R.L. *Factor analysis.* Toronto: Saunders, 1974.

Graham, F.K., & Kendall, B.S. Memory-for-Designs Test: Revised general manual. *Perceptual and Motor Skills,* 1960, *11,* 147–188.

Guilford, J.P. The structure of intellect. *Psychological Bulletin,* 1956, *53,* 267–293.

Guilford, J.P. Three faces of intellect. *American Psychologist.* 1959, *14,* 469–479.

Guilford, J.P. *The nature of human intelligence.* New York: McGraw-Hill, 1967.

Guilford, J.P., & Hoepfner, R. *The analysis of intelligence.* New York: McGraw-Hill, 1971.

Gutmann, D. On cross-cultural studies as a naturalistic approach in psychology. *Human Development,* 1967, *10,* 187–198.

Hakstian, A.R., & Cattell, R.B. The checking of primary ability structure on a broader basis of performances. *British Journal of Educational Psychology,* 1974, *44,* 140–154.

Halford, G.S. The impact of Piaget on psychology in the seventies. In P.C. Dodwell (Ed.), *New horizons in Psychology 2.* Middlesex, England: Penguin, 1972.

Halstead, W.C. *Brain and intelligence.* Chicago: The University of Chicago Press, 1947.

Harvard Educational Review. Reprint Series. No. 2, 1972.

Harvey, O.J., Hunt, D.E., & Schroder, H.M. *Conceptual systems and personality organization.* New York: Wiley, 1961.

Hawkins, P.R. The influence of sex, social class and pause-location in the hesitation phenomena of seven-year-old children. In B. Bernstein (Ed.), *Class codes and control* (Vol. 2). London: Routledge & Kegan Paul, 1973.

Haywood, H.C., & Tapp, J.T. Experience and the development of adaptive behavior. In N.R. Ellis (Ed.), *International review of research in mental retardation* (Vol. 1). New York: Academic Press, 1966.

Hearnshaw, L.S. Temporal integration and behavior. *Bulletin of the British Psychological Society*, 1956, *30*, 1–20.

Hebb, D.O. *The organization of behavior.* New York: Wiley, 1949.

Hebb, D.O. The American revolution. *American Psychologist*, 1960, *15*, 735–745.

Hess, W.R. Causality, consciousness and cerebral organization. *Science*, 1967, *158*, 1279–1283.

Hobbs, N. *The futures of children.* San Francisco: Jossey-Bass Publishers, 1975.

Horn, J.L. Organization of abilities and the development of intelligence. *Psychological Review*, 1968, *75*, 242–259.

Horn, J.L. Review of J.P. Guilford's *The nature of human intelligence. Psychometrika.* 1970, *35*, 273–277.

Horn, J.L. Theory of functions represented among auditory and visual test performances. In J.R. Royce (Ed.), *Contributions of multivariate analysis to psychological theory.* London: Academic Press, 1973.

Horn, J.L. Human abilities: A review of research and theory in the early 1970's. *Annual Review of Psychology*, 1976, *27*, 437–485.

Horn, J.L., & Cattell, R.B. Refinement and test of the theory of fluid and crystallized intelligence. *Journal of Educational Psychology*, 1966, *57*, 253–270.

Horn, J.L., & Knapp, J.R. On the subjective character of the empirical base of Guilford's structure of intellect model. *Psychological Bulletin*, 1973, *80*, 33–43.

Humphreys, L.G. Critique of Cattell's "Theory of fluid & crystallized intelligence: A critical experiment." *Journal of Educational Psychology*, 1967, *58*, 120–136.

Hunt, D.E. *Matching models in education.* Toronto: Ontario Institute for Studies in Education, 1971.

Hunt, D.E., & Sullivan, E.V. *Between psychology and education.* Hinsdale, Ill.: Dryden Press, 1974.

Hunt, E. What kind of computer is man? *Cognitive Psychology*, 1971, *2*, 57–98.

Hunt, E. The memory we must have. In R. Shank & K. Colby (Eds.), *Computer models of thought and language.* San Francisco: Freeman, 1973.

Hunt, E. Quote the Raven? Nevermore! In L. Gregg (Ed.), *Knowledge and cognition.* Potomac, Md.: Erlbaum, 1975.

Hunt, E. Varieties of cognitive power. In L. Resnick (Ed.), *The nature of intelligence.* Hillsdale, N.J.: Erlbaum, 1976.

Hunt, E., Frost, N., & Lunneborg, C. Individual differences in cognition: A new approach to intelligence. In G.H. Bower (Ed.), *The psychology of learning and motivation* (Vol. 7). New York: Academic Press, 1973.

Hunt, E., & Lansman, M. Cognitive theory applied to individual differences. In W.K. Estes (Ed.), *Handbook of learning and cognitive processes* (Vol. 1). Hillsdale, N.J.: Erlbaum, 1975.

Hunt, E., Lunneborg, C., & Lewis, J. What does it mean to be high verbal? *Cognitive Psychology*, 1975, *7*, 194–227.

Hunt, J. McV. *Intelligence and experience.* New York: Ronald Press, 1961.

Hunt, K. Syntactic maturity in school children and adults. *Monographs of the Society for Research in Child Development*, 1970, Serial No. 134, Vol. 35.

Ilg, F.L., & Ames, L.B. *School readiness: Behavior tests used at the Gesell Institute.* New York: Harper & Row, 1964.

Jakobson, R. Towards a linguistic typology of aphasic impairments. In A.V.S. D. Reuck & M. O'Connor (Eds.), *Disorders of language* (C.I.B.A. Symposium). London: Churchill, 1964.

Jakobson, R. *Studies on child language and aphasia.* The Hague: Mouton, 1971.

Jarman, R.F. Intelligence, modality matching and information processing. Unpublished Ph.D. dissertation. Department of Educational Psychology, University of Alberta, Edmonton, 1975.

Jarman, R.F. A method of construction of auditory stimulus patterns for use in cross-modal and intramodal matching tests. *Behavior Research Methods and Instrumentation,* 1977, 9, 22–25. (a)

Jarman, R.F. Patterns of cross-modal and intramodal matching among intelligence groups. In P. Mittler (Ed.), *Research to practice in mental retardation* (Vol. II). Baltimore, Md.: University Park Press, 1977. (b)

Jarman, R.F. Level I and Level II abilities: Some theoretical reinterpretations. *British Journal of Psychology,* 1978, 69, 257–269. (a)

Jarman, R.F. Patterns of cognitive ability in retarded children: A reexamination. *American Journal of Mental Deficiency,* 1978, 82, 344–348. (b)

Jarman, R.F. Cross-modal and intramodal matching: Relationships to simultaneous and successive syntheses and levels of performance among three intelligence groups. *Alberta Journal of Educational Research,* 1978, 24, 100–112. (c)

Jarman, R.F. Selection and validation of preschool screening instruments: Confirmatory analyses based on a test taxonomy. Paper given at the XIXth International Congress of Applied Psychology, Munich, 1978. (d)

Jarman, R.F. Simultaneous and successive cognitive processing in the Mueller-Lyer illusion. *Journal of Genetic Psychology,* in press. (a)

Jarman, R.F. Modality-specific information processing and intellectual ability. *Intelligence,* in press. (b)

Jarman, R.F., & Das, J.P. Simultaneous and successive syntheses and intelligence. *Intelligence,* 1977, 1, 151–169.

Jensen, A.R. Cumulative deficits in compensatory education. *Journal of School Psychology,* 1966, 4,, 37–47.

Jensen, A.R. How much can we boost IQ and scholastic achievement? *Harvard Educational Review,* 1969, 39, 1–123.

Jensen, A.R. Hierarchical theories of mental ability. In B. Dockrell (Ed.), *On intelligence.* Toronto: Ontario Institute for Studies in Education, 1970.

Jensen, A.R. A two-factor theory of familial mental retardation. Paper presented at the 4th International Congress of Human Genetics, Paris, September, 1971.

Jensen, A.R. *Educability and group differences.* New York: Harper & Row, 1973. (a)

Jensen, A.R. Level I and Level II abilities in three ethnic groups. *American Educational Research Journal,* 1973, 10, 263–276. (b)

Jensen, A.R. Interaction of level I and level II abilities with race and socioeconomic status. *Journal of Educational Psychology,* 1974, 66, 99–111. (a)

Jensen, A.R. Kinship correlations reported by Sir Cyril Burt. *Behavior Genetics,* 1974, 4, 1–28. (b)

Jensen, A.R. Cumulative deficit in IQ of blacks in the rural south. *Developmental Psychology,* 1977, 13, 184–191. (a)

Jensen, A.R. Did Sir Cyril Burt fake his research on heritability on intelligence? Part 2. *Phi Delta Kappan,* February 1977. (b)

Jensen, A.R., & Frederiksen, J. Free recall of categorized and uncategorized lists: A test of the Jensen hypothesis. *Journal of Educational Psychology*, 1973, *63*, 304–312.

Jinks, J.L., & Fulker, D.W. Comparison of the biometrical genetical MAVA and classical approaches to the analysis of human behaviour. *Psychological Bulletin*, 1970, *73*, 311–349.

Kagan, J. Reflection-impulsivity and reading ability in primary grade children. *Child Development*, 1965, *36*, 609–628.

Kagan, J., & Klein, R.E. Cross-cultural perspectives on early development. *American Psychologist*, 1973, *28*, 947–961.

Kagan, J., Klein, R.E., Haith, M.M., & Morrison, F.J. Memory and meaning in two cultures. *Child Development*, 1973, *44*, 221–223.

Kagan, J., Moss, H.A. & Sigel, I.E. Psychological significance of styles of conceptualization. In J.C. Wright & J. Kagan (Eds.) *Basic cognitive processes in children*. Monograph of the Society for Research in Child Development, 1963, Serial No. 86.

Kagan, J., Rosman, B.L., Day, D., Albert, J., & Phillips, W. Information processing in the child: Significance of analytic and reflective attitudes. *Psychological Monographs: General and Applied*, 1964, *78* (1, Whole No. 578).

Kagan, J., Sontag, L.W., Baker, C.T., & Nelson, V. Personality and IQ change. *Journal of Abnormal and Social Psychology*, 1958, *56*, 261–266.

Kahn, D., & Birch, H.G. Development of auditory-visual integration and reading achievement. *Perceptual and Motor Skills*, 1968, *27*, 459–468.

Kamin, L.J. *The science and politics of IQ*. New York: Wiley, 1974.

Kaufman, D. The relation of academic performance to strategy training and remedial techniques: An information processing approach. Unpublished Ph.D. dissertation. University of Alberta, Edmonton, Canada, 1978.

Kessel, F. The role of syntax in children's comprehension from age six to twelve. *Monographs of the Society for Research in Child Development*, 1970. Whole No. 139, Vol. 35.

Kimura, D. Right temporal-lobe damage: Perception of unfamiliar stimuli after damage. *Archives of Neurology*, 1963, *8*, 264–271.

Kimura, D. Spatial localization in left and right visual fields. *Canadian Journal of Psychology*, 1969, *23*, 445–458.

Kimura, D. The asymmetry of the human brain. *Scientific American*, 1973, *228*, 70–78.

Kirby, J.R. Information processing and human abilities. Unpublished Ph.D. Thesis, Department of Educational Psychology, University of Alberta, Edmonton, Canada, 1976.

Kirby, J.R., & Das, J.P. Comments on Paivio's imagery theory. *Canadian Psychological Review*, 1976, *17*, 66–68.

Kirby, J.R., & Das, J.P. Reading achievement, IQ, and simultaneous-successive processing. *Journal of Educational Psychology*, 1977, *69*, 564–570.

Kirby, J.R., & Das, J.P. Information processing and human abilities. *Journal of Educational Psychology*, 1978, *70*, 58–66. (a)

Kirby, J.R., & Das, J.P. Skills underlying two Raven's subscales. *Alberta Journal of Educational Research*, 1978, *24*, 94–99. (b)

Kirby, J.R., Jarman, R.F., & Das, J.P. Paradigmatic and syntagmatic clustering: Relation to simultaneous and successive processing. Unpublished manuscript, Department of Educational Psychology, University of Alberta, Edmonton, Canada, 1975.

Kirk, S.A., McCarthy, J.J., & Kirk, W. *Examiner's Manual: Illinois Test of Psycholinguistic Abilities (Rev. Ed.)*. Urbana, Ill.: University of Illinois Press, 1968.

Klahr, D. (Ed.) *Cognition and instruction*. Hillsdale, N.J.: Erlbaum, 1976.

Kolata, G.B. Childhood hyperactivity: A new look at treatments and causes. *Science*, 1978, *199*, 515–517.

Krywaniuk, L.W. Patterns of cognitive abilities of high and low achieving school children. Unpublished Ph.D. Thesis, Department of Educational Psychology, University of Alberta, Edmonton, Canada, 1974.

Lashley, K.S. The problem of serial order in behavior. In J.A. Jeffreys (Ed.), *Cerebral mechanisms in behavior: The Hixon Symposium.* New York: Wiley, 1951.

Lawson, M.J. An examination of the levels of processing approach to memory. Unpublished Ph.D. Thesis, Department of Educational Psychology, University of Alberta, 1976.

Lawson, M.J., & Jarman, R.F. A note on Jensen's theory of Level I ability and recent research on human memory. *British Journal of Educational Psychology,* 1977, *47,* 91–94.

Leong, C.K. An investigation of spatial-temporal information processing in children with specific reading disability. Unpublished Ph.D. Thesis, 1974, Department of Educational Psychology, University of Alberta, Edmonton, Canada.

Levine, R.A. Cross-cultural study in child psychology. In P. Mussen (Ed.), *Carmichael's manual of child psychology.* New York: Wiley, 1970.

Levy, J. Psychobiological implications of bilateral asymmetry. In S.J. Dimond & J.G. Beaumont (Eds.), *Hemisphere function in the human brain.* New York: Wiley, 1974.

Loevinger, J. Objective tests as instruments of psychological theory. *Psychological Reports,* 1957, *3,* 635–694.

Loevinger, J. Person and population as psychometric concepts. *Psychological Review,* 1965, *72,* 143–155.

Lomov, B.F. Present status of future development of psychology in the USSR in the light of decisions of 24th Congress of the Communist Party of the Soviet Union. *Voprosy Psikhologie,* 1971, *5,* 3–19 (Soviet Psychology, 1972, Summer, 329–358.)

Luria, A.R. *The role of speech in regulation of normal and abnormal behavior.* Oxford: Pergamon Press, 1961.

Luria, A.R. *Higher cortical functions in man.* New York: Basic Books, 1966. (a)

Luria, A.R. *Human brain and psychological processes.* New York: Harper & Row, 1966. (b)

Luria, A.R. *The origin and cerebral organization of man's conscious action: An evening lecture.* 19th International Congress of Psychology, London, 1969.

Luria, A.R. The functional organization of the brain. *Scientific American,* 1970, *222,* 3, 66–78.

Luria, A.R. Towards the problem of the historical nature of psychological processes. *International Journal of Psychology,* 1971, *6,* 259–272.

Luria, A.R. The frontal lobes and the regulation of behavior. In K.H. Pribram & A.R. Luria (Eds.), *Psychophysiology of the frontal lobes.* New York: Academic Press, 1973. (a)

Luria, A.R. The long road of a Soviet psychologist. *International Social Science Journal,* 1973, *25,* 71–87. (b)

Luria, A.R. Two basic kinds of aphasic disorders. *Lingua,* 1973, *115,* 57–66. (c)

Luria, A.R. *The working brain.* London: Penguin, 1973. (d)

Luria, A.R. Basic problems of language in the light of psychology and neurolinguistics. In E.H. Lenneberg & E. Lenneberg (Eds.), *Foundations of language development: A multidisciplinary approach* (Vol. 2). New York: Academic Press, 1975. (a)

Luria, A.R. *The man with a shattered world.* Hammondsworth, England: Penguin, 1975. (b)

Luria, A.R. *Cognitive development: Its cultural and social foundations.* Cambridge, Mass.: Harvard University Press, 1976.

Luria, A.R., & Artem'eva, E.Y. Two approaches to an evaluation of the reliability of psychological investigations. *Soviet Psychology,* 1970, *8,* 271–282.

Luria, A.R., & Majouski, L.V. Basic approaches used in American and Soviet clinical neuropsychology. *American Psychologist,* 1977, *32,* 959–968.

MacArthur, R.S. Some ability patterns: Central Eskimos and Nsenga Africans. *International Journal of Psychology*, 1973, *8*, 239–247.

MacArthur, R.S. Ecology, culture, and cognitive development: Canadian native youth. In L. Driedger (Ed.), *The Canadian ethnic mosaic: A quest for identity*. Englewood Cliffs, N.J.: Prentice-Hall, 1978.

Malpass, R.S. Theory and method in cross-cultural psychology. *American Psychology*, 1977, *32*, 1069–1079.

Manos, J. Children's cognitive abilities and their relation to socio-economic status and some personality characteristics. Unpublished Ph.D. Thesis, Department of Educational Psychology, University of Alberta, Edmonton, Canada, 1975.

Max-Muller, F. *Immanuel Kant: Critique of Pure Reason*. New York: Doubleday, 1966.

Maxwell, A.E. Factor analysis: Thomson's sampling theory recalled. *British Journal of Mathematical and Statistical Psychology*, 1972, *25*, 1–21.

McCarthy, J.J., & McCarthy, J.F. *Learning disabilities*. Boston: Allyn & Bacon, 1969.

McClelland, D.C. Testing for competence rather than for "intelligence." *American Psychologist*, 1973, *28*, 1–14.

McDaniel, E. The Purdue Motion Picture Tests of Visual Perception. In L. Cronbach & P. Drenth (Eds.), *Mental tests and cultural adaptation*. The Hague: Mouton, 1972.

McLaughlin, G.H. Psycho-logic: A possible alternative to Piaget's formulations. *British Journal of Educational Psychology*, 1963, *33*, 61–67.

McLeod, R.W. An exploratory study of inference and cognitive synthesis in reading comprehension with selected grade 4 readers. Unpublished Ph.D. Thesis, Department of Elementary Education, University of Alberta, Edmonton, Canada, 1978.

McNemar, Q. Lost: Our intelligence? Why? *American Psychologist*, 1964, *19*, 871–882.

Meichenbaum, D.H., & Goodman, J. Training impulsive children to talk to themselves: A means of developing self-control. *Journal of Abnormal Psychology*, 1971, *77*, 115–126.

Meier, J.H. Screening, assessment and intervention for young children at developmental risk. In N. Hobbs (Ed.), *Issues in the classification of children* (Vol. 2). San Francisco: Jossey-Bass, 1975.

Merrifield, P.R. Structuring mental acts. In B. Dockrell (Ed.), *On intelligence*. Toronto: Ontario Institute for Studies in Education, 1970.

Messer, S.B. Reflection-impulsivity: A review. *Psychological Bulletin*, 1976, *83*, 1026–1052.

Messick, S. Beyond structure: In search of functional models of psychological process. *Psychometrika*, 1972, *37*, 357–375.

Messick, S. Multivariate models of cognition and personality: The need for both process and structure in psychological theory and measurement. In J.R. Royce (Ed.), *Contributions of multivariate analysis of theoretical psychology*. New York: Academic Press, 1973.

Messick, S. The standard problem: Meaning and values in measurement and evaluation. *American Psychologist*, 1975, *30*, 955–966.

Milner, B. Interhemispheric differences in the localization of psychological processes in man. *British Medical Bulletin*, 1971, *27*, 272–277.

Molloy, G.N. Age, socioeconomic status and patterns of cognitive ability. Unpublished Ph.D. dissertation. University of Alberta, Edmonton, 1973.

Mulaik, S.A. *The foundations of factor analysis*. New York: McGraw-Hill, 1972.

Myers, C.S. Instinct and intelligence. *British Journal of Psychology*, 1910, *3*, 209–218.

Nebes, R.D. Hemispheric specialization in commissurotomized man. *Psychological Bulletin*, 1974, *81*, 1–14.

Neisser, U. *Cognitive psychology*. New York: Appleton-Century-Crofts, 1967.

Nelson, K. The syntagmatic–paradigmatic shift revisited: A review of research and theory. *Psychological Bulletin, 1977, 84,* 93–116.

O'Connor, N. The psychopathology of cognitive deficit. *British Journal of Psychiatry, 1976, 128,* 36–43.

O'Connor, N., & Hermelin, B. Inter- and intra-modal transfer in children with modality specific and general handicaps. *British Journal of Social and Clinical Psychology, 1971, 10,* 346–354.

O'Connor, N., & Hermelin, B. Modality-specific spatial coordinates in perception. *Psychophysics, 1975, 17,* 213–216.

O'Donnell, R.D., Griffith, W., & Norris, R. A transformational analysis of oral and written grammatical structures in the language of children in grades three, five and seven. *NCTE Research Report* No. 8, 1967.

Orn, D.E. Intelligence, socioeconomic status and short-term memory. Unpublished Ph.D. Thesis, Department of Educational Psychology, University of Alberta, Edmonton, Canada, 1970.

Ornstein, R.E. *The psychology of consciousness.* San Francisco: Freeman, 1972.

Orton, S.T. *Reading, writing and speech problems in children.* New York: W.W. Norton, 1937.

Paivio, A. Mental imagery in associative learning and memory. *Psychological Review, 1969, 76,* 241–263.

Paivio, A. *Imagery and verbal processes.* New York: Holt, Rinehart & Winston, 1971.

Paivio, A. Language and knowledge of the world. *Educational Researcher, 1974, 3,* 5–12.

Paivio, A. Imagery and synchronic thinking. *Canadian Psychological Review, 1975, 16,* 147–163.

Paivio, A. Concerning dual-coding and simultaneous-successive processing. *Canadian Psychological Review, 1976, 17,* 69–72.

Palkes, H., Stewart, J., & Freedman, J. Improvement in maze performance of hyperactive boys as a function of verbal-training procedures. *Journal of Special Education, 1971, 5,* 337–342.

Pascual-Leone, J. A mathematical model for the transition rule in Piaget's developmental stages. *Acta Psychologica, 1970, 63,* 301–345.

Pask, G. *The cybernetics of human learning and performance.* London: Hutchinson, 1975.

Pask, G., & Scott, B.C.E. Learning strategies and individual competence. *International Journal of Man-Machine Studies, 1972, 4,* 217–253.

Pavlov, I.P. *Lectures on conditioned reflexes* (Vol. 1). (Transl. W.H. Gantt.) New York: International Publishers, 1928.

Pavlov, I.P. *Lectures on Conditioned Reflexes* (Vol. 2). (Transl. W.H. Gantt.) New York: International Publishers, 1941.

Piaget, J. *Les mecanismes perceptifs.* Paris: Presses Universitaires de France, 1961.

Pick, H.L. Jr., Pick, A.D., & Klein, R.E. Perceptual integration in children. In L. Lipsitt & C.C. Spiker (Eds.), *Advances in child development and behavior* (Vol. 3). New York: Academic Press, 1967.

Pribram, K.H. *Languages of the brain.* Englewood Cliffs, N.J.: Prentice-Hall, 1971.

Pribram, K.H., & Luria, A.R. *Psychophysiology of the frontal lobes.* New York: Academic Press, 1973.

Price-Williams, D. Psychological experiment and anthropology: The problem of categories. *Ethos, 1974, 2,* 95–114.

Raven, J.C. *Coloured progressive matrices: Sets A, Ab, B.* London: H.K. Lewis, 1956.

Razran, G. Russian physiologist's psychology and American experimental psychology: A historical and systemic collation and a look into the future. *Psychological Bulletin,* 1965, *63,* 42–64.

Reese, H.W. Verbal mediation as a function of age level. *Psychological Bulletin,* 1962, *59,* 502–509.

Reid, L.S. Toward a grammer of the image. *Psychological Bulletin,* 1974, *81,* 319–334.

Repucci, N.D. Individual differences in the consideration of information among two-year-old children. *Proceedings of the Annual Convention of the American Psychological Association,* 1969, 257–258.

Resnick, L.B. Task analysis in instructional design: Some cases from mathematics. In D. Klahr (Ed.), *Cognition and instruction.* Hillsdale, N.J.: Erlbaum, 1976.

Rotter, J.B. Generalized expectancies for internal versus external control of reinforcement. *Psychological Monographs,* 1966, *80,* 1.

Ross, A.O. *Psychological aspects of learning disabilities and reading disorders.* New York: McGraw-Hill, 1976.

Rourke, B.P. Brain–behavior relationships in children with learning disabilities: A research program. *American Psychologist,* 1975, *30,* 911–920.

Royce, J.R. The conceptual framework for a multi-factor theory of individuality. In J.R. Royce (Ed.), *Multivariate analysis and psychological theory.* New York: Academic Press, 1973.

Satterfield, S.H. Neuropsychologic studies with hyperactive children. In D.P. Cantwell (Ed.), *The hyperactive child.* New York: Spectrum Publications, 1975.

Schonemann, P., & Steiger, J. Regression components analysis. *British Journal of Mathematical Statistics,* 1976, *29,* 175–189.

Schulhoff, C., & Goodglass, H. Dichotic listening, side of brain injury and cerebral dominance. *Neuropsychologia,* 1969, *7,* 149–160.

Schwebel, A.I., & Bernstein, A.J. The effects of impulsivity on the performance of lower-class children on four WISC subtests. *American Journal of Orthopsychiatry,* 1970, *40,* 629–636.

Scott, K.G. Learning theory, intelligence, and mental development. *American Journal of Mental Deficiency,* 1978, *82,* 325–336.

Scribner, S., & Cole, M. Cognitive consequences of formal and informal education. *Science,* 1973, *182,* 553–559.

Sechenov, I. *Selected physiological and psychological works.* Moscow: Foreign Languages Publishing House, 1878.

Semmes, J. Hemispheric specialization: A possible clue to mechanism. *Neuropsychologia,* 1968, *6,* 11–26.

Senf, G.M. Development of immediate memory for bisensory stimuli in normal children and children with learning disorders. *Developmental Psychology,* 1969, *6,* 1–28.

Shields, J. *Monozygotic twins.* Oxford: University Press, 1962.

Shipman, V.C. *Disadvantaged children and their first school experiences.* (ETS PR-72-18). Princeton, N.J.: Educational Testing Service, 1972.

Shipman, V.C., Barone, J., Beaton, A., Emmerich, W., & Ward, W. *Structure and development of cognitive competencies and styles prior to school entry.* (ETS PR-71-19). Princeton, N.J.: Educational Testing Service, 1971.

Shipman, V.C., Boroson, M., Bridgeman, G., Gant, J., & Mikovsky, M. *Notable early characteristics of high and low achieving Black Low-SES children.* (ETS PR-76-21). Princeton, N.J.: Educational Testing Service, 1976.

Shultz, T.R., & Pilon, R. Development of the ability to detect linguistic ambiguity. *Child Development,* 1973, *44,* 728–733.

Siegler, R.S. Three aspects of cognitive development. *Cognitive Psychology*, 1976, *8*, 481–520.

Smith, N.K. *Immanuel Kant's Critique of Pure Reason*. London: Macmillan, 1933.

Snow, R.E. Individual differences and instructional theory. Paper given at the annual meeting of the American Educational Research Association, New York, April 1977.

Sokolov, E.N. Brain functions: Neuronal mechanisms of learning and memory. In *Annual review of psychology* (Vol. 28), 1977.

Spearman, C. General intelligence objectively determined and measured. *American Journal of Psychology*, 1904, *15*, 202–293.

Spearman, C. *The nature of 'intelligence' and the principles of cognition*. London: Macmillan, 1923.

Spearman, C. *The abilities of man*. New York: Macmillan, 1927.

Sperry, R.W. Hemispheric deconnection and unity in conscious awareness. *American Psychologist*, 1968, *23*, 723–733.

Spicker, H.H. Intellectual development through early childhood education. *Exceptional Children*, 1971, *37*, 629–640.

Sprecht, H. Simultaneous successive processing, mathematics and reading achievement in low achieving high school students. Unpublished study. Centre for the Study of Mental Retardation, University of Alberta, Edmonton, Canada, 1976.

Stenhouse, D. *The evolution of intelligence*. London: Allen & Unwin, 1973.

Sternberg, R.J. *Intelligence, information processing and analogical reasoning: The componential analysis of human abilities*. Hillsdale, N.J.: Erlbaum, 1977.

Stroop, J.R. Studies of interference in serial verbal reactions. *Journal of Experimental Psychology*, 1935, *18*, 643–661.

Tarjan, G., & Eisenberg, L. Some thoughts on the classification of mental retardation in U.S.A. *American Journal of Psychiatry*, 1972, *128*, 14–18.

Tatsuoka, M.M. *Multivariate analysis: Techniques for educational and psychological research*. New York: Wiley, 1971.

Thomson, G.H. *The factorial analysis of human ability*. Boston: Houghton Mifflin, 1939.

Thorndike, E.L., Terman, L.M., Freeman, F.N., Colvin, S.S., Pintner, R., Pressey, S.L., Henmon, V.A.C., Pererson, J., Thurstone, L.L., Woodrow, H., & Haggerty, M.E. Intelligence and its measurement. A symposium. *Journal of Educational Psychology*, 1921, *12*, 123–147.

Thorndike, E.L., Bergman, E.O., Cobb, M.V., Woodyard, E., et al. *The measurement of intelligence*. New York: Columbia University Press, 1926.

Thorndike, R.L. Intellectual status and intellectual growth. *Journal of Educational Psychology*, 1966, *57*, 121–127.

Thurstone, L.L. *The nature of intelligence*. New York: Harcourt, Brace and World, 1926.

Thurstone, L.L. Primary mental abilities. *Psychometric Monographs*. No. 1, 1938.

Thurstone, L.L., & Thurstone, T.G. *SRA Primary Mental Abilities*. Chicago: SRA, 1962.

Tizard, J. A note on the international statistical classification of mental retardation. *American Journal of Psychiatry*, 1972, *128*, 25–29.

Triandis, H.C. Cultural influences upon cognitive processes. In L. Berkowitz (Ed.), *Advances in experimental social psychology*. New York: Academic Press, 1964.

Triandis, H.C. *The analysis of subjective culture*. New York: Wiley, 1972.

Tuddenham, R.D. A "Piagetian" test of cognitive development. In W.B. Dockrell (Ed.), *On intelligence*. Toronto: Ontario Institute for Studies in Education, 1969.

Tyler, L.E. *Individual differences*. New York: Appleton-Century-Crofts, 1974.

Tyler, L.E. The intelligence we test—an evolving concept. In L.B. Resnick (Ed.), *The nature of intelligence*. Hillsdale, N.J.: Erlbaum, 1976.

Vandenberg, S.G. Comparative studies of multiple factor ability measures. In J.R. Royce (Ed.), *Multivariate analysis and psychological* theory. New York: Academic Press, 1973.

Vernon, P.E. *The structure of human abilities.* London: Methuen, 1950.

Vernon, P.E. *Intelligence and attainment tests.* London: University of London Press, 1960.

Vernon, P.E. Abilities and attainments in the Western Isles. *Scottish Education Journal,* 1965, *48,* 948–950. (a)

Vernon, P.E. Ability factors and environmental influences. *American Psychologist,* 1965, *20,* 723–733. (b)

Vernon, P.E. Educational and intellectual development among Canadian Indians and Eskimos. *Educational Review,* 1966, *18,* 79–91, 186–195.

Vernon, P.E. *Intelligence and cultural environment.* London: Methuen, 1969.

Vernon, P.E. The distinctiveness of field independence. *Journal of Personality,* 1972, *40,* 366–391.

Vernon, P.E., Ryba, K.A., & Lang, R.J. Simultaneous and successive processing: An attempt at replication. *Canadian Journal of Behavioural Science,* 1978, *10,* 1–15.

Voronin, L.G. Stages in the evolution of higher nervous activity. *Soviet Psychology,* 1973, Spring, 93–111.

Wade, N. IQ and Heredity: Suspicion of fraud beclouds classic experiment. *Science,* 1976, *194,* 916–919.

Waller, J.H. Achievement and social mobility: Relationship among IQ score, education and occupation in two generations. *Social Biology,* 1971, *18,* 252–259.

Wechsler, D. *Manual for the Wechsler Intelligence Scale for Children-Revised.* New York: Psychological Corporation, 1974.

Wender, P.H. *Minimal brain dysfunction in children.* New York: Wiley-Interscience, 1971.

Wender, P.H. Hypothesis for a possible biochemical basis of minimal brain dysfunction. In R.M. Knights & D.J. Bakker (Eds.), *The neuropsychology of learning disorders: Theoretical approaches.* Baltimore, Md.: University Park Press, 1976.

Werner, H. *Comparative psychology of mental development.* New York: International Universities Press, 1948.

Weschler, D. *The measurement and appraisal of adult intelligence.* Baltimore, Md.: Williams & Williams, 1958.

Whimbey, A. *Intelligence can be taught.* New York: Dutton, 1975.

White, B.L., & Watts, J.C. *Experience and environment* (Vol. 1). Englewood Cliffs, N.J.: Prentice-Hall, 1973.

White, M.S. Laterality differences in perception: A review. *Psychological Bulletin,* 1969, *72,* 387–405.

White, P.O. A mathematical model for individual differences in problem solving. In A. Elithorn & D. Jones, *Artificial and human thinking.* Amsterdam: Elsevier, 1973.

White, R.T., & Gagné, R.M. Past and future research on learning hierarchies. *Educational Psychologist,* 1974, *11,* 19–28.

White, S.H. Evidence for a hierarchical arrangement of learning processes. In L.P. Lipsitt & C.C. Spiker (Eds.), *Advances in child development and behavior* (Vol. 2). New York: Academic Press, 1965.

Williams, N.H. Arousal and information processing in learning disabled children. Unpublished Ph.D. Thesis, Department of Educational Psychology, University of Alberta, Edmonton, Canada, 1976.

Witelson, S.F. Abnormal right hemispheric specialization in developmental dyslexia. In R.M. Knights & D.J. Bakker (Eds.), *The neuropsychology of learning disorders.* Baltimore, Md.: University Park Press, 1976.

Witkin, H.A. A cognitive style approach to cross-cultural research. *International Journal of Psychology,* 1967, *2,* 233–250.

Witkin, H.A., & Berry, J.W. Psychological differentiation in cross-cultural perspective. *Journal of Cross-Cultural Psychology,* 1975, *6,* 4–87.

Witkin, H.A., Lewis, H.B. Hertzman, M., Machover, K., Meissner, P.B., & Wapner, S. *Personality through perception.* New York: Harper, 1954.

Witkin, H.A., Moore, C.A., Goodenough, D.R., & Cox, P.W. Field-dependent and field-independent cognitive styles and their educational implications. *Review of Educational Research,* 1977, *47,* 1–64.

Wood-Gush, D.G.M. Comparative psychology and ethology. *Annual Review of Psychology,* 1963, *14,* 175–200.

Woodrow, H. The ability to learn. *Psychological Review,* 1946, *53,* 147–158.

Wyke, M., & Ettlinger, G. Efficiency of recognition in left and right visual fields. *Archives of Neurology,* 1961, *5,* 659–665.

Yalow, E., & Webb, N. Introspective strategy differences reflecting aptitude processes. Paper given at the annual meeting of the American Psychological Association, San Francisco, August, 1977.

Zeitlin, S. *Kindergarten screening: Early identification of potential high-risk learners.* Springfield, Ill.: Charles C. Thomas, 1976.

Zigler, E. Mental Retardation: Current issues and approaches. In L.W. Hoffman & M.L. Hoffman (Eds.), *Review of child development research* (Vol. 2). New York: R. Sage Foundation, 1966.

Index

EDUCATIONAL PSYCHOLOGY

continued from page ii